ENGLISH IN THE NEWS

ISSN 0769-3036 ISBN 2-7011-**1399**-7

ENGLISH IN THE NEWS

By

Éloi Le Divenach

Illustrations Punch

BELIN

8, RUE FÉROU - 75278 PARIS CEDEX 06

TABLE DES MATIÈRES

AVANT-PROPOS

Fondé sur la lecture de milliers d'articles de journaux et de magazines de langue anglaise, et sur une écoute quotidienne de la BBC (Radio 4), *English in the News* regroupe l'essentiel du vocabulaire de l'actualité telle que nous la présentent les médias. Les mots qui figurent dans cet ouvrage sont le fruit de ce long travail de recensement. Tous ont été lus ou entendus par nous dans la presse écrite ou audiovisuelle ; leur présence est ainsi garantie dans l'usage d'aujourd'hui.

Le vocabulaire retenu (environ 3 500 mots) a été organisé en rubriques. Notre souci de situer chaque mot dans sa zone d'utilisation habituelle nous a incité à faire quelques répétitions volontaires. Par exemple, on trouvera "to donate", "a donor", "a donation" dans le chapitre « Le Tiers Monde » comme dans le chapitre « La médecine ». "To attempt", "an attempt" figurent dans les chapitres « L'espace », « La médecine », « Les délits et les châtiments », « La politique » et « Le sport ».

Pour faciliter l'utilisation de l'ouvrage, le vocabulaire a été divisé en deux parties : le « Vocabulaire à haute fréquence » et le « Vocabulaire complémentaire », séparées par un ensemble de noms composés et d'expressions ou tournures idiomatiques que nous avons intitulé « Expressions ».

A la fin de chaque chapitre figurent quelques articles de journaux (une cinquantaine au total dans le livre). Ils sont suivis d'exercices qui permettent de mettre en pratique le vocabulaire acquis et de se familiariser avec la presse anglophone. L'utilisateur trouvera un corrigé en fin d'ouvrage et pourra ainsi évaluer sa performance dans les exercices.

L'ouvrage, ainsi conçu, permet l'acquisition systématique et graduée du vocabulaire de l'actualité. Pour tous ceux qui travaillent à entretenir ou à perfectionner leur anglais, soit par un travail individuel, soit dans le cadre de cours de langue, *English in the News* devrait constituer un outil précieux.

Il devrait aussi rendre de grands services aux élèves de second cycle de l'enseignement secondaire dans la préparation de leurs examens ainsi qu'aux étudiants des premières années de l'enseignement supérieur qui n'auraient pas encore acquis ce vocabulaire de l'actualité.

AVANT-PROPOS DE LA NOUVELLE ÉDITION

En raison de la demande sans cesse croissante dont *English in the News* est l'objet, nous avons jugé opportun de présenter une nouvelle édition pour mieux répondre à l'attente des utilisateurs.

Plus encore qu'une mise à jour, il s'agit d'une refonte complète de l'ouvrage, entraînant un renforcement général, tant pour les articles de journaux que pour les exercices et les séquences de vocabulaire.

A signaler, notamment, l'apparition d'un nouveau chapitre : *Les spectacles et les mass média* et la division en deux chapitres de chacun des chapitres *L'économie* et *La politique*.

English in the News s'adresse à tous ceux qui souhaitent et doivent acquérir le vocabulaire anglais de l'actualité, en particulier aux étudiants des premières années de l'enseignement supérieur.

Le corrigé placé à la fin du livre joue un rôle de guide sémantique, de test d'évaluation, de source d'information ; il incite l'utilisateur à la recherche personnelle.

Nous exprimons notre vive gratitude aux journaux qui nous ont permis de reproduire certains de leurs articles :
The Daily Telegraph
The Evening Post (Bristol)
The Financial Times
The Guardian
The Independent
The Sunday Times
The Times
The Western Morning News

et les agences de presse :
Associated Press
Reuter

CONSEILS D'UTILISATION

A tous nous conseillons de commencer par le « Vocabulaire à haute fréquence », choisi dans un chapitre quelconque du livre, en fractionnant l'étude de ce vocabulaire selon les possibilités ou les disponibilités de chacun. Étudier ensuite les articles situés en fin de chapitre en faisant les exercices qui les accompagnent. Enfin, vérifier le travail en le confrontant au corrigé situé à la fin de l'ouvrage. La lecture des journaux et des magazines ainsi que la compréhension des informations à la radio seront sensiblement améliorées par cette pratique.

Dans le cadre scolaire, la même méthode pourra être appliquée, aussi bien dans un travail individuel que dans un travail guidé par le professeur. Ceux qui intègrent l'actualité à leur enseignement savent que les possibilités d'exploitation sont innombrables. Contrairement à ce que l'on pourrait penser, les élèves ne rechignent pas à fournir l'effort nécessaire pour acquérir du vocabulaire, en particulier par des exercices, des débats, des exposés ou des dossiers.

La connaissance d'un vocabulaire spécifique permet des échanges plus riches sur les textes étudiés. Elle permet par ailleurs d'aborder certains sujets sans avoir recours aux « textes à thèmes » ; l'expérience prouve que ces derniers sont difficiles à utiliser en classe.

Enfin, cette connaissance doit faciliter la préparation des candidats aux examens oraux, en particulier à l'épreuve du baccalauréat ; rappelons qu'il est prévu d'introduire dans cette épreuve un document choisi par l'examinateur en dehors de la liste des textes étudiés.

Afin d'enrichir le travail de préparation, nous suggérons que l'étudiant, pour chaque exercice du type QCM ou « vrai/fraux », justifie sa réponse en se référant à l'article de journal concerné. Nous suggérons également d'entraîner les élèves à l'écoute de courts bulletins d'information d'une radio de langue anglaise. Cet exercice de compréhension complètera de façon profitable les exercices proposés dans *English in the News*.

ABRÉVIATIONS

Abréviations utilisées dans l'ouvrage :

EC	The European Community	**CE**	La Communauté Européenne
GB	Great Britain	**qch.**	quelque chose
sb.	somebody	**qn.**	quelqu'un
sth.	something	**fam.**	familier
US	the United States		

SIGNES PHONÉTIQUES

Sons voyelles

[i:] seat [i] sit [e] head [æ] bag [ɑ:] car [ɔ] clock

[ɔ:] four [u] put [u:] moon [ʌ] bus [ə:] bird [ə] about

Sons diphtongues

[ei] make [əu] so [ai] five [au] now [ɔi] toy [iə] near

[ɛə] chair [ue] pure

Sons triphtongues

[aiə] fire [auə] power [eiə] player

Sons consonnes

[b] book [d] down [f] four [dʒ] Jim [g] go [r] river

[ʃ] shop [k] cap [l] list [ɫ] well [m] mist [ʒ] measure

[n] narrow [p] part [t] top [s] simple [ð] this [j] yes

[v] above [w] where [z] pens [ŋ] long [θ] think

1

POLLUTION — LA POLLUTION

VOCABULAIRE A HAUTE FRÉQUENCE

General Background	Contexte général
to pollute /pə'lu:t/	polluer
pollution	la pollution
environment /in'vaiərənmənt/	l'environnement
an environmentalist /in,vaiərən'mentəlist/	un défenseur de l'environnement
nature conservation	la protection de la nature
a conservationist	un protecteur de la nature
to discharge	décharger, déverser
to dump	rejeter, déposer
to get rid of, to dispose of	se débarrasser de
disposal	la destruction, l'élimination
waste	les déchets
rubbish, refuse trash, garbage (US)	les ordures
litter	les détritus
a tip, a dump	une décharge, un dépôt
to escape	s'échapper
to leak	fuir, s'échapper
a sewer /'sju:ə/	un égout
sewage	les eaux usées
a sewage farm a sewage plant	une station d'épuration
a sewage system	un réseau d'assainissement
to treat	traiter
treatment	le traitement
a standard	une norme
to recycle	recycler
biodegradable	biodégradable
the greenhouse effect	l'effet de serre
global warming	le réchauffement du globe

Industry and Car Pollution	La pollution industrielle et automobile
chemistry /ˈkemistri/	la chimie
a chemical	un produit chimique
a gas	un gaz, une vapeur
exhaust fumes	les gaz d'échappement
to release	libérer, dégager
an emission	une émission, un rejet
a release	un dégagement, une émanation
sulphur /ˈsʌlfə/	le soufre
mercury	le mercure
lead /led/	le plomb
lead-free, unleaded	sans plomb
acid rain	la pluie acide
the ozone layer	la couche d'ozone

Farm Pollution	La pollution agricole
a pesticide	un pesticide
an insecticide	un insecticide
to spread	épandre
a fertiliser	un engrais
manure /məˈnjuə/	le fumier
nitrates /ˈnaitreits/	les nitrates
to spray	pulvériser
a spray	une pulvérisation
a crop	une récolte
intensive	intensif
factory farming	l'élevage hors-sol
farm produce	un produit agricole
organic farming	l'agriculture biologique

Oil Pollution	La pollution pétrolière
crude oil	le pétrole brut
an oil tanker	un pétrolier
a cargo	une cargaison
a tank	une cuve
to spill	(se) déverser
a spill	un déversement
an oil spill	une marée noire
a slick	une nappe
a detergent /diˈtə:dʒənt/	un détersif
marine life	le milieu marin
oiled	mazouté
to soil, to foul /faul/	salir, souiller
to clean up	nettoyer

Nuclear Pollution	La pollution nucléaire
a power plant a power station	une centrale
fuel	le combustible
enriched uranium	l'uranium enrichi
to cool	refroidir
a cooling system	un système de refroidissement
a breakdown	une panne
a fault	un défaut, une anomalie
faulty	défectueux
radiation /ˌreidiˈeiʃn/	les radiations
radioactivity	la radioactivité
radioactive	radioactif
a level	un niveau, une teneur
a reading	un relevé (de mesure)
a fall-out	une retombée
dust	la poussière
to process	traiter
to reprocess	retraiter
material	des matières
to bury	enfouir
burying	l'enfouissement
to store	stocker
storage	le stockage
a site	un emplacement, un site

Consequences	Les conséquences
a hazard	un risque
to affect, to hit	toucher, atteindre
to do harm to sth.	faire du mal à qch.
harmful	nuisible
safe, harmless	sans danger, inoffensif
noxious	nocif
to endanger	mettre en danger
to threaten /ˈθretn/	menacer
a threat	une menace
to poison	empoisonner
toxic, poisonous	toxique, empoisonné
a dose	une dose
a trace, a residue	une trace, un résidu
drinking water	l'eau potable
underground waters	les nappes souterraines
water supply	l'alimentation en eau
the food chain	la chaîne alimentaire
to damage	endommager
damage	les dégâts

to destroy	détruire
destruction	la destruction
a disaster	un désastre
a catastrophe / kəˈtæstrəfi/	une catastrophe
to contaminate	contaminer
a contamination	une contamination
to compensate	indemniser
compensation	une indemnité

EXPRESSIONS

to deplete the ozone layer	appauvrir la couche d'ozone
to pose a threat	constituer une menace
dumping at sea	les décharges en mer
to break down a slick	réduire une nappe
the balance of nature	l'équilibre de la nature

VOCABULAIRE COMPLÉMENTAIRE

General Background	**Contexte général**
the rainforest	la forêt tropicale
a pollutant	un polluant
ecology /iˈkɔlədʒi/	l'écologie
an ecologist	un écologiste
ecological /iːkəˈlɔdʒikl/	écologique
an ecosystem	un écosystème
strewn with / littered with	jonché de
a bottle bank	un conteneur de collecte du verre
sewage sludge	les boues d'épuration

Industry and Car Pollution	**La pollution industrielle et automobile**
to mix	(se) mélanger
a mixture	un mélange
an effluent	un effluent
sump oil	l'huile de vidange
carbon	le carbone
chlorofluorocarbons (CFCs)	les chlorofluorocarbones
a propellant	un propulseur

an aerosol	un aérosol
a substitute / an alternative	un produit de substitution / un produit de remplacement
depletion	l'appauvrissement
nitrogen	l'azote
an oxide	un oxyde
carbon dioxide	le gaz carbonique
catalytic	catalytique
asbestos	l'amiante
dioxin	la dioxine

Farm Pollution — La pollution agricole

a weedkiller	un désherbant
a herbicide	un herbicide
weeds	les mauvaises herbes
a fungicide	un fongicide
to apply	appliquer, mettre (sur)
an application	une application, un usage
slurry	le lisier
fish farming	l'élevage piscicole
a battery	une batterie (élevage)
animal feed	les aliments pour animaux
a hormone	une hormone
an additive	un additif
a preservative	un produit conservateur
a substance	une substance
anabolic steroids	les stéroïdes anabolisants

Oil and Nuclear Pollution — La pollution pétrolière et nucléaire

to flush, to swill tanks	dégazer
the hull	la coque
the hold	la soute
an oil rig	une plate-forme de forage
to drill	forer
offshore	au large
to drift	dériver
ashore	vers la côte
a containment boom	un barrage flottant
a skimmer vessel	une barge de récupération
spent fuel	le combustible usé
a reprocessing plant	une usine de retraitement
leukaemia /luːˈkiːmiə/	la leucémie
caesium /ˈsiːziəm/	le césium
a containment structure	une enceinte de confinement

the core	le cœur
a fast breeder	un surgénérateur
plutonium	le plutonium
to expose to	mettre en contact avec
exposure	l'exposition la mise en contact

Consequences	**Les conséquences**
to concentrate	concentrer
a concentration	une concentration
to build up	accumuler
a build-up	une accumulation
a living tissue /'tiʃu:/	un tissu vivant
cancer	le cancer
a carcinogen /kɑ:'sinədʒən/	un produit cancérigène
carcinogenic	cancérigène
wildlife	la faune et la flore
habitat	le biotope
long-term	à longue échéance
endangered species	les espèces menacées
extinct	disparu
a strain	une souche (d'espèce)
resistant	insensible, résistant

Practise your vocabulary.

1. What are the main causes of river, sea and air pollution?
2. How can our food become polluted?
3. Why do many people worry about nuclear waste?
4. Can you think of any major pollution disasters that have happened in France or elsewhere in the world?
5. An ever greater number of people are becoming aware that pollution is a major issue. Can you quote a few facts to support this claim?

Energy proposals

Plans to phase out nuclear power stations and introduce tax incentives to curb pollution and save fuel resources were announced yesterday by the Liberal Democrats in their energy Green Paper, which proposes developing wind, wave and tide power.

The Independent, March 1, 1990

Help for farms hit by fall-out

Hill farmers still suffering from restrictions imposed following the Chernobyl nuclear disaster a year ago are to get further government compensation.

Latest readings from the hills of Cumbria and North Wales show that radiation levels rose appreciably over the winter despite predictions from government scientists that they would fall.

About 450 farms and more than 300,000 sheep are still affected by the restrictions on movement and slaughter, and the number is increasing daily as this season's lambs are born.

Mr Michael Jopling, the Agriculture minister, told the annual meeting of the Young Farmers Association in Blackpool that an early announcement on compensation could be expected.

Readings taken last May after a radioactive raincloud from Chernobyl swept over Britain showed levels four times higher than the Government's safety limit.

There are still pockets where readings six times higher are being recorded, and showing no signs of falling.

The Guardian,
May 4, 1987

1 **Match each word (1-5) to its definition (A-E).**

1. fall-out
2. compensation
3. a reading
4. slaughter
5. level

A. the result given by a measuring instrument
B. that of the sea is the reference for the height of mountains
C. radioactive dust coming down from the atmosphere
D. money paid by someone responsible for a loss
E. killing animals for meat

2 **Read the article and say whether the following statements are true (T) or false (F).**

1. The Chernobyl disaster happened in 1987.
2. The farmers hit by the fall-out had already received some compensation.
3. It is easy to understand why hilly areas were most affected.

4. Bad weather brought down the radiation levels.
5. Scientists knew exactly how radiation levels might change.
6. The farmers were not allowed to sell their sheep freely.
7. The Agriculture minister didn't reveal the amount of compensation.
8. In fact, there was no real danger as shown in the radiation levels, at any time.
9. Reading the article makes us aware of the particularly dangerous features of nuclear pollution.

3 **Pick out the word used three times to show continuity and the two verbs meaning "going up".**

4 **"To compensate" and "to observe" are the verbs corresponding to the nouns "compensation" and "observation". Find the verbs corresponding to the nouns below.**

a) contamination b) multiplication c) destination
d) participation e) examination f) privatisation
g) demonstration h) organisation i) consideration
j) frustration k) preservation l) discrimination
m) education n) exaggeration o) provocation

5 **Read the article and find three different ways of expressing a future idea.**

6 **Test your knowledge. Only one statement of each pair is correct. Which one?**

A. In 1990, nuclear power stations were supplying France with about 75% of its electricity.
B. 40% of French electricity consumption was generated by nuclear power stations in 1990.

C. Most French reactors are pressurised water reactors.
D. Britain was a pioneer in the use of these reactors.

Dutch clean spill

The Dutch Coast Guard was cleaning up an oil spill 18 miles long and 700 yards wide yesterday. Dutch television said authorities believed the oil had been deliberately pumped into the North Sea by an unnamed ship. AP.

April 2, 1990

Milk banned

The Hague (Reuter) – The Netherlands banned the sale of milk and meat from 39 farms after milk was found to contain high levels of toxic dioxin from waste incineration plants near farmland.

March 1, 1990

HOPS THREATENED

By James O'Brien

Hop harvests are being threatened by an aphid which is becoming resistant to the sprays used to keep it under control.

Researchers at the Ministry of Agriculture experimental farm at Rosemaund, near Hereford, are now looking for a new combination of chemicals to fight the aphid invaders.

Unless an effective spray is found, hop growers may be faced with crop losses similar to those suffered in the 19th century because of the same creature, the Damson Hop Aphid.

A new range of insecticides was formulated in the 1940s and since then the aphid has survived four groups, a total of 15 separate spray types. Tests are being carried out on the last group, pyrethroids, which until recently had provided adequate results.

Mr Frederick Dickens, a technical officer in charge of the hop enterprise, said the spray in use at present was the "last bastion".

He said: "Once the aphid becomes totally resistant we shall have to look at a completely new insecticide which has yet to be developed. It is becoming a serious problem."

The aphids have made a heavy attack on the hop crop this year and they have been more difficult to control. Ladybirds and other natural predators of the aphid have failed to contain their numbers...

September 29, 1987

1 **Match the definitions (A-F) to the words (1-6).**

1. hops	A. brought to a more advanced stage so that it can be used
2. aphid	B. a small insect with red elytra marked with black spots

3. spray	C. the produce of cultivated plants, such as vegetables, fruit, etc.
4. crop	D. fine particles of a liquid sent through the air
5. developed	E. a plant whose flowers are used in the making of beer
6. ladybird	F. a small insect which feeds on plants

2 **Choose the appropriate endings for the following sentences.**

1. Chemical spray
A. had done some harm to the hops.
B. had done little harm to the aphids.
C. had made the hops more resistant.

2. At Rosemaund, researchers were
A. carrying out experiments on familiar chemicals.
B. trying to find an entirely new chemical.
C. combining their efforts for the first time.

3. What the third paragraph expresses is best defined by
A. a condition and an identity.
B. a resemblance and an identity.
C. a condition, a resemblance and an identity.

4. It seems that in their fight against aphids
A. they used the same chemical for too long.
B. they tried hard to be effective.
C. they didn't carry out enough tests.

5. Mr Frederick Dickens sounded
A. pessimistic.
B. optimistic.
C. unconcerned.

6. As regards pest control, this article mentions
A. only chemical means.
B. only organic means.
C. both organic and chemical means.

7. After reading the article, we get the impression
A. it concerns a minor incident.
B. pests are completely under control.
C. it reveals a worrying development.

3 Looking for words.

1. Write in full:
a) the 1940s b) the 1950s c) the 1960s.
2. Write in full:
a) the 70s b) the 80s c) the 90s.
3. The journalist wrote that ladybirds "had failed" to control the aphids. What are the two verbs he could have used if they had been successful?

"It's what Alfred would have wanted—he was such a keen ecologist."

2

THE ECONOMY I — L'ÉCONOMIE I

VOCABULAIRE A HAUTE FRÉQUENCE

Variations and Assessment	Variations et évaluations
to go up, to rise	monter
a rise in prices	une hausse des prix
inflation	l'inflation
inflationary	inflationniste
to drop, to fall / to come down	baisser, diminuer
a fall, a drop in prices	une baisse des prix
expensive, dear	cher
to cost	coûter
cost	le coût
costly	coûteux
cheap	bon marché
worth	la valeur
to be worth	valoir
a profit	un bénéfice
profit	le profit
profitable, economic	rentable
a benefit	un avantage, une allocation
to gain	gagner
a gain	un gain, une plus-value
a loss	une perte
loss-making / unprofitable / uneconomic	non rentable
economical	économique, économe
to survey	étudier
a survey	une étude, une enquête
a price index	un indice des prix
to assess, to estimate	évaluer
an assessment / an estimate	une évaluation
to value	évaluer, apprécier
face value	la valeur nominale
a figure	un chiffre
a billion	un milliard
to exceed	dépasser

a trend	une tendance
to grow	croître
growth	la croissance
a rate	un taux
to expand	(se) développer
expansion	l'expansion
to thrive, to prosper	prospérer
thriving, prosperous	prospère
prosperity	la prospérité
a boom	une vague de prospérité
to decline	décliner
a decline	un déclin, une baisse
a crisis	une crise
a recession	une récession
to improve	(s') améliorer
an improvement	une amélioration
to recover	reprendre, se rétablir
recovery	la reprise, le rétablissement

Measures / Les mesures

a policy	une politique
to increase, to raise	augmenter
an increase	une augmentation
to bring down	abaisser, diminuer
to reduce, to cut back	réduire
a reduction, a cut-back	une réduction
to curb	juguler, maîtriser
a curb	un frein
austerity	l'austérité
to restrict	restreindre
a restriction	une restriction
to devalue	dévaluer
a devaluation	une dévaluation
to subsidise	subventionner
a subsidy	une subvention
to boost	stimuler, relancer
a boost	une relance

Taxes / Les impôts

to tax	taxer, imposer
taxation	l'imposition, la taxation
income tax	l'impôt sur le revenu
a taxpayer	un contribuable
the rates	les impôts locaux (avant 1990)
the poll tax	les impôts locaux
the community charge	les impôts locaux

to collect	lever, recouvrer
a tax collector	un percepteur, un receveur

Money — L'argent

cash	les espèces
a banknote, a bill (US)	un billet de banque
a coin	une pièce
currency	les devises, la monnaie
to earn	gagner
earnings	les gains
to spend	dépenser
spending	les dépenses
expenses	les dépenses, les frais
to owe money	devoir de l'argent
to save	économiser
savings	les économies
to invest	investir
an investment	un investissement
an investor	un investisseur
a sum	une somme
an amount	un montant
to amount to	s'élever à, revenir à

Production — La production

to produce	produire
a product	un produit
production, output	la production
productivity	la productivité
farm produce	les produits agricoles
to manufacture	fabriquer
a manufactured product	un produit fabriqué
goods, wares	les marchandises
a warehouse	un entrepôt
a commodity	une marchandise primaire
supply	l'offre
demand	la demande
to consume	consommer
consumption	la consommation
a grade	une qualité, une catégorie

Trade and the EC — Le commerce et la CE

business	les affaires
a customer	un client
to sell retail	vendre au détail
a sale	une vente
to buy wholesale	acheter en gros

to purchase	acheter, acquérir
a purchase	un achat, une acquisition
to order	commander
an order	une commande
to supply sb. with sth. to provide sb. with sth.	fournir qch. à qn.
to charge	faire payer
a charge	les frais, un prix à payer
an invoice	une facture
a bill, a check (US)	une note, une addition
to bargain	marchander, négocier
a bargain	une (bonne) affaire
a (bargain) sale a clearance sale	les ventes de soldes
an auction	une vente aux enchères
to trade	faire du commerce
a market	un marché
to advertise	faire de la publicité
advertising	la publicité
an advertisement /əd'vɜ:tismənt/	une publicité
an adman	un publicitaire
to import /im'pɔ:t/	importer
an import /'impɔ:t/	une importation
to export /eks'pɔ:t/	exporter
an export /'ekspɔ:t/	une exportation
home trade	le commerce intérieur
foreign trade overseas trade	le commerce extérieur
to share	partager
a share	une part
a trade gap	un déficit commercial
a deficit	un déficit
a surplus	un excédent
an outlet	un débouché un point de vente
to compete with sb.	concurrencer qn.
competition	la concurrence
competitive	compétitif
competitiveness	la compétitivité
to protect	protéger
protectionism	le protectionnisme
a protectionist	un protectionniste
customs	la douane
a duty	un droit
a tariff	un tarif douanier
a barrier	une barrière
a quota /'kwəutə/	un quota
free trade	le libre-échange

a free trader	un libre-échangiste
to join sth.	adhérer à qch.
a summit	un sommet
a directive	une directive
a single market	un marché unique
to veto sth.	opposer son veto à qch.
a veto	un veto

EXPRESSIONS

it's worth trying	cela mérite d'être essayé
it sells well	cela se vend bien
to sustain a loss to suffer a loss	subir une perte
to plough back profits	réinvestir les bénéfices
to get value for money	en avoir pour son argent
to earn one's living	gagner sa vie
the standard of living	le niveau de vie
the cost of living	le coût de la vie
to fetch a high price	atteindre un prix élevé
to foot the bill	payer l'addition
the retail price index	l'indice des prix de détail
the consumer price index	l'indice des prix à la consommation
a package of measures	un ensemble de mesures
pay as you earn	le prélèvement à la source
value added tax	la taxe à la valeur ajoutée
to drive a hard bargain	ne pas faire de cadeau
the gross national product	le produit national brut
the gross domestic product	le produit intérieur brut
the balance of trade	la balance commerciale
the balance of payments	la balance des paiements
a current account deficit	un déficit de la balance des paiements courants
a monetary compensatory amount	un montant compensatoire monétaire
a co-responsibility levy	une taxe de co-responsabilité
the Exchange Rate Mechanism	le mécanisme des changes
the European Monetary System	le système monétaire européen
a European Member of Parliament	un député européen

VOCABULAIRE COMPLÉMENTAIRE

Variations and Assessment	Variations et évaluation
a profit margin	une marge bénéficiaire
cost effective	rentable, d'un bon rapport coût-performance
dirt cheap	très bon marché
to stagnate	stagner
stagnation	la stagnation
to slacken, to slow down	ralentir
a slack, a slow-down	un ralentissement
to dip	fléchir, baisser
a dip	un fléchissement
to slump	baisser brutalement
a slump	une chute brutale un marasme
to plummet	dégringoler
to collapse	s'effondrer
a collapse	un effondrement
a setback	un revers, une déconvenue
a recession	une récession
to look up to pick up	se redresser, reprendre
an upturn, an upswing	un redressement
a downturn, a downswing	un fléchissement
to flourish	prospérer
flourishing	florissant, prospère
to overheat	surchauffer
to soar	s'envoler
to shoot up	monter en flèche
to revive	reprendre
a revival	une reprise
to make up for sth.	compenser qch.
to offset	contrebalancer, compenser
in real terms	en argent constant
a spin-off	une retombée
an analyst	un analyste, conjoncturiste
a pundit	un expert
a prospect	une perspective
to forecast	prévoir
a forecast, an outlook	une prévision

## Measures and Taxes	## Les mesures et les impôts
the Budget	le budget
public expenditure	les dépenses publiques
monetary	monétaire
monetarism	le monétarisme
deflation	la déflation
deflationary	déflationniste
to levy	percevoir, prélever
a levy	un prélèvement, une taxe
a fee	un droit, une redevance
to squeeze	comprimer
a squeeze	une compression, une rigueur
to bite	faire de l'effet
to nationalise	nationaliser
nationalisation	la nationalisation
to privatise	privatiser
privatisation	la privatisation
regulation	la réglementation
deregulation	la déréglementation
an incentive	une mesure d'incitation
to grant	accorder
a grant	une aide financière
to finance, to fund	financer
funds	les fonds
to slash	réduire radicalement
a slash	une réduction radicale
to jack up	relever (les prix)
to hike prices (US)	relever les prix
a price hike (US)	une augmentation des prix
to index	indexer
index-linked	indexé
a tax haven	un paradis fiscal
tax relief	un dégrèvement fiscal
a tax allowance	un abattement fiscal
tax evasion	la fraude fiscale
to cap taxes	fixer un plafond à l'impôt
revenue	les rentrées fiscales

## Money	## L'argent
a hard currency	une devise forte
to waste	gaspiller
waste, wastage	le gaspillage
to squander	dilapider, gaspiller
to skimp	lésiner, économiser

thrift	l'épargne
thrifty	économe
a spendthrift	un panier percé
extravagant, profligate	dépensier, prodigue
extravagance, profligacy	la prodigalité

Production — La production

just-in-time production, zero stock production	la production à flux tendu
a shortage	une pénurie
a shortfall	une insuffisance, un manque
a glut	un engorgement
to contract	s'engager par contrat
a contract	un contrat
a contractor	un entrepreneur
enterprise	l'esprit d'entreprise
to subcontract	sous-traiter
a subcontractor	un sous-traitant
a tender	une soumission
to exhaust	épuiser
exhaustion	l'épuisement
a brand	une marque commerciale
a make	une marque, une fabrication
to target	cibler
a target	une cible
custom made	fait sur commande

Trade and the EC — Le commerce et la CE

a niche	un créneau, un marché
a shopper	un client de magasin
a good buy	un bon achat
barter	le troc
to haggle	marchander
to shop around	comparer les prix
to refund	restituer de l'argent
a refund	une restitution d'argent
a discount	une remise
a rebate	un rabais
into the bargain	par-dessus le marché
hard sell	l'agressivité de vente
to undercut, to undersell	vendre moins cher que
to net	encaisser des bénéfices
consumer goods	les biens de consommation
capital goods	les biens d'équipement
business premises	les locaux commerciaux

mail-order	l'achat par correspondance
a middleman	un intermédiaire
to insure /in'ʃuə/	assurer
insurance	l'assurance
to underwrite	souscrire
a policy	une police
a premium	une cotisation, une prime
invisibles	les exportations et les importations invisibles
an imbalance	un déséquilibre
to corner	accaparer
to fix prices	s'entendre sur les prix
price fixing	l'entente illicite
a contribution	une contribution une cotisation
an MEP, a Euro MP	un député européen
set-aside land	les terres incultes, gelées

BIGGEST SLUMP IN SHOP SALES SINCE 1979

By Anne Segal, Economics Correspondent

High street retailers suffered their biggest setback for 11 years last month when the volume of goods sold fell by 2.8 per cent despite early summer sales and the continued buoyancy of spending on food.

The last time spending fell faster was in July, 1979, when retail volumes crashed by a freak 9.9 per cent in the wake of the first Conservative Budget.

There was also a dip in spending this time a year ago, but that was caused by disruption on the rail, tube and buses.

The figures provided a welcome boost for [the] Chancellor, after several months in which consumers seemed impervious to his interest rate medicine. The drop is taken by analysts as evidence that the squeeze is finally working.

The steepness of the June downturn came as a surprise in the City where a decline of just 0.8 per cent had been forecast after the 1.4 per cent spending rise in May. The figures nevertheless provided further confirmation of the sluggish trends in retailing identified by the Confederation of British Industry just a few hours earlier...

The Daily Telegraph,
July 17, 1990

1 **Choose the appropriate explanation (A-J) for each of the following words or phrases (1-10).**

1. slump 2. setback 3. buoyancy 4. freak 5. in the wake of 6. dip 7. Chancellor 8. impervious 9. steepness 10. sluggish

A. slight temporary decline B. a tendency to rise C. heavy drop D. following immediately E. not influenced by F. slow-moving G. abnormal or extremely unusual H. it stops progress or development I. suddenness and importance J. British counterpart of the Finance Minister in other countries

2 **Choose the appropriate endings for the following sentences.**

1. To use the word "slump" for a 2.8 per cent fall was
A. an exaggeration.
B. quite appropriate.
C. rather surprising.

2. "Despite early summer sales and the continued buoyancy of spending on food" means
A. although business was good in early summer and food sold as usual...
B. although business was good in early summer and consumers bought less food...
C. although they had sales and food sold as usual...

3. 1979 seemed to be a key date as it was, directly or indirectly, mentioned
A. once.
B. twice.
C. three times.

4. Spending declined temporarily a year before because people
A. found it more difficult to go shopping.
B. had less money.
C. boycotted public transport.

5. The Chancellor's aim was to
A. increase consumer spending.
B. reduce consumer spending.
C. boost the economy.

6. The outlook given by City analysts was
A. quite accurate.
B. partly inaccurate.
C. entirely wrong.

7. Although it never appears in the article, one word should be at the back of the reader's mind. It is
A. inflation. B. deficit. C. devaluation.

3 **The relative value is often shown by a percentage, for example 25 per cent. It can also be indicated by a fraction, for example, one quarter or one fourth.**
Use the smallest numerator and write down in full the fractions corresponding to the following percentages.

A. 5% B. 10% C. 20% D. 33% E. 40% F. 50%
G. 60% H. 66%

BRITISH-MADE NISSANS WILL COUNT IN QUOTAS

By David Usborne and Michael Harrisson

The controversy over the status of Japanese cars made in Britain deepened yesterday after the European Commission confirmed that the vehicles would be counted in import quotas due to be negotiated with Japan.

Frans Andriessen, the EC Commissioner for Foreign Trade, who is to begin exploratory talks in Tokyo later this month, said he expected that "some account" would have to be taken of Japanese assembly lines in Britain when the new controls come in.

His position partially sides him with the French government, which argued fiercely at a ministers' meeting here on Monday that UK-assembled Japanese cars, at present Nissan models made in Sunderland, should be considered Japanese rather than of EC origin.

Mr Andriessen nevertheless insisted that while the Nissan cars may be brought into the quota calculations, there would be no question of impeding their sale throughout all Community countries, including France.

The EC now has to reach an arrangement with Japan, as bilateral quotas operated by Britain, France, Italy and Spain will become untenable when the single market starts in 1992.

Mr Andriessen envisages scrapping all national restrictions by then, but agreeing a set of voluntary export curbs which would apply for a transitional period. The Commission would expect the arrangements to last five years, the French and Italians would prefer five years more.

The Independent,
May 7, 1990

1 **Say whether the statements are true (T) or false (F).**

1. The negotiations with Japan will be carefully prepared.
2. The third paragraph takes up the idea of "some account".

3. Mr Andriessen indicated that the decision was not final.
4. Exports of Nissan cars from Japan itself will not be affected by the status problem.
5. All EC members had introduced quotas for the import of Japanese cars.
6. France favoured a five-year transitional period.
7. The words "foreign competition" underlie the whole passage.

2 **Match the explanations (A-F) to the words (1-6).**

1. status 2. side with 3. argued 4. fiercely 5. impeding 6. scrapping.

A. restricting, obstructing B. tried to prove C. abolishing D. legal position E. vehemently, intensely F. associate oneself with

3 **"To deepen" is to make deeper. In the same way, how would you say:**

1. to make blacker 2. to make darker 3. to make weaker 4. to make shorter 5. to make wider 6. to make higher 7. to make longer 8. to make worse 9. to make less

4 **Test your knowledge. Only one statement is correct. Which one?**

A. After devaluation exports become cheaper and imports get more expensive.
B. The effect of devaluation is to raise the prices of exports and bring down the prices of imports.

"There were no survivors, sir. I'm afraid we'll have to find another test market."

3

THE ECONOMY II — L'ÉCONOMIE II

VOCABULAIRE A HAUTE FRÉQUENCE

Real Estate	Les biens immobiliers
to own	posséder
ownership	la propriété
property	les biens
a landlord	un propriétaire immobilier
a tenant	un locataire
to let	donner en location
to rent	prendre en location
rent	le loyer
an estate agent / a realtor (US)	un agent immobilier
housing	le logement
a council house	une HLM

Wealth and Poverty	La richesse et la pauvreté
rich, wealthy	riche
well-off	aisé, bien nanti
poor	pauvre
the poverty line	le seuil de pauvreté
hard up, broke	fauché
a need	un besoin
the needy	les nécessiteux
misery	la misère
hardship	les difficultés matérielles
destitute	sans ressources, démuni
destitution	l'indigence
deprived	déshérité
deprivation	le dénuement
underprivileged	défavorisé
to assist	assister, aider
assistance, welfare	l'assistance, l'aide
the welfare system	l'aide sociale
the welfare state	l'État providence

Banking	**Les banques**
a bank	une banque
an account	un compte
a balance	un solde
a cheque book	un carnet de chèques
to draw money	tirer de l'argent
a draft	un retrait
to overdraw	tirer à découvert
an overdraft	un découvert
to borrow	emprunter
to lend	prêter
a loan	un prêt, un emprunt
a mortgage /ˈmɔːgidʒ/	un prêt immobilier
a debt	une dette
a debtor	un débiteur
credit	le crédit
a creditor	un créancier
to pay back, to repay	rembourser
a payment	un paiement, un versement
repayment	le remboursement
to settle	régler
a settlement	un règlement
overdue	un retard, échu
interest	l'intérêt
the exchange rate	le taux de change

Companies	**Les sociétés commerciales**
to set up	(s') établir
to establish	fonder
a firm, a business	une firme, une affaire
a multinational	une multinationale
to manage, to run	diriger, gérer
management	la direction, la gestion
a partner	un associé
a partnership	une société de personnes
a company, a corporation (US)	une société commerciale
a joint-stock company	une société par actions
the head office, the headquarters	le siège social
capital	le capital
a stake, a holding	une participation au capital
a chairman, a president (US)	un président

a managing director a chief executive	un directeur général
a director	un administrateur
a board of directors	un conseil d'administration
an executive	un cadre
an annual report	un rapport d'activité
a general meeting	une assemblée générale
an agenda	un ordre du jour
turnover	le chiffre d'affaires
a dividend	un dividende
to bid for	faire une offre pour
a bid	une offre
to take over	racheter prendre le contrôle de
a take-over bid	une offre publique d'achat

Ailing Companies — Les sociétés en difficulté

running costs	les frais de fonctionnement
overheads, fixed costs	les frais généraux
assets	l'actif
liabilities	le passif
cash flow	le flux de liquidités
a lame duck	un canard boîteux
to prop up	soutenir, étayer
to bail out	renflouer
mismanagement	la mauvaise gestion
to fail, to go bust to go bankrupt to go under, to collapse	faire faillite
a failure, a bankruptcy	une faillite
a receiver	un administrateur judiciaire
to wind up, to liquidate	liquider
liquidation	la liquidation

The Stock Exchange — La Bourse des valeurs

stock, securities	les valeurs, les titres
a share	une action
a bond	une obligation
to subscribe	souscrire
a deal	une transaction
a dealer	un opérateur
a bearer	un porteur
a stockbroker	un agent de change

to quote	coter
a quotation	une cote, un cours
to close	clôturer
close /kləuz/	la clôture
to open up	ouvrir en hausse
to close down	clôturer en baisse
to yield	rapporter
a yield	un rapport

Market Fluctuations — Les fluctuations du marché

steady	stable
firm	ferme
dull	inactif, maussade
volatile	nerveux, fébrile
to slide	baisser
a slide	une baisse
to fall back	se replier
a fall-back	un repli
a crash	un krach
to rally	se raffermir
a rally	un raffermissement
to level off	se stabiliser
to ease	se détendre
buoyant /ˈbɔiənt/	soutenu
brisk	actif, animé

EXPRESSIONS

to go on welfare	s'inscrire à l'aide sociale
to feel the pinch	sentir les effets de la rigueur
to tighten one's belt	se serrer la ceinture
to make ends meet	joindre les deux bouts
a balance of account	un solde de compte
a statement of account	un relevé de compte
to be in the red	être à découvert, en déficit
to be in the black	être créditeur
to go public	introduire en Bourse
to dabble on the Stock Exchange	boursicoter
to buy forward	acheter à terme
to sell short	vendre à découvert
an all-time high	un record à la hausse
an all-time low	un record à la baisse

the Securities and Exchange Commission (US) the Securities and Investment Board (GB)	la Commission des opérations de Bourse
to mount a take-over bid	lancer une OPA
to drive out of business	contraindre à la fermeture
to go out of business	cesser son activité
to file for bankruptcy to file under chapter 11 (US)	déposer son bilan
to go belly up (US)	faire faillite
to be placed into receivership to go into liquidation	entrer en liquidation

VOCABULAIRE COMPLÉMENTAIRE

Wealth, Poverty and Housing	**La richesse, la pauvreté et le logement**
affluent	fortuné
affluence	l'abondance, l'opulence
means	les moyens
means testing	l'évaluation des ressources
purchasing power	le pouvoir d'achat
down and out	sans le sou
dough /dəu/	le fric, l'oseille
National Insurance	la Sécurité sociale
social security	l'aide sociale
food stamps (US)	les bons de nourriture
a bread line a soup kitchen	une soupe populaire
a lease	un bail
a housing estate	un lotissement
a slum	un taudis
homeless	sans logis
to sleep rough	dormir dehors
housing benefit	l'allocation de logement
child benefit	les allocations familiales
planning permission	le permis de construire
town planning	l'urbanisme
a property developer	un promoteur immobilier

Banking | Les banques

the base rate	le taux de base
the discount rate	le taux d'escompte
the lending rate	le taux de l'argent
a flat rate	un taux uniforme
a composite rate	un taux composé
a merchant bank	une banque d'affaires
a building society	une mutuelle d'épargne-logement
a blank cheque	un chèque en blanc
a bounced cheque	un chèque refusé
a dud	un chèque sans provision
to default	ne pas honorer, se dérober
a cash point	un distributeur de billets
a credit card	une carte de crédit
a quid (fam. GB)	une livre sterling
a buck (fam. US)	un dollar
to loan	prêter
a loan shark	un usurier
a bad debt	une créance impayée
arrears /ə'riəz/	les arriérés
money supply	la masse monétaire

Companies | Les sociétés commerciales

a concern	une entreprise, une firme
to undertake	entreprendre
an undertaking	une opération entreprise
a limited partnership	une société en commandite
a private company	une société à responsabilité limitée
a public company	une société anonyme
a parent company	une société mère
a sister company	une société du même groupe
a holding	une société de portefeuille
an offshoot	une branche
a subsidiary	une filiale
a joint venture	une société mixte
a front company	une société écran
a deputy chairman a vice-president (US)	un vice président
working capital	les fonds de roulement
returns, proceeds	les recettes, les rentrées

corporate tax	l'impôt sur les sociétés
pre-tax profits	les bénéfices avant impôt
a balance sheet	un bilan comptable
an auditor	un commissaire aux comptes
to issue shares	émettre des actions
a share issue	une émission d'actions
a rights issue	une émission de droits d'attribution
a golden share	une action à droit particulier
to allot	attribuer
an allotment	une attribution
to float	lancer (une société, des actions)
a flotation	une émission financière
a high flier	une personne de haut vol
a Yuppie	un jeune cadre dynamique

Companies as Targets — Les sociétés pour cible

to amalgamate, to merge	fusionner
an amalgamation, a merger	une fusion
a management buy-out	un rachat par les cadres
a leveraged buy-out	un rachat avec emprunt
a bidder	un repreneur
a predator	un rapace boursier
a raider	un assaillant
a raid	une attaque, un assaut
a white knight	un chevalier blanc
a (friendly) suitor	un repreneur amical
an insider	un initié
insider dealing or trading	le délit d'initié
a watchdog	un conseil de surveillance

The Stock Exchange — La Bourse des valeurs

a stock market	une place boursière
a portfolio	un portefeuille (valeurs)
equities	les actions ordinaires
gilt-edged securities	les valeurs sans risque (obligations d'État)
blue chips	les actions des grandes sociétés
junk bonds	obligations de pacotille
a bull	un spéculateur à la hausse

a bear	un spéculateur à la baisse
the spot market	le marché au comptant
the futures market	le marché à terme•
to hedge	se couvrir (risque)
the Mercantile Exchange	la Bourse des marchandises

Practise your vocabulary.

1. How do shopkeepers earn their living?
2. How does competition work?
3. What consequences can competition have on firms?
4. What are some of the objectives of the European Community?
5. Explain how a loan works.

Ford buys more stock in Jaguar as price drops

London – Ford Motor Co., the US automobile giant, bought up millions of bargain-value shares in Britain's luxury carmaker, Jaguar plc, as stock prices tumbled worldwide.

Ford which is vying for the prestige-laden Jaguar name with its American rival, General Motors Corp., the world's biggest automobile manufacturer, said on Tuesday it had doubled its shareholding to 10.4 percent.

Ford said it had bought or agreed to buy 19.04 million Jaguar shares by the end of trading on Monday, when prices slumped by the biggest margin since the Black Monday collapse of October 1987.

Stephen Reitman, automobile-industry analyst at UBS/Phillips and Drew, a London brokerage house, said Ford had been buying heavily in New York, when stocks began sinking, and in London on Monday before markets began to recover.

Ford, the world's N° 2 carmaker, has said it aims to boost its stake in Jaguar to 15 percent, the maximum allowed by Britain's Conservative government when it privatised the former state-run firm in 1984. That restriction expires in 1990, but it could be withdrawn before then if Jaguar so requested.

Jaguar, its elite image built on exclusivity, high-powered engines and sports cars, has spurned Ford's advances as an "unwelcome surprise". Jaguar says it needs a cash injection but wants to stay independent...

Reuter,
October 18, 1989

1 **Match the explanations (A-E) to the words (1-5).**

1. tumbled
2. vying
3. laden
4. state-run
5. spurned

A. loaded
B. fell sharply and suddenly
C. nationalised
D. rejected as worthless
E. competing

2 **Say whether the following statements are true (T) or false (F).**

1. The low price of shares is underlined twice in the first paragraph.
2. Ford didn't seem anxious to keep a low profile.
3. Ford seems to have acted at the wrong time.
4. Ford already had a stake in Jaguar.
5. The total number of Jaguar shares runs to over 100 million.
6. Jaguar could do nothing against the government restriction.
7. Ford was acting as a white knight.

3 **Test your knowledge. Only one statement is correct in each pair. Which one?**

A. In the end, Jaguar was taken over by Ford.
B. Eventually, the successful bid for Jaguar was made by General Motors.

C. In Britain, the rate of interest usually varies for mortgages even after repayment of the loan has started.
D. Once set, the interest rate on mortgages remains constant.

4 **A name of a place can actually mean the people living and working there. For example, Wall Street is synonymous with the world of finance in New York City. Match the place names (1-10) with their synonyms (A-J).**

1. The City
2. New Scotland Yard
3. Westminster
4. N° 10 Downing Street
5. Whitehall

A. high-ranking officials in government offices
B. the Prime Minister and the Cabinet
C. the financial world in central London
D. London police headquarters
E. British Members of Parliament

6. The White House	F. Congress
	G. the Defense Department
7. Capitol Hill	H. the US President and Administration
8. Madison Avenue	I. the President and his aides
9. The Pentagon	J. advertising and public relations firms in New York
10. The Oval Office	

WALL STREET STOCKS FALL SHARPLY OVER FEARS ON TOKYO MARKET

Reuter in New York

Wall Street stocks fell sharply yesterday on worries about the falling Tokyo market and fears that a squeeze on credit in the United States might drive the economy into a recession.

The Dow Jones industrial average had fallen 47.52 points, or 1.73 per cent, to 2,680.71 by mid-afternoon, extending losses to a third successive session.

In the broader market, losing shares raced past gainers by a margin of more than four to one. The volume on the New York Stock Exchange was a brisk 121.2 million shares.

"The Japanese stock market fall is the main feature in Wall Street's decline," said Ken Ducey, senior vice-president at S.G. Warburg. He said there were concerns among bankers and Federal Reserve officials that a growing squeeze on credit could lead to a recession. "It's one market factor and a long-term one."

Japanese stocks fell yesterday, extending the year's losses to more than 23 per cent. The Nikkei average lost 964 points, or 3.1 per cent, after falling by 456 on Tuesday. On Wednesday Japanese markets were closed for a national holiday.

Wall Street has long regarded the Tokyo market as overvalued especially relative to US stock prices, and analysts here have long said a fall was overdue. Investors were unsettled, however, by the degree of Tokyo's losses.

March 23, 1990

1 **Say whether the following statements are true (T) or false (F).**

1. All the blame was laid on Tokyo for the fall in Wall Street.
2. The article quotes very accurate figures.
3. It was the first fall in the Dow Jones.
4. Business was very slack on the Stock Exchange as prices were dropping.
5. Ken Ducey thought the trend would be short-lived.
6. The first quarter of 1990 was especially bad for Japanese stocks.
7. This fall in stock prices wasn't really unexpected.

2 **Looking for words. Read the article first and then:**

1. Pick out three nouns showing that investors were not completely confident about market prospects.
2. Pick out five nouns with a negative undertone as regards the economic situation or the trend in the market.
3. Find two verbs expressing a sense of direction and both associated with the same noun.

3 **"Overvalued" and "overdue" can be divided into two parts, the first one being "over". Find the adjectives constructed in the same way which correspond to the following explanations.**

1. receive too much money for one's work 2. is asked to pay too high a price 3. too much money has been taken out of this account 4. the river banks are under water 5. is really delighted 6. didn't wake up in due time 7. they were not strong enough to resist 8. too many people applied for shares in the issue

4 **Stockmarkets publish an index to show the trend. It is an average of a number of stocks; some may go up and others down on the same day. Choose the appropriate stock market (A-E) for each of the indexes or averages (1-5).**

1. The Dow Jones average	A. Paris
2. The Nikkei average	B. Frankfurt
3. The FT/SE 100 Share Index (Footsie)	C. New York
4. The CAC 40 index	D. Tokyo
5. The DAX index	E. London

5 Fill in each blank with a word from the following list. Use each word once only. Verbs are given in the infinitive.

further nearly slump down currencies early
to report

RECORD US TRADE DEFICIT HITS DOLLAR

By Steve Levinson, Economics Correspondent

Central banks around the world moved to check another ____________ in the dollar yesterday, after the United States ____________ that its trade deficit in October was a record £17.6bn.

Despite concerted central bank intervention, the dollar dropped sharply against other major ____________. It closed in London at a record low of Yen 129.40, and lost ____________ three pfennigs to close at DM1.6365. It fell ________ in New York and by ____ afternoon there was _____ to DM1.6245.

The Independent,
December 11, 1987

4

THE THIRD WORLD — LE TIERS MONDE

VOCABULAIRE A HAUTE FRÉQUENCE

Development and Population	Le développement et la population
to develop	(se) développer
under-developed	sous-développé
developing	en voie de développement
industrialised	industrialisé
to settle	s'installer
a settlement	un peuplement, une colonie
a refugee /ˌrefjuːˈdʒiː/	un réfugié
a camp	un camp
literacy	l'alphabétisation
illiteracy	l'analphabétisation
literate	alphabétisé
illiterate	analphabète

Production	La production
to feed on, to live on	se nourrir de, vivre de
to supply sb. with sth. to provide sb. with sth.	fournir qch. à qn.
a supply	un approvisionnement
rainfall	les précipitations
a pump	une pompe
a well	un puits
to drill, to bore	forer
to irrigate	irriguer
irrigation	l'irrigation
to grow, to cultivate	faire pousser, cultiver
to produce	produire
farm produce	les produits agricoles
farming	l'agriculture
to farm	cultiver
to plough	labourer

to sow	semer
seeds	les semences
a crop	une récolte
a harvest	une moisson
livestock	le cheptel
a flock of sheep	un troupeau de moutons
a herd of cattle	un troupeau de bétail
to graze	paître
grazing land / pasture land	les pâturages
self-sufficient	auto-suffisant
self-sufficiency	l'auto-suffisance
raw materials	les matières premières
a commodity	une marchandise primaire

Famine — La famine

a desert	un désert
drought /draut/	la sécheresse
a shortfall	une insuffisance
a shortage	une pénurie
a lack	un manque
scarce	rare, peu abondant
scarcity	la rareté, la disette
hunger	la faim
hungry	affamé
underfed	sous-alimenté
malnutrition	la malnutrition
malnourished	malnutri
to starve	manquer de nourriture
starvation	le manque de nourriture
an area	une zone, une région

Aid — L'aide

funds	les fonds
to collect, to raise	recueillir, collecter
relief	les secours
relief workers	les équipes de secours
a charity	une organisation caritative
a voluntary agency	une agence bénévole
a voluntary organisation	une organisation humanitaire
a relief organisation	une organisation d'aide
relief aid / humanitarian aid	l'aide humanitaire
to donate	faire don
a donation	un don
a donor	un donateur

a consignment, a shipment	un envoi
to deliver	livrer
a delivery	une livraison
a tool	un outil
equipment	l'équipement
a project a scheme /ski:m/	un projet
to advise	conseiller

EXPRESSIONS

to wear out the soil	épuiser le sol
the standard of living	le niveau de vie
the poverty line	le seuil de pauvreté
help with no strings attached	l'aide sans contrepartie

VOCABULAIRE COMPLÉMENTAIRE

Population	**La population**
a nomad	un nomade
nomadic	nomade *(adj.)*
a hut	une hutte
a cabin	une case
a shack	une cabane
a shanty town	un bidonville
forced resettlement	l'exode forcé
an influx	un afflux
an exodus	un exode

Production	**La production**
famished	affamé
a protein /'prəuti:n/	une protéine
a deficiency	une carence
topsoil	la terre végétale
to erode	éroder
erosion	l'érosion
staple food	la nourriture de base
food crops	les cultures vivrières
cash crops	les cultures de rente
a swarm of locusts	un essaim de criquets
to plague	tourmenter, affliger
a plague, a scourge /skə:dʒ/	un fléau

fallow land	la terre en jachère
to exploit	exploiter
exploitation	l'exploitation
deforestation	le déboisement
to fell, to chop down	abattre
reforestation	le reboisement
barren	stérile, aride
to desertify	désertifier
desertification	la désertification
a resource /ri'sɔ:s/	une ressource
soya bean, soybean (US)	le soja
cocoa	le cacao
sugar cane	la canne à sucre
manioc, cassava	le manioc
to plunder	piller
plunder	le pillage

Outside Aid — L'aide extérieure

to appeal to	faire appel à
an appeal	un appel
a campaign	une campagne
a volunteer /ˌvɔlən'tiə/	un volontaire
a convoy	un convoi
a hand-out	une aumône
to grant	accorder
a grant	une aide financière
tied aid	l'aide liée
untied aid	l'aide non liée
a string	une contrepartie
to pay back, to repay	rembourser
repayment	le remboursement
to reschedule	rééchelonner
to write off (a debt)	annuler (une dette)
to cooperate	coopérer
self-help	l'auto-assistance

Specific Diseases — Les maladies spécifiques

sanitation	les installations sanitaires
rampant	très répandu
cholera	le choléra
malaria /mə'lεəriə/	la malaria, le paludisme
typhus /'taifəs/	le typhus
leprosy	la lèpre
a leper /'lepə/	un lépreux

FIVE MILLION PEOPLE IN DANGER AS ETHIOPIAN FOOD CRISIS GROWS

From Blaine Harden in Addis Ababa

Ethiopia is moving inexorably towards another food emergency with an estimated five million people at risk after the failure of the rains in the north and central highlands.

The government last week requested about one million tons of food aid from Western donors, who agree that the sudden and severe drought in June and July has rendered the country vulnerable to another famine. Rainfall in some areas was as low or lower than 1984 and 1985.

The US embassy in Addis Ababa has sent an emergency request to Washington asking that 115,000 tons of food be sent here immediately. The EEC and the UN World Food programme are considering requests for immediate shipment of another 85,000 tons of food. It takes four or five months for food supplies to reach the highlands.

The government has warned that unless about 200,000 tons of food aid arrives by the end of the year, the northern regions of Eritrea and Tigre will go hungry and the masses of destitute and starving people will try to migrate.

A US Government survey last month reported a total crop failure in Eritrea and a 75 per cent crop loss in Tigre.

The head of the Government's Relief and Rehabilitation Commission, Mr Berhanu Jembere, sent a letter last week to a senior UN official here requesting food aid for next year...

The Guardian,
September 14, 1987

1 Match the explanations (A-C) to the words (1-3).

1. failure	A. made it known in advance
2. warned	B. detailed investigation
3. survey	C. the opposite of success

2 Choose the appropriate endings for the following sentences.

1. The emergency was created by

A. overpopulation.

B. drought.
C. nomadism.

2. The Ethiopian Government
A. wanted no outside aid.
B. wasn't aware of the shortage.
C. drew attention to the issue.

3. One of the major problems facing donors was
A. delivery.
B. production.
C. coordination.

4. Famine would cause people
A. to protest.
B. to move.
C. to plunder.

5. The US Government survey made it plain that the situation was
A. not an emergency.
B. under control.
C. a disaster.

6. Famine risks in Ethiopia seemed to be
A. comparatively well monitored.
B. a new issue.
C. largely ignored.

3 **Fill in the blanks with the following words. Use each word only once. Put the verbs in the correct form.**

relief starvation to supply to chop down
home sale migration fuel

1. The plan was __________ food to people in their ______ regions and avoid __________ to famine camps.
2. Because wood is the most important source of ______, the remaining forests are being __________ either for use in cooking food or for __________ in the market-place.
3. __________ officials in Addis Abada foresee mass ______ on the scale of the famine of 1984-85.

4 **Test your knowledge Only one statement is correct in the pair below. Which one?**

1. About 70% of the world's population lived in developing countries in 1990.
2. Developing countries accounted for about 30 % of the world's population in 1990.

STIRRINGS IN TEA AS STRUCTURE OF MARKET CHANGES

By Michael Prest

Tea is good evidence for the much-maligned thesis that developing country commodity producers have suffered over a long period from falling terms of trade for important exports. Put simply, they have to exchange steadily more tea for each unit of manufactured imports.

Behind the statistics lies a simple contradiction: world tea consumption is growing only slowly, while productivity has risen considerably. As one of the classic cash crops, tea has benefited from the "green revolution" in agricultural productivity. Tea drying and manufacturing, important parts of the business, were forced to become more efficient by the oil price shocks of the 1970s.

World tea consumption is rising by about 2.8 per cent a year, rather faster than population growth. The crop fell from 2.27 million tonnes in 1985, to 2.23 million the year after and is estimated to have been 2.3 million tons in 1987, when it probably exceeded consumption.

The balance between supply and demand in this market is fine because tea is a very responsive crop, unlike coffee or cocoa. Tea is a perennial bush, so different shoots can be picked roughly once a fortnight. Within the longer term productivity trend, therefore, output can respond quite quickly to changes in demand.

What has altered the market is the almost continuous undersupply of good quality teas. Without the demand for medium to higher qualities, which is a function of greater prosperity, average tea prices might be even lower.

The Independent,
February 1, 1988

1 Match the explanations (A-F) to the words (1-6)

1. stir 2. evidence 3. maligned 4. exceeded
5. shoots 6. fortnight

A. given a bad reputation B. new growth of a plant
C. two weeks D. indication, sign that proves
E. move a spoon round in liquid F. was higher than

2 **Say whether the following statements are true (T) or false (F).**

1. The journalist makes a play on words in the headline.
2. Care is taken to make the meaning plain (first paragraph).
3. Tea is a drink, therefore it is a food crop.
4. No energy is needed in the production of tea.
5. People are drinking less and less tea.
6. It is comparatively easy for tea-growers to meet demand.
7. More good quality teas are needed.
8. We are made aware of the link between demand and price level.

3 **Looking for words. Read the article and pick out:**

1. A key word in the first paragraph – the main export of developing countries.
2. A noun and an adjective, in the second paragraph, constantly used in the world of competition.
3. The name of a fundamental law in a free-market economy (fourth paragraph).

4 **Practise your vocabulary.**

1. What are the main difficulties that Third World countries have to face?
2. How can industrialised countries contribute to the development of the Third World?
3. Would it be a good thing to send our crop surpluses on a regular basis to reduce malnutrition?
4. Can you think of any reasons why outside aid isn't always as generous as it pretends to be?
5. How can Third World countries be affected by the pollution problems in the industrialised world?

5

EMPLOYMENT L'EMPLOI

(voir Variations et évaluation p. 24)

VOCABULAIRE A HAUTE FRÉQUENCE

Industries and Workplaces	**Les industries et les lieux de travail**
to employ	employer
a firm, a business	une entreprise
a plant, a factory	une usine
a steelworks	une aciérie
coal-mining	les charbonnages
shipbuilding	la construction navale
a shipyard	un chantier naval
management	la direction, la gestion
to manage, to run	diriger, gérer

Employment and Employees	**L'emploi et les employés**
to train	former
vocational training	la formation professionnelle
skilled	qualifié
unskilled	non qualifié
labour	la main-d'œuvre
to qualify for	(se) rendre apte à
qualifications	les qualifications
a workman, a worker	un ouvrier
the labour force the workforce, the staff	le personnel
a blue collar worker	un ouvrier
a white collar worker	un employé
a technician	un technicien
an engineer /ˌendʒiˈniə/	un ingénieur
an executive	un cadre
a job	un emploi

wages	les salaires hebdomadaires
a salary	un salaire mensuel
pay	la paie, le salaire
a bonus	une prime
working conditions	les conditions de travail
the working population	la population active
a job centre	une agence pour l'emploi
a situation, a post	une situation, un poste
a vacancy	une offre d'emploi
job seeking or hunting	la recherche d'un emploi
to apply for	être candidat à
an application	une demande
a C.V.	un C.V.
to interview	recevoir
an interview	un entretien
a self-employed worker	un travailleur indépendant
self-employment	le travail indépendant
to retire /ri'taiə/	prendre sa retraite
retirement	la retraite
early retirement	la retraite anticipée
a pension	une pension, une retraite
a pensioner	un retraité

Ups and Downs — Les variations

advanced technology high technology	la technologie avancée
an order	une commande
an order book	un carnet de commandes
a robot /'rəubɔt/	un robot
productive	productif
productivity	la productivité
to compete with sb.	concurrencer qn.
competition	la concurrence
competitive	compétitif
competitiveness	la compétitivité
overtime	les heures supplémentaires
short time working	le chômage partiel
part time working	le travail à temps partiel
temporary employment	le travail intérimaire
manning levels	les effectifs
overmanning	le sureffectif

Consequences	Les conséquences
a job loss	une perte d'emploi
to axe, to shed jobs	supprimer des emplois
redundant	licencié
to make redundant	licencier
a redundancy	un licenciement
a redundancy payment	une indemnité de licenciement
to lay off (US)*	licencier
a lay-off (US)	un licenciement
a closure, a shut-down	une fermeture
to create	créer
a creation	une création

Unemployment	le chômage
unemployed, on the dole	au chômage
out of work, jobless	sans emploi
to register	s'inscrire
to be eligible for to be entitled to	avoir droit à
to claim sth.	percevoir qch.
a claimant	un bénéficiaire
unemployment benefit	l'allocation de chômage
income support	l'allocation complémentaire
a school-leaver	un jeune sorti de l'école
to issue figures	publier des chiffres
to adjust	corriger
an adjustment	une correction
seasonal distortion	les variations saisonnières
to retrain	recycler
a scheme /ski:m/	un plan
a course	un stage

EXPRESSIONS

a low-paid job	un emploi mal rétribué
a dead-end job	un emploi sans avenir
to work overtime	faire des heures supplémentaires
to go out of business	cesser son activité, fermer
driven out of business	contraint à la fermeture
to give notice to sb.	donner son préavis à qn.

* Cette signification a tendance à se répandre en Grande-Bretagne.

to give a new job to sb.	reclasser qn.
a temporary employment agency	une agence de travail intérimaire
a seasonally-adjusted figure	un chiffre corrigé des variations saisonnières
to attend a crash course	suivre un stage intensif
on-the-job training	la formation permanente

VOCABULAIRE COMPLÉMENTAIRE

Employment and Employees	L'emploi et les employés
an apprentice	un apprenti
apprenticeship	l'apprentissage
a factory hand	un ouvrier
a casual worker	un ouvrier intérimaire
the labour market	le marché de l'emploi
a graduate	un diplômé universitaire
a skill	une compétence technique
a shift	une équipe de travail
to engage, to take on to hire	engager, embaucher
a prospect	une perspective
a career /kəˈriə/	une carrière
secure	stable, sûr
job security	la sécurité de l'emploi
fringe benefits	les avantages divers
perks	les à-côtés
flexible	flexible
flexibility	la flexibilité
a workaholic	un bourreau de travail
to skive	tirer au flanc
moonlighting	le travail au noir

Ups and Downs	Les variations
work sharing	le partage du travail
turnover	la rotation
natural wastage	les départs en retraite et les départs volontaires
compulsory redundancies	les licenciements secs
to refurbish	rénover
refurbishment	la rénovation
to computerise	informatiser

computerisation	l'informatisation
to automate	automatiser
automation	l'automatisation
robotisation	la robotisation

Consequences	**Les conséquences**
to restructure	restructurer
restructuring	la restructuration
to run down	réduire l'activité
a run-down	une réduction d'activité
to streamline / to slim down	dégraisser
a development area	une zone de conversion

OVERWORKING KILLS JAPANESE BOSSES

By Robert Whymant in Tokyo

A growing number of Japan's top executives are dying at work from stress and overwork, prompting medical officials to appeal for a less frenzied pace of work to be adopted.

The problem attracted attention after the sudden death on July 12 of Yoshio Ohno, president of a leading cosmetic firm, Shiseido. His immediate predecessor had died in office from a heart complaint three years earlier.

Ohno's death, from pneumonia, brought to eight the number of presidents and chairmen of top corporations who have succumbed to what are known as "business war deaths" so far this year. Last year the figure was 34. Most of them were younger than 65-year-old Ohno, and the most common cause was heart failure.

But doctors who have studied these cases say stress and impossible work schedules in up to 24-hour days were at least aggravating factors, if not directly responsible.

"It must have been years of accumulated fatigue", said a colleague of Ohno, citing the president's 20 trips to France alone in one year.

Like Ohno, the president of Seiko Epson, Ichiro Hattori, 55, thought he was fit, and even took time off for exercise. But on May 26 he suddenly collapsed and died while playing golf.

Friends said Hattori was under great strain in coping with the strong yen, which slashed the watch and computer firm's export earnings...

The Daily Telegraph,
July 17, 1987

1,000 jobs at tractor firm axed

One thousand jobs at Massey-Ferguson, the Coventry tractor makers, are to be cut, staff were told yesterday.

The company asked for 800 volunteers for redundancy from its hourly-paid workforce by July.

It also wants to lose 200 white-collar staff by the same date.

The cuts will leave the company with 2,500 people, 4,000 fewer than in 1978.

An announcement from the company also warned that it wanted to cut wage rates to improve its chances in the worldwide farm machinery market.

Massey-Ferguson once produced 80,000 machines a year, but declining markets have halved that output.

There has been a lasting decline in world demand for new tractors.

The company remained the world market leader in tractor production with 18.2 per cent of the market last year, and had increased its world share of new markets for the past three years.

The company has spent more than £22 million at Coventry, its largest tractor-making plant, in the last five years. It plans to spend a further £5-6 million this year on modernisation.

April 17, 1987

1 **Say whether the following statements are true (T) or false (F).**

1. It was bad news for the staff.
2. The company hoped to get some cooperation from its employees.
3. The 1,000 workers made redundant were all manual workers.
4. The company had a workforce of 4,000 in 1978.
5. Massey-Ferguson produced 40,000 tractors in 1986.
6. The firm was in trouble mainly because of foreign competition.
7. They planned to increase spending on modernisation.
8. Management thought no other remedy than an increase in productivity would be needed.
9. The process described in the article is a typical one.

2 **Looking for words. Read the article and find synonyms for:**

1. to shed 2. labour force 3. reductions 4. to boost 5. formerly 6. production 7. works.

3 **An adjective expressing a colour can take on a special meaning in association with a noun, as in "white-collar staff". Such is the case in the following list and you have to match a number (1-9) and a letter (A-I).**

1. blue-collar worker	A. a comparatively new university
2. red carpet	B. bureaucratic methods, official formalities
3. redbrick	C. treatment received by very important people
4. green belt	D. person regarded as worthless by others
5. red light area	E. non-striking worker
6. blackmail	F. protected area of countryside around a city
7. black sheep	G. a lot of prostitutes in such a district
8. blackleg	H. manual worker
9. red tape	I. threats made to obtain something

4 **Fill in each blank with a word from the following list. Use each word once only. Verbs are given in the infinitive.**
executives unemployment pace overwork quarter to computerise seasonally-adjusted labour staff

1. Government plans ___________ the social security system are being dangerously rushed to cut _________ by a ___________ , a union alleges today.
2. A growing number of Japan's top ___________ are dying at work from stress and ___________ , prompting medical officials to appeal for a less frenzied _________ of work.
3. ___________ in October fell to below 10 per cent of the ___________ force for the first time since July 1982. The ___________ total of adult jobless fell by 58,400 to 2,714,000 or 9.8 per cent.

Ford restores merit pay

The Ford Motor Company has told its salaried workers in the US and Canada that merit pay will be restored because of the company's belief that the worst of the auto sales slump is over. The move affects about 55,000 workers.

The Guardian, April, 2, 1990

UK'S FUTURE "DEPENDS" ON JOB TRAINING

by Ngaio Crequer, Education Editor

Britain's prosperity depends on a complete change of attitude by young people to the need for training, John MacGregor, Secretary of State for Education, said yesterday.

He was speaking at the end of a visit to West Germany to discover why the Germans are so successful at encouraging people to undertake vocational training.

"The Germans told us that their economic miracle was due to their emphasis on the skilled worker", Mr MacGregor said. "In the world of the future you will not get a job unless you have qualifications and skills and the aptitude to acquire them. Training is crucial to our prosperity."

He said there was a tradition in Germany that it was important and necessary to get qualifications. He called on Britain to change its attitude. In the UK, 90 per cent of the 16-year-olds are involved in education or training, but this falls to 68 per cent at the age of 17 and drops to 35 per cent at 18. In West Germany the figures are 96 per cent at 16, 92 per cent at 17 and 80 per cent at 18.

Only 4 per cent of German pupils leave school without a school leaving certificate. The overwhelming majority of pupils go on to take a combination of work and vocational training. Mr MacGregor said that a recent UK survey showed that 40 per cent of people at work did not expect to receive any training and did not even see it had any relevance...

The Independent,
June 14, 1990

1 **Match the explanation (A-D) to the words (1-4).**

1. undertake
2. emphasis
3. overwhelming
4. relevance

A. that cannot be resisted
B. take up, start
C. connection with something
D. special importance given to something.

2 **Choose the appropriate endings for the sentences.**

1. Mr MacGregor addressed himself to

A. the unemployed.

B. teenagers.
C. middle-aged people.

2. The article was published in June 1990
A. but one obsolete term appears twice.
B. and every word is still valid.
C. but one obsolete term appears once.

3. According to Mr MacGregor, what you will have to acquire to get a job is shown by
A. one word.
B. two words.
C. three words.

4. Training in Germany is given
A. solely in schools.
B. both in schools and in firms.
C. solely in firms.

5. In Britain, working people are
A. completely unaware of the need to train on the job.
B. fully aware of the need to train on the job.
C. largely unaware of the need to train on the job.

3 **"Careless" is the opposite of "careful", but some of the adjectives ending in "less" or "ful" do not have their opposites constructed in this way. Can you pick them out in the following list?**

1. painless 2. successful 3. pitiful 4. heartless
5. ruthless 6. joyless 7. plentiful 8. mindless
9. dutiful 10. eventful 11. jobless 12. spotless
13. powerful 14. defenceless 15. merciful
16. countless 17. fearless

4 **Practise your vocabulary.**

1. How do people set about looking for a job?
2. What things may be important to people when they think of the sort of job they would like to have?
3. What changes have taken place in a lot of firms over the past decade?
4. Why do some employers sometimes find it difficult to recruit new workers even in times of heavy unemployment?
5. Describe the situation of people that are made redundant.
6. Can governments take any measures to reduce unemployment?

6

DISPUTES AND TENSION — CONFLITS ET TENSIONS

(voir *Variations et évaluation* p. 24)

VOCABULAIRE A HAUTE FRÉQUENCE

The World of Labour	Le monde du travail
a wage earner	un salarié
a trade union a labor union (US)	un syndicat ouvrier
a member	un adhérent
a trade unionist	un syndicaliste
a local branch	une section locale
a shop steward	un délégué syndical
management	la direction
a pay claim	une revendication salariale
a mass meeting	une assemblée générale
a rally	un rassemblement
to ballot	consulter par vote
a ballot	une consultation

International Tension	La tension internationale
tense, strained	tendu
a relationship a relation	une relation
a chill	un refroidissement
a strain	une tension
to deteriorate	se dégrader
a deterioration	une dégradation
detente	la détente
to ease	se détendre
a summit	un sommet
a conference	une conférence
a bloc	un bloc

a pact	un pacte
to violate	violer
a violation	une violation
to impose	imposer
a sanction	une sanction
a boycott	un boycott
an embargo /imˈbɑ:gəu/	un embargo

Negotiations — Les négociations

a delegate	un délégué
to talk	s'entretenir, discuter
a talk	un entretien, une discussion
to claim	revendiquer, affirmer
a claim	une revendication une affirmation
to demand	exiger
a demand	une exigence
to organise, to stage	organiser
to consider	examiner, étudier
a consideration	un examen, une étude
to bargain, to negotiate	négocier
the bargaining table the negotiating table	la table des négociations
an agenda	un ordre du jour
an issue	une question, un problème
to propose	proposer
a proposal	une proposition
to offer	offrir
an offer	une offre
a step	une mesure une disposition
a move	une décision une initiative
a gesture	un geste
a formula /ˈfɔ:mjulə/	une formule

Disagreement — Le désaccord

to reject, to turn down	rejeter, décliner
a rejection	un rejet
to refuse	refuser
a refusal	un refus
a stalemate	un point mort
a deadlock	une impasse
an obstacle, a hurdle	un obstacle
to disagree	être en désaccord
to warn	avertir, mettre en garde

a warning	un avertissement
to threaten /'θretn/	menacer
a threat	une menace
to break off	rompre
to break down	(se) rompre, échouer
to walk out	quitter la salle
a walk-out	une sortie, un départ
to fail to	ne pas réussir à
a failure	un échec

Industrial Disputes — Les conflits sociaux

to walk out	débrayer
a walk-out	un débrayage
to stop work	cesser le travail
a work stoppage	un arrêt du travail
to strike to go on strike	se mettre en grève
a strike	une grève
a non-striker	un non-gréviste
a scab	un jaune
to disrupt	perturber
a disruption	une perturbation
a picket	un piquet (de grève)
to picket	installer un piquet
to suspend	mettre à pied, suspendre
a suspension	une mise à pied
to dismiss, to sack	renvoyer, limoger
a dismissal, a sacking	un renvoi

A Settlement — Un règlement

to resume	reprendre
a resumption	une reprise
to compromise	transiger
to give in, to yield	céder
to grant	accorder
to draw up, to work out	établir, élaborer
a compromise	un compromis
a breakthrough	une avancée
a term	une condition
to accept	accepter
an acceptance	une acceptation
to agree	être d'accord
an agreement, a deal	un accord
to manage to to succeed in	réussir à
to solve, to resolve	résoudre, solutionner
to overcome	surmonter

a difference	une divergence un différend
to settle	régler
a spokesperson	un(e) porte-parole
a statement	une déclaration

Ending a Strike	**La fin d'une grève**
a peace formula	une formule d'apaisement
a pay settlement a pay deal	un accord salarial
a pay award	une augmentation de salaire
to call off a strike	terminer une grève

EXPRESSIONS

Trades Union Congress	la Fédération des syndicats
to press a claim to lodge a claim	déposer une revendication
to come to a halt	s'arrêter (production)
to come to a standstill	être paralysé
to refer to arbitration	soumettre à l'arbitrage
to take industrial action	entamer une action revendicative
to cross the picket line	franchir le piquet de grève
to call out a strike	appeler à la grève
the strike won't go ahead	la grève n'aura pas lieu
to sequestrate the assets	placer les avoirs sous séquestre
to fight to the bitter end	lutter jusqu'au bout
to enter into negotiations	entamer des négociations
a round of talks	une série d'entretiens
to come to a deadlock	aboutir à une impasse
to break the deadlock to break the stalemate	sortir de l'impasse
to pave the way	préparer la voie
to prepare the ground	préparer le terrain
to strike a deal	conclure un accord
to come to an agreement to reach an agreement	parvenir à un accord
an across-the-board increase	une augmentation générale uniforme
to put to a vote	soumettre au vote
to report for work to turn up for work	se présenter à l'embauche

to be back to normal	être de retour à la normale
to break off diplomatic links	rompre les liens diplomatiques
to sever diplomatic ties	rompre les relations diplomatiques
a show of strength	une démonstration de force
a trial of strength a test of strength	une épreuve de force
gunboat diplomacy	la diplomatie de la canonnière
to make representations	élever une protestation
to issue a statement	publier une déclaration

VOCABULAIRE COMPLÉMENTAIRE

The World of Labour	Le monde du travail
collective bargaining	la négociation collective
the shopfloor	les ouvriers, la base
rank and file	la base
an official	un responsable
closed shop	le monopole de l'embauche
organised labour	les ouvriers syndiqués
a pay packet	une enveloppe de paie
a pay check (US)	une paie, un salaire
working conditions	les conditions de travail
working hours the working week	la durée du travail
works patterns	les tableaux de service
safety standards	les normes de sécurité

International Tension	La tension internationale
to go sour	se gâter
to escalate	monter, faire monter
escalation	l'escalade
a breach	une rupture
a diplomat /ˈdipləmæt/	un diplomate
diplomacy /diˈpləuməsi/	la diplomatie
diplomatic	diplomatique
an embassy	une ambassade
an ambassador /æmˈbæsədə/	un ambassadeur

at large, roving	itinérant
a hot line	un téléphone rouge
to normalise	normaliser
normalisation	la normalisation
an envoy	un envoyé, un émissaire
an emissary	un émissaire
a counterpart an opposite number	un homologue
the West Bank	La Cisjordanie
the Gaza Strip	la bande de Gaza
the Near East	le Proche-Orient
the Middle East	le Moyen-Orient

Negotiations — Les négociations

a stand, a stance	une attitude, une position
to founder	achopper
a sticking point a stumbling block	un point d'achoppement un blocage
to be bogged down to be mired down	s'enliser
a counterproposal	une contre-proposition
a row /rau/	une querelle
a pre-condition	un préalable
to thrash out	élaborer par discussion
a draft	un projet
a draft agreement	un protocole d'accord
a framework	un cadre
a showdown	un bras de fer
confrontation	l'affrontement
a deadline	une limite de temps une date butoir
behind the scenes backstage	dans les coulisses
to attempt to	tenter de
an attempt	une tentative
to mediate	servir d'intermédiaire
a mediator	un médiateur
to defuse	désamorcer
to placate, to appease	apaiser
an appeasement	un apaisement
to conciliate	concilier
conciliation	la conciliation
conciliatory /kən'siliətəri/	conciliant
to trade off for	échanger contre
a trade-off	un échange, un arrangement
a bargaining chip	une monnaie d'échange
an accord	un accord

Industrial Disputes — Les conflits sociaux

a grievance /'gri:vəns/	une doléance
pace	les cadences
working practices	l'organisation du travail
job demarcation	le domaine de compétence
to consult	consulter
a consultation	une consultation
strike pay	l'allocation de grève
a blackleg	un jaune
a strike breaker	un briseur de grève
a lightning strike	une grève éclair
a selective strike	une grève limitée, ponctuelle
an all-out strike	une grève totale
a token strike	une grève d'avertissement
a go-slow, a work-to-rule	une grève du zèle
a sympathy strike	une grève de solidarité
a sit-in	une grève avec occupation
an official strike	une grève préparée, légale
an unofficial strike	une grève spontanée
a wildcat strike	une grève sauvage
a rolling strike	une grève tournante
an indefinite strike	une grève illimitée
a hunger strike	une grève de la faim

Consequences — Les conséquences

to cripple, to paralyse	paralyser
to lay off	mettre en chômage technique
lay-off	le chômage technique
to black	mettre sur la liste noire
a court ruling	une décision de justice
to discipline	punir, sanctionner
to fire	virer
an industrial tribunal	un conseil de prud'hommes
unfair dismissal	le licenciement abusif
to reinstate	réintégrer
reinstatement	la réintégration

Ending a Strike — La fin d'une grève

to crumble	s'effriter
to drift back	retourner progressivement
a drift-back	un retour progressif

Practise your vocabulary.

1. What part do trade unions play in the world of labour?
2. What are some of the changes that took place in international relations during the late 1980s and early 1990s?
3. What are some of the typical features of negotiations in an industrial dispute?
4. What are the various reasons why workers go on strike?
5. What can strikers do, while they are on strike, to draw attention to their problems?

BAe PLANT ENDS 23-WEEK DISPUTE

By Martin Whitfield, Labour Correspondent

One of the longest strikes in British manufacturing ended yesterday when 1,200 workers at British Aerospace's Kingston plant in south-west London, voted to accept a deal for a 37-hour week.

The 23-week dispute was part of the engineering unions' campaign for shorter working time, but dragged on despite deals at the company's factories at Chester and Preston.

One of the main stumbling blocks was the planned abolition of tea breaks to compensate for the two-hour reduction in the working week. A compromise means that the 15-minute breaks will be cut to 10 minutes with the afternoon rest scrapped next year. The strike halted production of fuselages for the Harrier jump jet.

Dave Gollop, secretary of the union negotiating committee, maintained that the stoppage was worthwhile despite the fact that workers only received £75-a-week in strike pay. "It has been a real struggle but we have stuck it out because we believe that all engineering workers should have shorter hours," he said.

Talks are continuing at other BAe plants with the likelihood that all the company's 40,000 manual workers will have secured agreement for 37-hour working before the end of the year...

The Independent,
April 25, 1990

1 **Match the explanation (A-G) to the words (1-7).**

1. engineering
2. drag on
3. stumbling block
4. scrap
5. worthwhile
6. stick it out
7. secure

A. obstacle, sticking point
B. not a waste of time
C. construction of cars, machines, planes, etc.
D. (fight) to the end
E. obtain, succeed in getting
F. abolish
G. go on, continue, be prolonged

2 **Choose the appropriate endings for the following sentences.**

1. The strike came to an end
A. without a ballot.
B. before a ballot.
C. after a ballot.

2. The strike was called out over
A. working hours.
B. wages.
C. safety standards.

3. The last obstacle to overcome
A. was typically British.
B. could appear in any country.
C. sounded European.

4. The formula ending the strike was
A. a victory for management.
B. a victory for the unions.
C. a good example of bargaining.

5. During the strike, production was
A. reduced.
B. brought to a standstill.
C. improved.

6. The striking workers
A. lost a considerable amount of money.
B. lost no money.
C. saved some money.

7. Industrial action at the various plants of British Aerospace
A. was well-coordinated.
B. lacked coordination.
C. obtained the same results everywhere at the same time.

3 **Three different sentences have been cut into parts and the parts scrambled. Put them back into the right order. (Capitals have been removed at the beginning of each of the sentences.)**

stopped at Crewe yesterday / after 40 workers walked out / production of Rolls Royce cars / in working time / fish and chips / when told to stop eating

to attend the funeral / the men had been given / of a colleague / time off

back to the factory / time for lunch / because they didn't have / fish and chips / they brought

BUSH BACKS DOWN ON SOVIET SANCTIONS

From Colin Hughes in Washington and Helen Womack in Moscow

President George Bush yesterday stepped back from imposing economic sanctions against the Soviet Union over its blockade of Lithuania, saying action by the United States would risk undermining progress towards freedom elsewhere in Eastern Europe.

In Moscow, Mikhail Gorbachev continued to turn the screws: he left a Lithuanian team of would-be negotiators kicking their heels yesterday, and further built up the pressure on the secessionist Baltic state by tightening border controls to prevent any circumvention of his economic blockade.

Mr Bush made it plain that he would prefer Lithuanian leaders to reach a negotiated settlement with Moscow that would allow peaceful and gradual progress towards independence.

This is the second time in recent weeks that the US has turned away from a confrontation with Moscow over Lithuania. Although Mr Bush said that limited economic sanctions were still under consideration it seems increasingly improbable that any serious gesture will be made.

US officials had encouraged an expectation that the White House was on the point of announcing a package of very restrained sanctions but the proposals under discussion stopped well short of any real breach in relations; Mr Bush has no intention of cancelling his summit with Mr Gorbachev in the US in June, nor does he want to upset the prospect of an arms agreement this year...

The Independent,
April 25, 1990

1 **Match the explanations (A-H) to the words (1-8).**

1. undermine 2. turn the screws 3. would-be 4. kick one's heels 5. circumvention 6. package 7. breach 8. upset

A. be kept waiting B. weaken at the base C. separate items in a single unit D. cause to be disturbed E. intended to be F. break, rupture G. getting round something H. increase pressure

2 **Say whether the following statements are true (T) or false (F).**

1. President Bush had never talked about sanctions before.

2. Mr Bush had other countries in mind when he took his stand.

3. Mikhail Gorbachev also seemed ready to back down.

4. Mr Bush thought Lithuanian leaders had not shown enough restraint.

5. Mr Bush was likely to change his mind.

6. Mr Bush was keen to maintain a good relationship with Moscow.

3 **Looking for words. Read the article and pick out:**

1. Two adjectives showing that, even when contemplating sanctions, President Bush was very cautious.

2. One noun, usually associated with a state of war, showing that Lithuania and Moscow were having a serious dispute.

3. Four verbs showing Mr Gorbachev's determination to make things worse for Lithuanian rebels.

4. A verb showing that the words "United States" are treated differently in English and in French.

5. "To undermine" can be divided into two parts: "under" and "mine". The affix "under" meaning from a lower position. Find the verbs built in the same way and corresponding to the following explanations :
A. to offer goods or services at a lower price (2 verbs). B. to experience, to pass through C. to form the basis of a theory D. to emphasize, to stress (2 verbs) E. to start a piece of work and intend to carry it out to the end F. to commit oneself to buying newly issued shares.

7

MEDICINE LA MÉDECINE

VOCABULAIRE A HAUTE FRÉQUENCE

Health and Disease	La santé et la maladie
ill, sick	malade
an illness, a sickness a disease	une maladie, un mal
to suffer from	souffrir de
pain	la douleur
painful	douloureux
sore	endolori
a sore throat	un mal de gorge
a headache	une migraine
to hurt	faire mal
temperature, fever	la fièvre
a fit	un accès, une attaque
a fit of coughing	une quinte de toux
critical	critique
a condition	un état
healthy	bien portant
a virus /ˈvaiərəs/	un virus
bacteria /bækˈtiəriə/	les bactéries
contagious, catching	contagieux
to pass on, to transmit	transmettre
to develop, to contract	attraper, contracter
an outbreak	un début d'épidémie
an epidemic	une épidémie
a case	un cas
a cold	un rhume
measles /ˈmi:zlz/	la rougeole
flu, influenza /ˌinfluˈenzə/	la grippe
to spread	se répandre, s'étendre
to infect	infecter
an infection	une infection
to contaminate	contaminer
contamination	la contamination
a carrier	un porteur
a malignant tumour	une tumeur maligne
cancer	le cancer
leukaemia /lu:ˈki:miə/	la leucémie
Aids	le Sida
an Aids sufferer	un malade du Sida

HIV positive	séropositif
the immune system	le système immunitaire
to faint, to pass out	s'évanouir
to come to	reprendre connaissance
disabled	handicapé
a heart attack	une crise cardiaque
a heart failure	une défaillance cardiaque
a nervous breakdown	une dépression nerveuse
a victim	une victime
mentally handicapped	handicapé mental
life expectancy	l'espérance de vie
euthanasia /ˌjuːθəˈneiziə/	l'euthanasie

Organs and Tissues — Les organes et les tissus

blood	le sang
a cell	une cellule
a blood cell	un globule
a blood sample	une prise de sang
blood pressure	la tension artérielle
a kidney	un rein
the liver	le foie
a breast	un sein
a lung	un poumon
the brain	le cerveau
the womb /wuːm/	l'utérus
a nerve	un nerf
a chromosome /ˈkrəuməsəum/	un chromosome
a gene /dʒiːn/	un gène
genetic engineering	le génie génétique

Health Service and Treatment — Les services de santé et le traitement

a general practitioner	un médecin généraliste
a surgeon	un chirurgien
surgery hours	les heures de consultation
a surgery	un cabinet médical
a chemist, a pharmacist	un pharmacien
a nurse	une infirmière
an outpatient	un malade de jour
a ward	une salle, un service
an emergency	une urgence
to examine	examiner
an examination	un examen
to check	vérifier

a check-up	un contrôle
to diagnose /ˈdaiəgnəuz/	diagnostiquer
a diagnosis	un diagnostic
a test	une analyse
to detect	déceler, dépister
detection	le dépistage
to screen	examiner pour dépister
screening	examen de dépistage
to prescribe	prescrire
a prescription	une ordonnance
a medicine, a drug	un médicament
a pill	une pilule
a tablet	un comprimé, un cachet
a tranquilliser	un tranquillisant
to treat	traiter, soigner
to respond	réagir
efficient	efficace
a side effect	un effet secondaire
to relieve	soulager
a relief	un soulagement
to cure	guérir
a cure	une guérison, un remède
a remedy	un remède
incurable	incurable
to save	sauver
to recover	se rétablir
a recovery	un rétablissement
a diet	un régime
a slimming diet	un régime amincissant

Operations — Les opérations

surgery	une intervention
to perform	effectuer
to undergo	subir
an operating theatre	une salle d'opération
intensive care	les soins intensifs
a transfusion	une transfusion
to remove	enlever
a removal	une ablation
to transplant /trænsˈplɑːnt/	transplanter
a transplant /ˈtrænsplɑːnt/	une transplantation
to donate	faire un don
a donor	un donneur
a recipient	un receveur
to reject	rejeter
a rejection	un rejet

Research	**La recherche**
a survey	une étude, une enquête
to research	faire de la recherche
a scientist	un scientifique
a laboratory	un laboratoire
to carry out	effectuer
an experiment	une expérience
to discover	découvrir
a discovery	une découverte
findings	les résultats (recherche)
to develop	mettre au point
development	la mise au point
a breakthrough	une percée, une avancée

Childbearing	**La maternité**
sterile, infertile	stérile
childless	sans enfant
to fertilise	féconder
in vitro fertilisation	la fécondation in vitro
a test tube	une éprouvette
sperm	le sperme
to inseminate	inséminer
insemination	l'insémination
an embryo /ˈembriəu/	un embryon
pregnant	enceinte
a pregnancy	une grossesse
a fœtus /ˈfi:təs/	un fœtus
a surrogate mother	une mère porteuse
surrogacy /ˈsʌrəgəsi/	la substitution
to deliver	accoucher
a delivery	un accouchement

EXPRESSIONS

to be on a diet	suivre un régime
to be confined to bed	être cloué au lit
to take a sample	faire un prélèvement
a sexually transmitted disease	une maladie sexuellement transmissible
to have an X-ray	passer une radio
to be operated on	subir une opération
he is making good progress	son état s'améliore

to be doing well	être en bonne voie
to change one's mind to change heart	changer d'avis
to be in two minds	hésiter
to make up one's mind	se décider
to take heart	prendre courage
to see eye to eye with sb.	voir du même œil que qn.
to rack one's brain	se creuser la tête

VOCABULAIRE COMPLÉMENTAIRE

Health and Disease	**La santé et la maladie**
sound	sain
a deficiency	une carence
stamina	le tonus
a complaint	une affection
acute	aigu
chronic	chronique
a germ	un germe
a microbe /ˈmaikrəub/	un microbe
a bug	un microbe, un virus
bronchitis	la bronchite
pneumonia	la pneumonie
hepatitis /ˌhepəˈtaitis/	l'hépatite
diabetes /ˈdaiəbi:ti:z/	le diabète
asthma /ˈæsmə/	l'asthme
arthritis /ɑ:ˈθraitis/	l'arthrite
rheumatism /ˈru:mətizəm/	le rhumatisme
multiple sclerosis	la sclérose en plaques
meningitis /meninˈdʒaitis/	la méningite
rabies /ˈreibiz/	la rage
a stroke	une attaque d'apoplexie
cholesterol	le cholestérol
a symptom	un symptôme
a sick note	un certificat de maladie
sick leave	un congé de maladie
a growth	une grosseur, une tumeur
cancerous	cancéreux
a stage	un stade
mercy killing	l'euthanasie
a haemophiliac /ˌhi:məuˈfiliæk/	un hémophile
food poisoning	l'intoxication alimentaire
salmonella	la salmonellose
listeria	la listeriose

Organs and Tissues	Les organes et les tissus
a vessel	un vaisseau
a vein	une veine
an artery	une artère
coronary	coronaire
the belly, the tummy	le ventre
the bladder	la vessie
bone marrow	la moëlle des os
the uterus	l'utérus
an intestine	un intestin
the bowels	les entrailles
the cervix	le col de l'utérus
cervical	du col de l'utérus
a gland	une glande
a mole	un grain de beauté

Health Service and Treatment	Les services de santé et le traitement
a physician	un médecin
a consultant	un chef de clinique
a leading specialist	un spécialiste éminent
a junior doctor	un interne
a sister	une infirmière chef
a unit	un service
a clinic	une clinique un service de consultation
a nursing home	une maison de santé
a mental hospital	un hôpital psychiatrique
terminal care	les soins palliatifs
antibiotics /ˌæntibaiˈɔtiks/	les antibiotiques
to vaccinate	vacciner
a vaccine	un vaccin
to eradicate	éradiquer
a smear /smiə/	un frottis (vaginal)
a biopsy /ˈbaiɔpsi/	une biopsie
chemotherapy	la chimiothérapie
radiation therapy	radiothérapie
a serum	un sérum
a report, a bulletin	un bulletin
to pull through	s'en sortir

Operations	Les opérations
surgical	chirurgical
cosmetic/plastic surgery	la chirurgie esthétique
under anaesthetic	sous anesthésie

a bypass	un pontage
to implant	implanter
an implant	un implant
a pioneer /ˌpaiəˈniə/	un pionnier
to graft	greffer
cross-species	inter-espèces
a graft	une greffe
a pacemaker	un stimulateur
a respirator	un respirateur
a dialysis machine	un rein artificiel

Childbearing	**La maternité**
to conceive	concevoir
conception	la conception
an ovary /ˈəuvəri/	un ovaire
ovulation	l'ovulation
Fallopian tubes	les trompes
periods	les règles
semen /ˈsi:mən/	la semence
a miscarriage	une fausse couche
stillborn	mort-né
newborn	nouveau-né
Caesarian section	une césarienne
an offspring	un descendant
to breastfeed	nourrir au sein
to bring up	élever
premature	prématuré
twins	des jumeaux
triplets	des triplés
quadruplets	des quadruplés
abnormal	anormal
malformed	malformé
malformation	la malformation
a disability	un handicap
a wheelchair	un fauteuil roulant

Practise your vocabulary.

1. What is meant by a transplant operation?
2. What sort of transplant operations can you think of?
3. Does high technology play an important part in medicine?
4. What are some consequences of progress in medicine?
5. Why does the use of embryos give rise to so much controversy?
6. What are the typical features of Aids as a disease?
7. How is Aids transmitted?
8. What arguments are used for and against euthanasia?

FRENCH PLEA OVER ROMANIA CHILD AIDS EPIDEMIC

Ian Traymor in Bucharest

A French medical team yesterday called for an international campaign to combat an Aids emergency among Romanian infants, as it became clear that a likely cause of the epidemic – repeated use of non-disposable syringes – was continuing.

Following investigations into reports of an alarmingly high incidence of Aids among children in Bucharest hospitals and orphanages, Dr Jacques Lebas of Medecins du Monde called on the international community to provide disposable needles, Aids detection kits, and medical training as well as funds.

"In the prevention field, this is an emergency. We cannot wait for confirmation by our epidemiology study," said Dr Lebas. "In African countries, the epidemic among children is not as bad as it is here."

He described the limited data on the spread of the disease as "explosive".

Statistics compiled by Bucharest's Institute of Virology, and believed by the French team following cross-checking in Paris, show that 367 of 1,025 infants tested in hospitals and orphanages are HIV positive. Sixty per cent of the hospitalised children have developed symptoms of Aids.

Romania's Aids problem was not admitted by the Ceaucescu regime and all research was suppressed.

Testing and blood-screening measures are now being implemented under the leadership of the Institute of Virology, but the project is a daunting one and the French doctors urged immediate foreign help...

The Guardian,
February 6, 1990

1 Match the explanations (A-D) to the words (1-4).

1. plea 2. orphanage 3. implement 4. daunt

A. home for children who have lost their parents
B. urgent appeal C. intimidate, dishearten
D. put into effect

2 **Say whether the following statements are true (T) or false (F).**

1. The epidemic was already under control when the article was written.
2. The French team said that only materials and funds were needed.
3. African countries compared favourably with Romania.
4. 367 children were Aids sufferers.
5. The late disclosure of the problem was not surprising.
6. Romanian doctors were in charge of the project.

3 **Looking for words. Read the article and pick out:**

A. Two adjectives showing that French doctors accepted the findings of the investigations (first paragraph).
B. A word showing that they had taken steps to confirm the findings (fifth paragraph).
C. One reaction showing that Aids is sometimes looked upon as a shameful disease.
D. Words or phrases in the passage that are equivalents for "drive", "supply" "under way" and "scheme".
E. The opposites of "support", "elderly people", "denial", "exhaustive" and "dismissed".

4 **Fill in each blank with a word from the following list. Use each word once only. Verbs are given in the infinitive.**

breast to treat cells screeening marrow illness volunteers elderly to develop to test

1. The first objective would be to __________ an Aids vaccine from the virus. It would then be __________ on chimpanzees and finally on human __________
2. The patient is __________ with drugs which kill off all the diseased white blood __________ and the bone __________ which contains leukaemic cancer cells.
3. Routine __________ of middle-aged and __________ women in the South-West for __________ cancer will begin next year to reduce death from the __________

5 **Two different sentences have been cut into parts and the parts scrambled. Put them back into the right order. (The capital letter has been removed at the beginning of the second sentence.)**

and doctors are optimistic about her recovery / is improving / who is suffering from serious pneumonia / Elizabeth Taylor /
in Santa Monica / 58-year-old actress / is in the intensive care unit / the seven-times married / California

DOCTORS SET TO TRANSPLANT BRAIN TISSUE

by Neville Hodgkinson, Medical Correspondent

British scientists have helped to pioneer research that will lead later this year to the first transplant of human brain tissue.

The operation, on a patient with Parkinson's disease, will involve removing brain cells from a human embryo at about 10 weeks of development and injecting them deep into the patient's brain. It is to take place in Sweden where, after a public debate, doctors have decided that the potential benefits outweigh ethical concerns over the use of stillborn or aborted human embryonic material.

An important factor in this decision has been the striking success of experiments in London and Cambridge using the same techniques on animals. The research has shown that when fœtal brain cells are transplanted into rats and monkeys whose brains have been damaged experimentally, the cells not only take root and grow but connect up with other cells to make good the deficiencies, physically and behaviourally.

The technique works only with fœtal brain cells, which have not yet taken on a specific task and still have flexibility of development...

The Sunday Times,
January 18, 1987

1 **Match the explanations (A-F) to the words (1-6).**

1. set to 2. pioneer 3. involve 4. outweigh
5. stillborn 6. abort

A. dead at birth B. have a greater value or importance C. expel a fœtus from the mother's womb
D. ready to, start to E. include, contain as a part
F. initiate, lead the way

2 **Choose the appropriate endings for the following sentences.**

1. With regard to brain tissue transplants, British scientists
A. were the only ones to carry out research.
B. weren't interested in research.
C. were playing an important part in research.

2. According to this medical correspondent, the first transplant would take place
A. in 1987.
B. in 1990.
C. later than 1987.

3. To perform the operation, doctors would
A. entirely remove the patient's brain.
B. introduce new cells into the patient's brain.
C. remove a part of the patient's brain.

4. Swedish doctors seemed
A. to have no moral objection to the transplant.
B. to put aside their moral objections.
C. to have come to no conclusion.

5. When reading the description of the experiments carried out in London and Cambridge, animal rights activists would feel
A. outraged.
B. reassured.
C. indifferent.

6. The new cells transplanted into the patient's brain
A. only replace the defective cells.
B. also improve the defective cells.
C. have no effect on defective cells.

7. In the article, the phrase : "cells from a human embryo at about 10 weeks of development" is
A. fully explained.
B. still unexplained.
C. only partly explained.

3 Match the words (1-5) with their appropriate definitions (A-E).

1. brain-drain
2. brain teaser
3. brainchild
4. brains trust
5. brainwashing

A. group of experts
B. rejection of old beliefs under pressure
C. emigration of scientists
D. difficult problem
E. original idea

8

SPACE — L'ESPACE

VOCABULAIRE A HAUTE FRÉQUENCE

Getting Ready	Les préparatifs
a rocket	une fusée
a spacecraft / a spaceship	un vaisseau spatial
a shuttle	une navette
on board, aboard	à bord
a cabin	une cabine
a spaceman	un spationaute
an astronaut	un astronaute
a spacesuit	un scaphandre
a crew	un équipage
a manned flight	un vol habité
to check	vérifier
the countdown	le compte à rebours
a computer	un ordinateur
a schedule /ˈʃedjuːl/	un horaire
on schedule	comme prévu
nominal	impeccable
to put off, to postpone	reporter, ajourner
a postponement	un ajournement
to cancel	annuler
a cancellation	une annulation
a fault	un défaut, une anomalie
defective, faulty	défectueux
to work	marcher, fonctionner

Lift-off	Le décollage
to ignite	allumer, mettre à feu
ignition	l'allumage, la mise à feu
to launch	lancer
a launch	un lancement, un tir
a launching-pad	un pas de tir
to blast off, to lift off	décoller
a blast-off, a lift-off	un décollage, un envol

fuel	le carburant
a tank	un réservoir
a booster	un propulseur d'appoint
to soar	s'élever, s'élancer
a stage	un étage
to separate	se séparer
to fall off	se détacher
to orbit	tourner en orbite
an orbit	une orbite
to go into orbit	se mettre en orbite
to monitor, to track	suivre la trace de

In space — Dans l'espace

a stage	une étape
a flightpath	une trajectoire de vol
a weather satellite	un satellite météo
a spy satellite	un satellite espion
weightlessness	l'apesanteur
a pull	une attraction
a laboratory	un laboratoire
to carry out	effectuer
an experiment	un expérience
a process /ˈprəuses/	un procédé, une méthode
a cargo	une cargaison
a payload	une charge utile
a pay-off, a spin-off	une récompense, une retombée
a drug	un médicament
the cargo bay, the hold	la soute
a panel	un panneau
a device	un dispositif
to retrieve, to recover	récupérer, reprendre
retrieval, recovery	la récupération
a spacewalk	une sortie dans l'espace
a spacewalker	un piéton de l'espace
a lifeline	un filin, une ligne de vie
a backpack	un fauteuil de l'espace
to steer /stiə/	diriger, gouverner
to manœuvre /mənˈu:və/	manœuvrer
a manœuvre	une manœuvre

Return — Le retour

to complete	terminer
to re-enter	rentrer
re-entry	la rentrée

the atmosphere	l'atmosphère
to land	atterrir
landing	l'atterrissage
a base	une base

EXPRESSIONS

to be behind schedule	être en retard
to be out of order	être en panne
there was something wrong with...	il y avait quelque chose qui n'allait pas dans...
they had some trouble with...	ils ont des ennuis avec...
to put something right	remédier à quelque chose

VOCABULAIRE COMPLÉMENTAIRE

Flight	**Le vol**
space sickness	le mal de l'espace
lunar	lunaire
a module	un module
a capsule	une capsule
a retro-rocket	une rétrofusée
a rendez-vous	un rendez-vous
to dock	arrimer
to link up	relier
a docking, a link-up	un arrimage
to team up	s'assembler
a back-up system	un système de secours
remote control	le contrôle à distance
an orbiting station	une station orbitale
a tracking station	une station de repérage
a meteorite /ˈmi:tjərait/	un météorite

Missions	**Les missions**
geostationary	géostationnaire
to relay	relayer
a telescope	un télescope
to probe	sonder
a probe	une sonde
an antennae /ænˈtenə/	une antenne
outer space	le cosmos
a planet	une planète

a galaxy	une galaxie
the solar system	le système solaire
gravitation	la gravitation
gravity	la pesanteur
vacuum	le vide

Space record likely by cosmonauts

Two Soviet cosmonauts aboard a new type of spacecraft docked with the Mir orbiting station at the weekend and prepared for what Western experts expect to be the longest stay in space.

Moscow Radio said Cdr Yury Romanenko and Flight Engineer Laveikin were in good health. The Soyuz TM-2 craft, a new generation space vehicle launched early on Friday had performed a unique automatic docking involving several U-turns to reduce speed about 220 miles above Earth.

The craft spent two days reaching Mir instead of the usual one to save fuel during the link-up. Inside Mir the crew found salt and bread, a traditional Russian greeting, left for them by the previous crew.

Reuter,
February 2, 1987

Practise your vocabulary.

1. Can you describe a shuttle flight from beginning to end?
2. Why is the launching date often postponed?
3. Can you point out some of the main differences between the American and the Soviet space programmes?
4. How is space competition likely to increase in the future?
5. What are some of the uses of satellites?
6. Why might some people be opposed to space programmes?

Blast off

Cape Canaveral (Reuter) – The shuttle Discovery blasted off with the revolutionary Hubble Space Telescope that will seek to solve the mysteries of the universe. The shuttle was launched after a two-week delay because of a problem with a power unit.

April 25, 1990

EUROPE POISED TO JOIN THE SPACECRAFT POWERS

By Michael Cross

Europe is poised to take the expensive decision to join the United States and Soviet Union as a front-rank space power, with its own capacity for putting people into orbit. But many uncertainties remain about how the 13-member European Space Agency will go about it.

British and French engineers are promoting two different re-usable space planes, Hermes and Hotol, as Europe's future space vehicle. The two craft are often seen as rivals: in fact they are almost as different as spacecraft can be.

Hermes, originally a French concept, was designed as a quick way of putting people into space, either on independent missions or to visit the space station which NASA plans to put in orbit by the late 1990s, with existing technology. Hotol was designed as an unmanned satellite launcher, based on a complete technological departure.

Hermes will ride into orbit on an Ariane V rocket, the most powerful version of Europes's disposable satellite launcher, and glide back to a runway on Earth. Hotol would be the first single-stage spacecraft to fly into orbit.

Space enthusiasts now hope that Europe can handle both projects, with Hermes providing valuable experience for a second generation of spaceplanes...

The Independent,
June 15, 1987

1 **Match the explanations (A-F) to the words (1-6)**

1. poised to	A. build for a purpose
2. go about	B. be able to carry out
3. design	C. ready to
4. disposable	D. planes land on it
5. runway	E. not used a second time
6. handle	F. set to work on

2 **Choose the appropriate endings for the following sentences.**

1. The major obstacle to overcome in becoming a front-rank space power is

A. competition.
B. uncertainty.
C. cost.

2. When compared to the European Community, in 1990, the European Space Agency included

A. more countries.
B. fewer countries.
C. the same number of countries.

3. The two space planes seemed to be fundamentally different,

A. so they had no common feature.
B. and yet they had one common feature.
C. and yet they had several common features.

4. Hermes would be

A. totally independent from the Americans.
B. partly associated with the Americans.
C. completely associated with the Americans.

5. The difference between Hermes and Hotol would appear

A. on getting into orbit.
B. on re-entry into the atmosphere.
C. on landing.

6. Space enthusiasts thought that

A. Hermes would fly last.
B. both spacecraft would fly at the same time.
C. Hermes would fly first.

3 Looking for words. Read the article and find:

A. A synonym for "an orbiting station"
B. The words underlining the unique features of Hotol (paragraph three).

"Do you think there's somewhere up there where they don't play football?"

4 "Engineering" means applying scientific principles to the design, construction and maintenance of engines, cars, machines, etc. The word is often associated with an adjective, for example "electrical engineering". Find the adjectives that would be used in the same way for the following activities:

1. building machines and engines 2. building roads and bridges 3. building plants and machinery for chemistry 4. building aircraft 5. the use of genes (medicine)

Ulysses speeds towards sun as shuttle crew experiment

The solar probe Ulysses whizzed past the moon yesterday while American space officials boasted of a flawless mission of the shuttle Discovery that began on Saturday.

Ulysses released from the shuttle's cargo bay on Saturday, was speeding at almost 600 miles per minute towards an intended orbit between Mars and Jupiter, where it will survey the sun's polar regions for the first time.

"Everything is clicking right," said Jeff Carr, a spokesman for the National Aeronautics and Space Administration in Houston. "There are no systems failures or other problems."

Ground controllers at the NASA Jet Propulsion Laboratory in Pasadena, California, yesterday began extending remote controlled antennae which the satellite will use from 1992 to send back information on sunspots, flares, and other solar phenomena.

Their main mission accomplished, Discovery's five astronauts yesterday turned attention to shipboard experiments.

An experimental voice activated control system for the shuttle's television cameras refused to recognise the mission specialist, apparently because the sound of his speech had been changed by the absence of gravity.

Crossing about 160 miles above the Atlantic, the astronauts observed tropical storm Klaus, which hit the Caribbean as a hurricane earlier in the week. Meteorologists will use their photographs to learn more about the Earth's weather pattern...

Reuter in Cape Canaveral,
October 8, 1990

1 **Match the explanations (A-E) to the words (1-5).**

1. whiz
2. boast
3. flawless
4. survey
5. click right

A. fall easily into place
B. move or go rapidly
C. detailed inspection
D. perfect
E. speak proudly

2 **Say whether the following statements are true (T) or false (F).**

1. The reader knows about the exact nature of Ulysses right from the beginning.
2. No mention was made of the way Ulysses was launched.
3. Getting into orbit might still give rise to some problems for the probe.
4. Jeff Carr was feeling both proud and relieved.
5. It will take a long time before Ulysses can send back information.
6. Discovery had a seven-member crew.
7. The only disappointment reported was surprising.
8. Part of the mission data was due to sheer coincidence.
9. Only two places in the US were involved in the flight, Houston and Pasadena.

3 **Looking for words. Read the article and:**

A. Find equivalents for "hold", "on-board" and "weathermen".
B. Fill in the blank with the appropriate word: as we are told that there were no system failures, the shuttle must have had a ____________ system for the voice-activated control system.

4 **Test your knowledge. Only one statement is correct in each pair. Which one?**

A. The space age began with the launching of a Soviet satellite in 1957.
B. The first satellite to be launched was American and the event took place in 1960.

C. An American astronaut was the first to fly in orbit round the earth in 1964.
D. The first manned flight was made by a Soviet cosmonaut in 1961.

E. The first successful launching of *Ariane* took place in 1979.
F. *Ariane* was launched successfully for the first time in 1982.

9

POLITICS I — LA POLITIQUE I

VOCABULAIRE A HAUTE FRÉQUENCE

Political Parties	Les partis politiques
to join sth.	adhérer à qch.
a member	un adhérent, un membre
membership	les adhérents, l'adhésion
a policy	une politique
a politician	un homme politique
radical	radical, maximaliste
extreme /iks'tri:m/	extrême
an extremist	un extrémiste
moderate	modéré
left-wing, leftist	de gauche
right-wing, rightist	de droite
Tory, Conservative	conservateur
Labour	travailliste
a programme	un programme
a view, an opinion	une opinion
a multi-party system	le multipartisme
a one-party system	le système du parti unique
a coalition	une coalition

Before the Election	Avant l'élection
an opinion poll	un sondage d'opinion
to publish	publier
to survey	interroger (échantillon)
a figure	un chiffre
a rating	une cote
a lead /li:d/	une avance
to trail	avoir du retard
a margin	une marge
popular	populaire
popularity	la popularité

dissatisfaction	le mécontentement
a referendum	un référendum
local	locale, municipale
general, legislative	législative
presidential	présidentielle
an election	une élection
a by-election	une élection partielle
to fight	disputer
to stand for, to run for	se présenter à, être candidat à
a candidate	un candidat
a constituency	une circonscription
a deposit	une caution
a campaign	une campagne
to pledge	promettre
a pledge	une promesse

Elections — Les élections

a ballot	un scrutin
a ballot paper	un bulletin de vote
polling day	le jour des élections
a polling station	un bureau de vote
a ballot box	une urne
to vote	voter
a vote	une voix, un suffrage
a voter	un électeur
a round	un tour (de scrutin)
turn-out, polling	la participation
to count	dépouiller
counting	le dépouillement
a seat	un siège
to elect	élire
to win	remporter
a win, a victory	une victoire
overwhelming	écrasant
close	serré
to retain	conserver
a defeat	une défaite
an overall majority	une majorité absolue
to swing	faire pencher, virer
a swing	un revirement, transfert
to shift	changer, se déplacer
a shift	un changement, déplacement
results	les résultats
the outcome	le résultat, la conclusion

The United States	Les États-Unis
a primary	une primaire
a caucus	un comité de primaire
a convention	une convention
a delegate	un délégué
nomination	la désignation
Congress	Le Congrès
a congressman	un membre du Congrès
the Senate	le Sénat
a senator	un sénateur
the House of Representatives	la Chambre des représentants
a representative	un représentant
to inaugurate	investir
inauguration	l'investiture

EXPRESSIONS

to be in the lead	être en tête
they are 2 points ahead	ils ont 2 points d'avance
the run-up to an election	la période pré-électorale
to call an election	provoquer une élection
to hold an election	procéder à une élection
to go to the country	en appeler aux électeurs
to field a candidate	présenter un candidat
to jump on the bandwagon	prendre le train en marche
to got to the polls	aller aux urnes
to cast a vote	déposer un bulletin
to concede defeat	admettre la victoire
to hold the balance of power	détenir la minorité de blocage
to be sworn in	prêter serment

VOCABULAIRE COMPLÉMENTAIRE

Political Parties	Les partis politiques
the leading role	le rôle dirigeant
an apparatus	un appareil
the political spectrum	l'éventail politique
a watershed	une ligne de partage
the rank and file the grass roots	la base
an activist	un militant

influential	influent
reactionary	réactionnaire
progressive	progressiste
a hard liner	un dur
a conference	un congrès
to chair	présider
a rival	un rival
rivalry	la rivalité
to split	éclater
a split	une rupture
a rift	un fossé, une faille
in-fighting	les luttes internes
a tendency	une tendance
to fall apart	éclater, se séparer
to break away	se détacher
a breakaway group	un groupe dissident
a fringe party	un groupuscule
the loony left	la gauche irresponsable

Before the Election — Avant l'élection

a pollster, a poll taker	un sondeur
the don't knows	les indécis
to conduct	organiser
a straw poll	une consultation improvisée
a standing	une position, un classement
a showing	une performance
to lag	être à la traîne
neck and neck	au coude à coude
a constituent	un électeur (circonscription)
proportional representation	la représentation proportionnelle
an election manifesto	un manifeste électoral
a platform	une plate-forme
bread an butter issues	les questions matérielles
to canvass	faire du porte à porte
a rostrum	une tribune
to heckle	harceler
to smear /smiə/	diffamer
a smear campaign	une campagne de diffamation
character assassination	atteinte à la réputation
mudslinging	les coups bas
dirty tricks	les magouilles
to stand against sb.	se présenter contre qn.

to contend, to contest	disputer
a contender, a contestant	un concurrent
a safe seat	un siège sûr
a stronghold	un bastion, un fief
a marginal seat	un siège menacé
to commit	engager
a commitment an undertaking	un engagement
to vow to /vau/	s'engager à
propaganda /ˌprɔpəˈgændə/	la propagande
an image	une image

Elections — Les élections

a run-off election	un deuxième tour avec deux candidats
to register	s'inscrire
to poll	recueillir
the poll	les suffrages
a polling-booth	un isoloir
the electorate	l'électorat
an exit poll	un sondage à la sortie
returns	les résultats partiels
a tally	un décompte
to recount	recompter
a recount	un nouveau décompte
to declare	proclamer (résultats)
a declaration	une proclamation
an absolute majority	une majorité absolue
a landslide victory	une victoire écrasante
a groundswell	une lame de fond
a share of the vote	un pourcentage de voix
a hung Parliament	un Parlement sans majorité
a mandate	un mandat (contrat)
a term	un mandat (durée)
wilderness, the limbo	le désert (politique)
fraud	la fraude
to rig	truquer
ballot rigging	le trucage électoral

The United States — Les États-Unis

presidency	la présidence
the incumbent president	le président en exercice
the outgoing president	le président sortant
a ticket	un ticket électoral
an elector	un grand électeur

Practise your vocabulary.

1. What are the main categories into which political parties can be classified?
2. How are political parties organised?
3. What are the main features of opinion polls?
4. What happens during an election campaign?
5. What are the typical features of polling day?
6. What happens in the evening after the polls have closed?

TORIES BITTER IN WAKE OF EASTBOURNE

By Nicholas Timmins, Political Correspondent

Recriminations over the disastrous Conservative showing in Eastbourne broke out in the party ranks yesterday as Charles Kennedy, the Liberal Democrat president, said his party's by-election triumph "put us back on the political map".

The result which saw a Conservative majority of nearly 17,000 turned into a 4,500 lead for the Liberal Democrats also stunned Labour. The party came within three votes of losing its deposit in its second worst by-election result since the Second World War.

After the Liberal Democrat's first by-election win this parliament and the first after the trauma of the Alliance merger, Paddy Ashdown said the result showed the party to be "a decisive force in defeating Thatcherism".

There were 200 seats where his party ran the Tories second, he said, dozens of which were now vulnerable. "Labour's claim to be the only alternative capable of standing up to the Conservatives is fatally damaged by this".

Both Labour and the Tories dismissed suggestions that the result marked a return to three-party politics which, on the showing of the 1980s, would benefit the Tories. In both 1983 and 1987 a divided opposition helped the Conservatives to win.

All parties will be watching closely for evidence of the tactical voting that was apparent – without the help of opinion polls during the campaign – in Eastbourne. While it was not decisive, the squeeze of Labour's vote, down from 8.8 to 5 per cent, boosted the Liberal Democrats.

The Independent, October 20, 1990

EASTBOURNE BY-ELECTION RESULT

David Bellotti (Lib Dem) .... 23,415 (50.8 per cent)
Richard Hickmet (Con) 18,865 (40.9)
Charlotte Atkins (Lab) 2,308 (5)
David Aherne (Green) 553 (1.2)
Theresa Williamson (Liberal) 526 (1.1)
Lindi St Claire (Corrective) 216 (0.5)
John McAuley (NF) 154 (0.3)
Eric Page (Ironside) 35 (0.07)
Liberal Democrat majority: 4,550, Electorate: 75,904, Total Vote: 46,115, Poll: 60.75 per cent, Swing: 20.05 Conservative to Liberal Democrat. 1987 general election result: Ian Gow (C) 33,587 (59.9 per cent); Peter Driver (Liberal Alliance) 16,664 (29.7); Ashok Patel (Lab) 4,928 (8.8); Ruth Addison (Green) 867 (1.5); Con majority: 16,923 (30.2 per cent). Electorate: 74,144, Total Vote: 56,046, Poll: 75.6 per cent.

1 Match the explanations (A-G) to the words (1-7).

1. in the wake of 2. showing 3. stun 4. trauma 5. merger 6. stand up to 7. squeeze
A. emotional shock B. reduction, compression
C. confront, resist D. appearance, performance
E. after, following F. shock, confuse the mind
G. combination of two to make one

2 Say whether the statements are true (T) or false (F).

1. We know the exact nature of the election right from the beginning of the article.
2. It was not a dramatic swing.
3. The deposit is lost when the candidate does not poll 5 per cent of the vote.
4. The merger between the Liberals and the Social Democratic party was a painful process.
5. "His party ran the Tories second" means that the Liberal Democrats came before the Tories.
6. Labour and the Tories agreed on one point.
7. Tactical voting means that voters cast their votes to defeat a candidate.

3 Fill in the blanks with the appropriate words.

1. If three parties get about the same number of seats, no party has an __________ majority and it leads to a __________ Parliament.
2. A way out of this situation, to get a parliamentary majority, can be to form a __________ government with two parties.

3. The merger was painful because David Owen, the SDP leader, refused to ________ the Liberal Democrats.
4. Margaret Thatcher resigned in 1990, she has now become a __________ Prime Minister.

4 **Test your knowledge. Only one statement is correct in the pair below. Which one?**

A. At a general election in the United Kingdom, the candidate who gets the most votes is elected straight away.
B. To be elected in the United Kingdom, a candidate must get an overall majority in the first round at a general election.

Seaga facing defeat in poll

Kingston: Jamaicans began voting yesterday in municipal elections that opinion polls forecast will bring a defeat for the Jamaica Labour Party of Mr Edward Seaga, the Prime Minister.

Around 970,000 people are eligible to vote in 187 constituencies, the first local elections since early 1981, and the results will be seen as a test of Mr Seaga's unpopular economic austerity policies.

Mr Michael Manley, leader of the opposition People's National Party, has said a PNP victory should prompt the Prime Minister into calling national elections, not due till 1988.

Mr Seaga says he does not regard yesterday's vote as a referendum on his economic policies and defended them in his final election broadcast on Monday night.

"Happily, there are now clear signs that those sacrifices, far from being in vain, were the investment we all needed to make in order that all of us can look forward with growing confidence to a more rewarding and secure future," he said.

Mr Seaga said no one could contest that Jamaica was "witnessing an unprecedented revitalisation of the economy in all its major sectors."

The Prime Minister who announced in May an expansionary 1986-87 budget that broke with austerity policies followed under successive International Monetary Fund programmes, forecast economic growth this year after a 5 per cent drop in 1985...

Reuter,
July 30, 1986

1 **Match the explanations (A-F) to the words (1-6).**

1. forecast 2. eligible 3. prompt 4. look forward to 5. reward 6. witness
A. be the reason causing somebody to do something.
B. recompense for a service C. be present at an event
D. predict, say in advance E. having the right qualifications F. anticipate with pleasure

2 **Say whether the following statements are true (T) or false (F).**

1. Election results in Jamaica come out very rapidly.
2. Apparently, local elections take place in Jamaica every five years.
3. The leader of the opposition was ready to take advantage of the situation.
4. There was some contradiction in the Prime Minister's attitude.
5. The Prime Minister didn't admit Jamaicans had been through some hardship.
6. The Prime Minister showed great optimism for the future.
7. It is clear from the article that Jamaica had been in financial difficulties for some years.

3 **Fill in the blanks with words taken from the article.**

1. Heavy rain in some areas is ____________ for tomorrow.
2. His lack of confidence ____________ him to refuse the offer.
3. Low demand brought about a ____________ in prices.
4. Most MPs leave London and travel back to their ____ for the weekend.
5. We all ____________ to meeting you next summer.
6. A lot of ____________ is needed to modernise our manufacturing industry.
7. He was ____________ for his patience: he won the seat after standing unsuccessfully three times.

4 **Two different sentences have been cut into parts and the parts scrambled. Put them back into the right order. (Punctuation and the capital letter at the beginning of the second sentence have been removed.)**

Nepal lifts ban on political parties

1. is lifting a 30-year-old-ban / were killed during prodemocracy demonstrations / on political parties / Nepal / on Friday / where at least 50 people.
2. who had earlier / the move was announced / met opposition leaders/from the palace of King Birendra

10

POLITICS II — LA POLITIQUE II

VOCABULAIRE A HAUTE FRÉQUENCE

Power	**Le pouvoir**
to set up, to establish	établir, installer
a regime	un régime
a dictator	un dictateur
a dictatorship	une dictature
to liberalise	libéraliser
liberalisation	la libéralisation
a say	une voix au chapitre
a status	un statut
a constitution	une constitution
constitutional	constitutionnel
democracy /di'mɔkrəsi/	la démocratie
democratic /ˌdemə'krætik/	démocratique
a republic	une république
office	les fonctions
powerful	puissant
to rule	diriger, gouverner
the ruling party	le parti au pouvoir
rule	l'autorité, l'administration
majority rule	le gouvernement de la majorité
self-rule	l'autonomie
a state	un État
a statesman	un homme d'État

Parliament	**Le Parlement**
a Member of Parliament (MP)	un député
the House of Commons	la Chambre des députés
the House of Lords	la Chambre des lords
a committee	une commission
to sit	siéger
a sitting	une séance
to put forward	proposer, soumettre

to table	déposer
a motion	une motion
a bill	un projet de loi
a private member's bill	une proposition de loi
to amend	amender
an amendment	un amendement
to reject	rejeter
a rejection	un rejet
to abolish	abolir
abolition	l'abolition
to carry	faire passer
to defeat	repousser
to adopt	adopter
an adoption	une adoption
a law	une loi

Debate — Les débats

to debate	débattre
an issue	une question, un problème
to propose	proposer
a proposal	une proposition
to discuss	discuter
a discussion	une discussion
to approve of sth.	approuver qch.
approval	l'approbation
to praise sth.	faire l'éloge de qch.
to criticise	critiquer
criticism	la critique
to argue	argumenter, faire valoir
to state	déclarer
a statement	une déclaration
to advocate	prôner
an advocate	un défenseur, un partisan
to support, to back	soutenir
support, backing	le soutien
to favour	être partisan de
confidence	la confiance
to agree to sth.	consentir à qch.
to agree with sb.	être d'accord avec qn.
an agreement	un accord
to disagree with sb.	être en désaccord avec qn.
a disagreement	un désaccord
a difference	une divergence
to explain	expliquer
an explanation	une explication
to contradict	contredire
a contradiction	une contradiction

to deny	nier
a denial	un démenti
to claim	affirmer
a claim	une affirmation
to maintain	continuer d'affirmer
to complain	se plaindre
a complaint	une plainte, une réclamation
to advise	conseiller
advice	les conseils
to press sb. to	pousser qn. à
pressure	la pression
to urge	exhorter
to blame sb. for sth.	reprocher qch. à qn.
to blame sth. on sb.	rendre qn. responsable de qch.
blame	la responsabilité
to protest /prə'test/	protester
a protest /'prəutest/	une protestation
a controversy	une polémique
controversial	controversé, polémique
to contest	contester
to oppose sth.	s'opposer à qch.
an opponent	un opposant
opposition	l'opposition
to challenge	défier
a challenge	un défi
to denounce	dénoncer
denunciation	la dénonciation
to accuse	accuser
an accusation	une accusation
to condemn	condamner
to outrage	provoquer l'indignation de
an outrage	un scandale
a row /rau/	une querelle, une dispute
a crisis /'kraisis/	une crise
a division	un vote au Parlement
to abstain	s'abstenir
abstention	l'abstention

Government — Le gouvernement

to govern	gouverner
to appoint	nommer
an appointment	une nomination
a minister	un ministre (à l'étranger)
a minister of state	un secrétaire d'État
a junior minister	un ministre délégué

the Prime Minister	le Premier ministre
a cabinet	un cabinet
to deal with sth.	s'occuper de qch.
to tackle sth.	s'attaquer à qch.
to handle sth.	traiter, gérer qch.
to implement	mettre en œuvre
an implementation	une mise en œuvre
a move	une démarche, une initiative
a step	une disposition, une mesure
a stand, a stance	une position
an objective	un objectif
an aim	un but
to back down	faire marche arrière
to climb down	faire des concessions
a climb-down	une reculade
to yield, to give in	céder
to reform	réformer
a reform	une réforme
to reshuffle	remanier
a reshuffle	un remaniement
a setback	un revers, une déconvenue
to bring down	faire chuter
to overthrow, to topple	renverser
an overthrow	un renversement
downfall	la chute
to resign /ri'zain/	démissionner
resignation	la démission
to hand in	remettre
the former Prime Minister	l'ancien Premier ministre

EXPRESSIONS

to take office	entrer en fonction
to remove from office	démettre de ses fonctions
the ousted president	le président déchu
to sponsor a bill	introduire une proposition
to go to the vote	être soumis au vote
to put to the vote	soumettre au vote
to come to power	accéder au pouvoir
to bring into force	mettre en application
to come under pressure	subir des pressions
to bow to pressure	céder aux pressions
to address an issue	aborder un problème

to take issue with sb.	engager une controverse avec qn.
to be critical of	trouver à redire à
to take sb. to task	prendre qn. à partie
to level a charge at sb.	lancer une accusation contre qn.
to be at loggerheads	être en conflit
to come under fire	être vivement critiqué
to pour scorn on	tourner en dérision
to carry a lot of clout	avoir beaucoup d'influence

VOCABULAIRE COMPLÉMENTAIRE

Power	**Le pouvoir**
dictatorial	dictatorial
parliamentary	parlementaire
a junta /ˈdʒʌntə/	une junte
tyranny	la tyrannie
a tyrant	un tyran
a despot	un despote
despotism	le despotisme
totalitarian	totalitaire
to purge	purger
a purge	une épuration, une purge
a monarchy	une monarchie
a monarch /ˈmɔnək/	un monarque
influence peddling	le trafic d'influence

Parliament	**Le Parlement**
a session	une session
the Speaker	le Président de la Chambre
a whip	un chef de groupe
a front-bencher	un député porte-parole
a back-bencher	un député de la base
question time	la séance des questions
to sponsor	présenter (une proposition)
the sponsor	l'auteur (d'une proposition)
to endorse	endosser
an endorsement	un endossement
to legislate	légiférer
legislation	la législation
a framework	un cadre (de discussion)

a draft	une ébauche, un avant-projet
a loophole	une faille, une lacune
to outlaw	mettre hors la loi
an Act	une loi
to lobby	faire pression
a lobby	un groupe de pression
a surgery	une permanence (de député)
a deputy	un député (à l'étranger)

Debate — Les débats

to stress sth. / to insist upon sth.	insister sur qch.
to emphasise	bien préciser
to underline	souligner
to highlight	mettre en valeur
to prop up	étayer, soutenir
to vindicate	justifier, donner raison à
vindication	confirmation du bien-fondé
to placate	apaiser
unanimous	unanime
unanimity	l'unanimité
consensus	le consensus
to alter	modifier
an alteration	une modification
to repeal	abroger
a repeal	une abrogation
to antagonise sb.	provoquer l'hostilité de
to incense	mettre en fureur
an outcry	un tollé
an uproar	un tapage
turmoil	les remous
to barrack	chahuter
to castigate	fustiger
to lambast	éreinter, fustiger
a scathing attack	une attaque cinglante
a stooge	un fantoche
a puppet	un pantin
a pawn	un pion
to filibuster	faire de l'obstruction
a guillotine	une limitation des débats
to rescind	révoquer, résilier
a turning-point	un tournant
a watershed	un moment décisif
to turn around / to turn about	faire volte-face

a turn-around an about-turn, a U-turn	une volte-face
to cover up	étouffer
a cover-up	un étouffement (scandale)
the Dispatch Box	la tribune du gouvernement
a White Paper	un avant-projet de loi
to censure	censurer
censure	la censure parlementaire
a no-confidence motion	une motion de censure
to defeat	mettre en minorité
a casting vote	une voix prépondérante
to assemble	se réunir
to adjourn	suspendre, reporter
an adjournment	une suspension, un report
to convene /kən'vi:n/	convoquer (parlement)
recess /ri'ses/	les vacances parlementaires
to re-assemble	rentrer (parlementaires)
to dissolve /di'zɔlv/	dissoudre
dissolution	la dissolution

The United States — Les États-Unis

an aide	un collaborateur
bipartisan	bipartite
to veto sth. /'vi:təu/	opposer son veto à qch.
a veto	un veto
to override sth. to overrule sth.	passer outre à qch. annuler, casser qch.
to impeach	mettre en accusation
an impeachment	une mise en accusation
the State Department	le ministère des Affaires étrangères
the Secretary of State	le ministre des Affaires étrangères
the Attorney General	le ministre de la Justice
the Supreme Court	la Cour suprême

Government — Le Gouvernement

the Queen's speech	le discours du Trône
provisional	provisoire
interim	intérimaire
caretaker	chargé des affaires courantes
a portfolio	un portefeuille
to shake up	réaménager, remodeler
a shake-up	un réaménagement

a decree	un décret, une ordonnance
a by-law	un arrêté municipal
a package of measures	un ensemble de mesures
to review	réexaminer
a review	un réexamen
a body	un organisme
a watchdog	un comité de vigilance
an ombudsman	un médiateur
a record	un bilan
to achieve	accomplir
an achievement	une réalisation
to mishandle sth.	se montrer maladroit
to scrap	mettre au rebut
to phase in	introduire progressivement
to phase out	abandonner progressivement
to undermine	saper
to step down	se désister
to stand down	se démettre
devolution	la régionalisation
a Cabinet meeting	un conseil de cabinet
the Shadow Cabinet	le contre-gouvernement
the Lord Chancellor	le ministre de la Justice
the Home Secretary	le ministre de l'Intérieur
the Education Secretary	le ministre de l'Éducation
the Foreign Secretary	le ministre des Affaires étrangères
the Foreign Office	le ministère des Affaires étrangères
The Treasury	le ministère du Budget

1 Practise your vocabulary.

1. How is a government formed after a general election in Britain?
2. What are some of the tasks of Parliament?
3. In which way do members of the ruling party and members of the opposition take part in a debate?
4. How does a government work (machinery, procedures, etc.)?
5. How can a government be brought down by Members of Parliament?
6. What decisions can a Prime Minister take in a time of crisis?

2 **Test your knowledge. Only one statement is appropriate in each pair. Which one?**

A. In Britain, opinion polls can be conducted up to polling day.

B. Opinion polls are not allowed in Britain within a week of polling day.

C. Elections take place on a Sunday in Britain.

D. Polling day is always on Thursday in Britain.

LAWSON QUITS GOVERNMENT

By Philip Stephens, Political Editor in London

Mr Nigel Lawson threw Mrs Margaret Thatcher's Government into turmoil yesterday by resigning as Chancellor of the Exchequer over his differences with the Prime Minister on exchange rate policy.

In a move which forced a dramatic cabinet reshuffle, stunned Conservative MPs and raised questions at Westminster over Mrs Thatcher's long-term future, Mr Lawson effectively walked out of N° 11 Downing Street.

In a curt letter to the Prime Minister, he said he could no longer serve as Chancellor while she retained Sir Alan Waters – a strong critic of Mr Lawson's advocacy of full British membership of the European Monetary System – as her personal economic adviser. Within two hours, Sir Alan announced his own resignation.

Mrs Thatcher immediately appointed Mr John Major, the Foreign Secretary to replace Mr Lawson and the Government emphasised that its economic strategy would remain unchanged. Mr Major had served for two years under Mr Lawson as Chief Secretary to the Treasury and his appointment was seen as an attempt by Mrs Thatcher to emphasise the continuity of policy.

Hours later, Mr Douglas Hurd, the Home Secretary, was appointed to replace Mr Major, while Mr David Waddington, the Chief Whip, was appointed Home Secretary.

Amid tense scenes at Westminster, senior Conservative MPs counselled against panic. But they and Government ministers were acknowledging that Mrs Thatcher now faced perhaps the most difficult political crisis of her more than 10 years in office...

The Financial Times,
October 27, 1989

1 **Match the explanations (A-E) to the words (1-5).**

1 turmoil 2. stun 3. curt 4. acknowledge 5. Whip

A. brief, abrupt B. recognise, admit the truth of C. person in charge of party discipline in Parliament D. shock, surprise E. agitation, tumult

2 **Say whether the following statements are true (T) or false (F).**

1. Mr Nigel Lawson would be called the Finance Minister in most countries outside the United Kingdom.
2. When in office, Mr Nigel Lawson was Mrs Thatcher's next-door neighbour.
3. His resignation had only two immediate consequences.
4. The journalist got it right about Mrs Thatcher's future.
5. The affair resulted in a triumph for Sir Alan Waters.
6. Mr Major was well-qualified because he was Foreign Secretary.
7. Mrs Thatcher was anxious to reassure the world of finance.
8. This affair is a good example of a reshuffle.
9. The disarray created among Conservative MPs is mentioned three times.
10. Mrs Thatcher came to office in June 1979
11. Two of the men who took part in the leadership battle after Mrs Thatcher's resignation are mentioned in the article.

3 **Looking for words. Read the article and find synonyms for:**

A. disagreement B. shake-up C. to keep
D. to stress E. power

2. The nouns corresponding to "to appoint", "to resign", "to refuse" and "to attempt" are "appointment", "resignation", "refusal" and "attempt".
Find the nouns corresponding to the following verbs: to protest, to abolish, to amend, to approve, to overthrow, to state, to abstain, to acknowledge, to deny, to claim, to complain, to argue, to advise and to explain.

4 **Test your knowledge. Only one statement is appropriate in the pair below. Which one?**

4. Britain became a member of the European Monetary system in 1988.
B. Britain entered the European Monetary System in 1990.

BUSH ABANDONS "NO NEW TAXES" PLEDGE

From Colin Hughes in Washington

George Bush yesterday took the politically risky step of abandoning his pledge not to raise taxes. He accepted in writing that "tax revenue increases" would be an essential part of any package to bridge the ever-growing United States federal budget deficit.

Throughout his 1988 campaign for the presidency, Mr Bush reiterated his promise to American voters as if it were an incontrovertible refrain: "Read my lips; no new taxes." Yesterday, however, he bowed to the overriding view of American economists that there was no political or financial alternative.

At first Mr Bush's use of the phrase "tax revenue increase" were taken to be weasel words, implying that the White House might somehow be hoping either to increase the tax take without levying "new" or higher taxes, or laying the responsibility for an unpopular tax hike on the Democrats. But there was no doubt among the Democrat leaders who have spent several weeks now in joint negotiations with the administration over a budget deficit reduction package. Mr Bush, they affirmed, had withdrawn his campaign pledge.

President Bush has therefore opened the way to direct talks with Congress over how the extra taxes might be raised. Some Republicans have sought to argue that Mr Bush's campaign phrase applied only to income tax, and that purchase taxes – such as petrol or cigarette tax raises – would not strictly breach his "read my lips" promise. Those options are the most probable outcome...

The Independent,
June 27, 1990

1 Match the explanations (A-G) to the words (1-7).

1. package 2. bridge 3. incontrovertible 4. weasel words 5. bow to 6. levy 7. hike

A. rise, increase B. evasive or misleading speech
C. impose, collect D. that cannot be disputed
E. submit to, accept F. separate items in a single unit
G. reduce, curb

2 **Choose the appropriate endings for the following statements.**

1. The phrase "tax revenue increases" is used because the economic situation was
A. getting better.
B. getting worse.
C. unchanged.

2. Mr Bush had to change his mind because
A. most experts agreed it was unavoidable to do so.
B. it was politically advisable to do so.
C. his supporters expected him to do so.

3. The phrase: "tax revenue increases" was
A. readily accepted by the media.
B. immediately dismissed by the media.
C. cautiously reported by the media.

4. The journalist had
A. no idea what the final decision would be.
B. a fairly accurate idea of the result.
C. only a vague idea of the result.

5. Republicans tried to
A. emphasise the implications.
B. ignore the implications.
C. minimise the implications.

6. This article implies that Congress
A. plays no part in drawing up the Budget.
B. plays only a small part in drawing up the Budget.
C. plays a major part in drawing up the Budget.

3 **Looking for words.**

1. What words could be used to describe a phrase used repeatedly during a campaign, like "no new taxes"?
2. Read the passage and find a noun which means "an increase" in American English. Although it is commonly used as a verb in British English (twice in the article), it seldom appears as a noun.
3. Pick out one verb (third paragraph) showing that the journalist takes care to point out he is reporting other people's opinion and not his own.

11 RELIGION LA RELIGION

VOCABULAIRE A HAUTE FRÉQUENCE

Religions	Les religions
religious /ri'lidʒəs/	religieux
a Jew	un juif
Jewish	juif
a Christian	un chrétien
a Roman Catholic	un catholique
a Protestant	un protestant
Islam /'izlɑ:m/	l'islam
a Moslem, a Muslim	un musulman
a Sikh	un sikh
a god	un dieu
a goddess	une déesse
faith	la foi
faithful	fidèle
to obey sb.	obéir à qn.
obedience	l'obéissance
to worship	adorer, vénérer
a worshipper	un fidèle
to follow	suivre
a follower	un adepte
to believe	croire
a belief	une croyance
a creed	un credo, les principes
a dogma	un dogme
a verse	un verset
a doctrine	une doctrine
to endoctrinate	endoctriner
endoctrination	l'endoctrinement
a denomination	une confession religieuse
a non-believer	un incroyant
an atheist	un athée
a pagan, a heathen /'hi:ðən/	un païen
an idol /'aidl/	
supernatural	
to save	

salvation	le salut
tolerance	la tolérance
tolerant	tolérant
intolerance	l'intolérance
intolerant	intolérant
to persecute	persécuter
persecution	la persécution
a fundamentalist	un intégriste
fundamentalism	l'intégrisme

Worship — La pratique religieuse

a cathedral /kəˈθiːdrəl/	une cathédrale
a churchgoer	un pratiquant
an abbey	une abbaye
a mosque /mɔsk/	une mosquée
a temple	un temple
a chapel	une chapelle, un temple
a sanctuary	un sanctuaire
to pray	prier
a prayer	une prière
to celebrate	célébrer
a celebration	une célébration
mass	la messe
a service	un office
to bless	bénir
a blessing	une bénédiction
the congregation	l'assemblée des fidèles
the choir /kwaiə/	le chœur
a hymn	un cantique
to preach	prêcher
a sermon	un sermon
the pulpit	la chaire
a saint	un saint
holy	saint
evil /ˈiːvl/	le mal
to sin	pécher
a sin	un péché
blasphemy	le blasphème
a soul	une âme
to convert	convertir
a conversion	une conversion
a disciple	un disciple

Christianity — Le christianisme

Christ /kraist/	le Christ
the Lord	le Seigneur
the Holy Spirit	le Saint-Esprit

the Blessed Virgin	la Sainte Vierge
the Bible	la Bible
the Gospel	l'Évangile
Easter	Pâques
Whitsun	la Pentecôte
Anglican	anglican
an angel	un ange
to damn	damner
a devil	un diable
Satan /ˈseitən/	Satan
heaven	le ciel
hell	l'enfer
a cross	une croix
to cross oneself	se signer

The Servants — Les serviteurs

an ayatollah /aiəˈtɔlə/	un ayatollah
a rabbi /ˈræbai/	un rabbin
clergy	le clergé
a clergyman	un ecclésiastique
a priest	un prêtre
a vicar	un curé
a parish	une paroisse
a parishioner	un paroissien
a parson, a minister, a pastor	un pasteur
ministry	le ministère religieux
a deacon	un diacre
a bishop	un évêque
an archbishop	un archevêque
a cardinal	un cardinal
the Pope	le pape
to ordain	ordonner
an ordination	une ordination

Cults — Les sectes

to join sth.	adhérer à qch.
a cult	une secte, un culte
a sect	une secte
a member	un membre, un adhérent
membership	les adhérents
a Freemason	un franc-maçon
Freemasonry	la franc-maçonnerie
a Jehovah's Witness	un Témoin de Jéhovah
to recruit /riˈkru:t/	recruter
a recruit	une recrue
recruitment	le recrutement

EXPRESSIONS

a born-again Christian	un chrétien régénéré
a place of worship	un lieu de culte
the Established Church	l'Église officielle
to make a hell of a noise	faire un boucan du diable
a hell of a lot of...	un tas de...
they had a hell of a time	ils en ont bavé
What the hell does she want?	Que peut-elle bien vouloir?

VOCABULAIRE COMPLÉMENTAIRE

Religions and Cults	**Les religions et les sectes**
the Koran	le Coran
Muhammad, Mohammed	Mahomet
a Shiite, a Shiah, a Shia	un chiite
a Druse	un druze
a Sunni	un sunnite
Mecca	la Mecque
Buddha	Bouddha
Buddhism	le bouddhisme
a Buddhist	un bouddhiste
Hinduism	l'hindouisme
a Hindu	un hindouiste
a guru /ˈguru:/	un gourou
a prophet	un prophète
a prophecy	une prophétie
prophetic	prophétique
a martyr	un martyr
martyrdom	le martyre
a saviour	un sauveur
a miracle	un miracle
miraculous	miraculeux
a godsend	un don du ciel
devout /diˈvaut/	dévot
a persuasion	une confession, religion
a devotee	un fervent, un adepte
to lapse	ne plus pratiquer
to curse	maudir
a curse	une malédiction

Worship	La pratique religieuse
to practise	pratiquer
practice	la pratique
a synagogue /ˈsinəgɔg/	une synagogue
a shrine	un lieu saint
a rite	un rite
a sacrament	un sacrement
sacramental	sacramentel
a pilgrim	un pèlerin
a pilgrimage	un pèlerinage
an altar	un autel
an address	une allocution
to fast	jeûner
Ramadan /ˌræməˈdɑ:n/	le ramadan
to swear	jurer
a swear-word, an oath	un juron
to tempt	tenter
temptation	la tentation
sacrilege	un sacrilège
to consecrate	consacrer
a consecration	une consécration
to desecrate	profaner
desecration	la profanation
a crusade	une croisade
sectarian	sectaire, confessionnel

Christianity	Le christianisme
The Messiah /miˈsaiə/	le Messie
the Scriptures	les Écritures
a lesson	une lecture des Écritures
a Testament	un Testament
the Apostles	les apôtres
Christendom	la chrétienté
celibacy	le célibat
a diocese /ˈdaiəsis/	un diocèse
the Holy See	le Saint-Siège
Ecumenism /ˌi:kjuˈmenizm/	l'œcuménisme
Ecumenical	œcuménique
a flock	un troupeau
the fold	le bercail
Lent	le Carême
to baptise, to christen	baptiser
a christening	un baptême
Communion	la communion
your neighbour	votre prochain

The Servants	Les serviteurs
lay	laïque
a layman	un laïc
secular	séculier
the Pontiff	le souverain pontife
a primate	un primat
a curate	un vicaire
a dog collar	un col ecclésiastique
the vicarage, the rectory	le presbytère
a churchwarden	un conseiller paroissial
a missionary	un missionnaire
a chaplain	un aumônier
a monk	un moine
a monastery	un monastère
a nun	une religieuse
to take vows	prononcer des vœux
a religious order	un ordre religieux
theology	la théologie
a theologian	un théologien
a theocracy	une théocratie

Practise your vocabulary.

1. Can you name some of the features that most religions have in common?

2. What can religious intolerance lead to?

3. Are there any conflicts in which religion plays an important part in the world today?

4. Where does fundamentalism appear today? Can you find any explanations for it?

5. What issues are often raised in Christian churches nowadays?

6. What comfort can people find in religion?

7. How can it be explained that so many people are recruited into cult membership?

8. Why do cults sometimes meet with strong opposition?

9. What religious difficulties may immigrants encounter in their adopted country?

WAVE OF PROTESTS AWAITS POPE IN US

From Christopher Thomas, Washington

Details are being completed for the Pope's visit to the United States in September, a trip already beset by controversy, anger and worry at a time when the rift between American Catholics and the Vatican has never been wider.

A top-level American delegation is in Rome this week to discuss plans for the trip and to alert the Vatican about the problems and protests the Pontiff will encounter. He will meet demonstrations at every stop, from feminists, homosexuals, teachers and anti-Catholics.

There are fears among Catholics that what the National Conference of Catholic Bishops called a "growing and dangerous disaffection" within the American Church could be accelerated by the Pope's visit and his emphasis on the reimposition of traditional orthodoxy.

There are 52 million American Catholics, a quarter of the population, but church attendance is low. Many of the faithful have been disillusioned by Rome's disciplining of nuns, theologians and bishops who have stepped out of line.

The Vatican's sweeping new proposals urging governments to ban medical intervention in reproduction has added a further dimension to the rift. Legal experts are warning of interminable fights in the courts if state legislatures or judges attempt to impose laws supporting the Vatican's position on such "illicit" techniques as surrogate motherhood, embryo and sperm banks, artificial insemination and test-tube fertilisation...

The Times,
March 18, 1987

1 Match the explanations (A-E) to the words (1-5).

1. beset 2. rift 3. attendance 4. discipline
5. surrogate

A. punish or correct B. number of people present
C. dissension, difference of opinion D. substitute
E. trouble, harass

2 **Say whether the following statements are true (T) or false (F).**

1. The visit was to take place within a year.
2. Relations between the Vatican and American Catholics were getting better.
3. The trip would be well-prepared.
4. The Pope was too liberal for American Catholics.
5. In the article, we get a rough idea of the total US population.
6. American Catholics are regular churchgoers.
7. All major legislation in the US is passed in Washington.
8. Scientific progress has led to controversy among Catholics.

"Unfortunately, our country's just gone over to Fundamental Islam."

3 **Looking for words.**

1. Pick out two words showing that a dangerous tendency was developing among American Catholics.
2. Find a phrase denoting a lack of discipline among top-level Catholics in the US.
3. The word "bank" usually means an institution offering a number of financial services. But, as in a "sperm bank", it can also indicate a facility for storing. What do you call a place where the following are stored?
A. a lot of information
B. empty containers made of glass for recycling
C. plasma for transfusions

4 **Fill in the blanks with the appropriate words from the following list. Verbs are given in the infinitive.**

atheists to attend to practise faith survey belief findings Catholics

CATHOLIC POLL SHOCK

From Jane Walker in Madrid

A ____ published by the Catholic Church in Spain yesterday showed that, contrary to popular ____ , less than half of Spaniards are ____ , and less than 20 per cent ____ mass regularly.

The ____ showed that only 46 per cent of those questioned, fewer than nine million, said that they were practising Catholics. Thirty-nine per cent said they were believers but did not ____ their religion, and 5 per cent were ____ . Only 7 per cent of those queried said they would be willing to die for their ____

The Guardian, April 2, 1986

5 **Test your knowledge. Only one statement is correct in the pair below. Which one?**

A. Abortion was a major issue in the US during the eighties.
B. During the eighties in the US, abortion was only a minor issue.

ABOLISH LAWS OF BLASPHEMY URGES LEGAL REFORM GROUP

By A. J. McIlroy

Abolition of the crime of blasphemy in the wake of controversy over Salman Rushdie's book, *The Satanic Verses*, was urged today by a Committee of Justice, the British section of the International Commission of Jurists.

In a report on freedom of expression and the law, the committee of leading lawyers, civil servants, academics, and media figures opposed extending the blasphemy laws to include Islam.

"Mr Rushdie has been threatened with death for outraging Muslim feelings and there have been proposals that protection of criminal law should be extended to include Islam," the committee said.

"We are strongly against such proposals. Notwithstanding the possible religious discrimination and other political difficulties, we favour the abolition of blasphemy."

The committee, chaired by Lord Deedes, former editor of *The Daily Telegraph,* was concerned that the threat of disorder or crime was in itself a restriction on freedom of expression.

"Many bookstores have refused to display or even to stock The Satanic Verses after threats of violence.

"We accept that restriction on freedom of expression by the authorities may be necessary to prevent a breach of the peace.

"But we agree with the interpretation of the European Court of Human Rights that a failure to protect from violence those peacefully exercising their right to freedom of expression can itself be a violation of that right"...

The Daily Telegraph,
April 9, 1990

1 Match the explanations (A-G) to the words (1-7).

1. in the wake of
2. urge
3. civil servant
4. academic

A. university or college teacher
B. cause profound indignation
C. preside over
D. after, following
E. offence against public order

5. outrage

6. chair

7. breach of the peace

F. someone who works for a government department

G. strongly recommend

2 **Say whether the following statements are true (T) or false (F).**

1. Blasphemy was a criminal offence at the time.
2. The blasphemy law did not apply to Islam.
3. The main topic in the article is freedom of religion.
4. The blasphemy law would protect Salman Rushdie if it was extended to Islam.
5. The committee underlined other restrictions to freedom of expression.
6. Bookstores refused to display or stock *The Satanic Verses* because its contents might have been against the law.
7. Apparently, it is difficult to find the correct balance between the maintenance of public order and freedom of expression.

3 **The word "book" is often used as a modifier or in combination with another noun, as in "bookstore". Match the definitions (A-F) to the words (1-6) in the following list.**

1. a bookkeeper
2. a bookseller
3. a bookworm
4. a bookmaker
5. a bookcase
6. a bookmark

A. a piece of furniture containing books

B. it is placed between the pages to indicate a place

C. one who keeps records of business transactions

D. you can buy books from him

E. one who takes bets on horse races

F. one who is very fond of reading

12

ENTERTAINMENT AND THE MASS MEDIA — LES SPECTACLES ET LES MASS MÉDIA

VOCABULAIRE A HAUTE FRÉQUENCE

The World of Entertainment	Le monde des spectacles
to entertain	divertir, amuser
to act	jouer
an actor	un acteur
an actress	une actrice
to interpret /in'tɜ:prit/	interpréter
an interpretation	une interprétation
to play (a part, a role)	jouer un rôle
a part, a role	un rôle
the leading part, the lead	le rôle principal
a supporting role	un rôle secondaire
a character	un personnage
a character part	un rôle de composition
an artist	un artiste
a plot	une intrigue
a director	un metteur en scène
to cast	choisir la distribution
a cast	une distribution
to produce	produire
a production	une production
a performance	une représentation
the setting, the scenery	le décor
a designer	un décorateur
to design /di'zain/	dessiner, concevoir
to release	sortir, publier
a release	une sortie, une parution
a comedian	un comédien, un comique
a conjuror	un prestidigitateur
a trick	un tour
an act	un numéro
a circus	un cirque
a show	une revue, un spectacle
ballet	le ballet
ballet dancing	la danse classique
a ballerina	une ballerine
a pantomime	un spectacle musical de Noël

Success and failure	Le succès et l'échec
fame	la célébrité
the box office	le guichet, la caisse
a hit	un succès, un tube
a flop	un four
a fanatic, a fan	un admirateur
an idol /ˈaidl/	une idole
a masterpiece	un chef-d'œuvre
a review	une critique
a reviewer, a critic	un critique
an award	une récompense
to nominate	nommer
a nominee	un candidat désigné
an Oscar winner	un lauréat des Oscars

The Theatre	Le théâtre
a play	une pièce de théâtre
a playwright	un auteur dramatique
a tragedy	une tragédie
a comedy	une comédie
a drama	un drame
to stage	monter (une pièce)
the stage	la scène
to rehearse /riˈhəːs/	répéter
a rehearsal	une répétition
an act	un acte
act two	le deuxième acte
the interval	l'entracte
a curtain call	un rappel

Cinema and Television	Le cinéma et la télévision
a screen	un écran
to screen	projeter
a motion picture (US) a film, a movie	un film
a silent movie	un film muet
the feature film	le film principal
an animated cartoon	un dessin animé
a filmmaker	un cinéaste
to shoot	tourner
a shot	un plan
a cameraman	un opérateur
to edit	monter
an editor	un monteur
editing	le montage

a sequence	une séquence
the soundtrack	la bande sonore
a scenario /si'nɑ:riəu/	un scénario
a script, a screenplay	un scénario détaillé
a scenarist a screenwriter	un scénariste
to star	avoir pour vedette
a star	une vedette
a studio	un studio
pornography /pɔ:'nɔgrəfi/ porn	la pornographie
pornographic /pɔ:nə'græfik/	pornographique
a documentary	un documentaire
a detective film	un film policier
a thriller	un film à suspense
a horror movie	un film d'horreur
to dub	doubler
an undubbed film	un film en version originale
subtitles	les sous-titres

Music — La musique

a concert	un concert
an orchestra /'ɔ:kistrə/	un orchestre
to conduct	diriger (un orchestre)
a conductor	un chef d'orchestre
a concerto /kən'tʃə:təu/	un concerto
a symphony	une symphonie
a sonata /sə'nɑ:tə/	une sonate
a piece	un morceau
a score	une partition
classical	classique
a bar	une mesure
a tune	un air
an instrument	un instrument
a band	une formation, un groupe
lyrics	les paroles
a musical (comedy)	une comédie musicale
to record /ri'kɔ:d/	enregistrer
a record /'rekɔ:d/	un disque
a single	un 45 tours
a maxi single	un super 45 tours
an album	un album
a compact disc	un disque compact
a record shop	un magasin de disques
a record company	une maison de disques

a cassette	une cassette
the charts	le hit-parade
a group	un groupe

Journalism — Le journalisme

a journalist a newspaperman	un journaliste
a news agency	une agence de presse
to report	signaler, faire savoir
reporting	le reportage
an article	un article
the *Times* editor	le directeur du *Times*
the sports editor	le rédacteur sportif
a correspondent	un correspondant
a free lance	un journaliste indépendant
a column	une chronique
a columnist	un chroniqueur
the leading article the leader	l'éditorial principal
an editorial	un éditorial
to publish	éditer
a publisher	un éditeur
a proprietor, an owner	un propriétaire
to investigate	enquêter
an investigation	une enquête
to reveal	révéler
a revelation	une révélation
the popular press	la presse à sensation
a tabloid	un journal de petit format
the quality papers	les journaux sérieux
a copy	un exemplaire
an issue	un numéro (publication)
a headline	un titre
a banner headline	une manchette
the front-page	la une
advertisements	les publicités
classified advertisements	les petites annonces
circulation	le tirage

Radio and Television — La radio et la télévision

to broadcast	émettre
a broadcast, a programme	une émission
to listen in to	écouter (la radio)
a listener	un auditeur
a frequency	une fréquence
a wavelength	une longueur d'ondes
to watch TV, to view	regarder la télé

a viewer	un téléspectateur
a video	un enregistrement vidéo
a station	une station
a channel	une chaîne
a network	un réseau
the news	les informations
a news bulletin, a newscast	un bulletin d'information
a newsreader, a newscaster	un présentateur de journal
to announce	annoncer
an announcer	un speaker
to comment	commenter
a comment	un commentaire
a commentator	un commentateur
to present	présenter
a presenter	un présentateur
a TV crew	une équipe de télé
peak time, prime time	les heures de grande écoute
the ratings	l'indice d'écoute
audience	l'audience
a slot	une tranche horaire
a commercial	une annonce publicitaire
a spot	une coupure publicitaire
a series	une série
a serial	un feuilleton
a soap opera	un feuilleton mélo

Events — Les événements

to cover	couvrir
coverage	la couverture
live	en direct
a summary	un résumé
a source	une source
a leak	une fuite
a topic	un sujet, un thème
current affairs	l'actualité
sensational	sensationnel
sensationalism	recherche du sensationnel
off the record	hors antenne, en privé
to distort	déformer
distortion	la déformation
bias /ˈbaiəs/	le préjugé, le parti pris
biased, one-sided	partial, partisan
unbiased, objective	impartial, objectif
a news conference	une conférence de presse
a statement	une déclaration
a communique /kəmˈju:nikei/	un communiqué

EXPRESSIONS

to be a sell-out	se jouer à guichets fermés
an award-winning film	un film primé
to be presented with an award	recevoir une distinction
to be in the limelight	être sous les projecteurs
to bring to the screen	porter à l'écran
a box-office attraction	un spectacle à grand succès
to play the piano	jouer du piano
to sing out of tune	chanter faux
What's on tonight?	Que peut-on voir ce soir?
the top of the ratings	la tête du classement
to hit the headlines	faire les gros titres
to be given front-page treatment	faire la une des journaux
to give prominence to	mettre en vedette
to fuel rumours	alimenter la rumeur
to carry an exclusive tag	porter la mention "en exclusivité"
to appear on television	paraître à la télévision
to go on television	se montrer à la télévision
to be glued to the TV set	être rivé devant la télé
to be on the air	être à l'antenne
to name sources	révéler ses sources
contempt of court	outrage à magistrat
letters to the editor	le courrier des lecteurs
in order to sell copy	pour augmenter les tirages

VOCABULAIRE COMPLÉMENTAIRE

The World of Entertainment	**Le monde des spectacles**
characterisation	la peinture des caractères
costumes	les costumes
make-up	le maquillage
to impersonate /im'pə:səneit/	imiter
an impersonator	un imitateur
to audition	auditionner

an audition	une séance d'essai
a theatre buff	un mordu, un cinglé de théâtre
a slapstick comedy	une comédie bouffonne
glamour	l'éclat, la séduction
a festival	un festival
a rerun	une reprise
a preview	une avant-première

The Theatre — Le théâtre

a cue	une réplique
a dress rehearsal	une répétition générale
the first night	la première
limelight	les feux de la rampe
stagecraft	l'art de la scène
stage fright	le trac
a stage manager	un régisseur
a repertory company	une troupe du répertoire
an understudy	une doublure
in the wings, backstage	dans les coulisses

Radio and Television — La radio et la télévision

a press review	une revue de presse
a repeat	une rediffusion
the tube, the box	la téloche
a newsflash	un flash d'information
an anchorman	un présentateur
a host	un animateur
a chat show	une conversade
a phone-in	un programme à ligne ouverte
a quiz	un jeu avec questions
a quizmaster	un meneur de jeu
a radio car	une voiture émettrice
an aerial /ˈɛəriəl/	une antenne
cable	le câble
to tune in to	se brancher sur
to zap	zapper

Cinema and Television — Le cinéma et la télévision

an animated feature	un dessin animé de long métrage
a full-length film	un long métrage

a filmgoer, a cinemagoer	un cinéphile
a television film	un téléfilm
to adapt	adapter
an adaptation	une adaptation
a take	une prise de vue
a close-up	un gros plan
location	les extérieurs
an extra	un figurant
a set	un plateau
a stunt	une cascade
a stuntman	un cascadeur
the props	les accessoires
a propman	un accessoiriste
an X-rated film	un film classé X
a U-rated film	un film pour tous
footage	le métrage
in slow motion	au ralenti
a reel	une bobine
a trailer	une bande annonce
the credits	le générique
an episode	un épisode
a sequel	une suite
an impresario /ˌimprəˈsɑːriəu/	un imprésario
gore	l'hémoglobine
a video nasty	une cassette porno et/ou très violente

Journalism — Le journalisme

a tycoon	un magnat
a newshound	un reporter
to highlight	mettre en relief
the highlights	les points importants
to feature	figurer, faire figurer
a feature	un article de fond
a dispatch	une dépêche
a note	un billet
obituaries	la rubrique nécrologique
the agony column	le courrier du cœur
the agony aunt	le journaliste du courrier du cœur
the gossip column	les commérages
a gossip columnist	un chroniqueur mondain
a chief editor	un rédacteur en chef
to contribute to	collaborer à
a contributor	un collaborateur
a broadsheet	un journal grand format
a rag	une feuille de chou

the gutter press	la presse à scandales
a hack	un pisse-copie
an inset	un encart
a cartoon	un dessin humoristique
a cartoonist	un dessinateur humoristique
a caption	une légende
a comic strip	une bande dessinée
the lay-out	la mise en page
a press cutting	une coupure de journal
an excerpt	un extrait
a pull-out supplement	un supplément détachable
news in brief	les nouvelles brèves
miscellaneous news	les faits divers
newsprint	le papier journal

Events / Les événements

a development	une évolution de situation
to hype	matraquer
media hype	le matraquage des médias
to fabricate	inventer, fabriquer
a news blackout	un refus d'informer
to gag	bâillonner
a gag	un bâillon
to censor	censurer
censorship	la censure
propaganda /ˌprɔpəˈgændə/	la propagande
disinformation	la désinformation
an authoritative source	une source autorisée
a reliable source	une source sûre
a press release	un avis à la presse
to brief	mettre au courant
a press briefing	un point de presse
lurid reporting	reportage à sensation
muck raking	la recherche du sordide
to pander to sb.	flatter bassement les goûts de qn.
libel /ˈlaibəl/	la diffamation écrite
defamatory	diffamatoire
to slander	calomnier
slander	la calomnie
to sue /su:/	poursuivre en justice
a breach of privacy	une atteinte à l'intimité, la vie privée
damages	des dommages-intérêts

Practise your vocabulary.

1. What are the essential steps that must be taken before one can start shooting a film?
2. Can your name some of the Oscars that are awarded every year?
3. Describe a visit to the cinema or to the theatre.
4. Does keen competition between the various TV channels influence the nature of programmes?
5. Can you think of any events in which the mass media played a leading role?
6. What sort of difficulties did reporters encounter during the Gulf war?

TODAY IS MURDOCH'S FOR £38M

By Peter Fiddick, Media Editor

Mr Rupert Murdoch's News International group has bought the *Today* newspaper from Mr Tiny Rowland's Lonrho group for £38 million cash. It will be the third owner in the 16-month life of the daily whose founder, Mr Eddy Shah, claimed that it would break the mould of Fleet Street.

Because News International already controls four national newspapers, the acquisition has to be approved by the Secretary for Trade and Industry, Lord Young. Under the terms of the deal, clearance has to be obtained by 4 pm today, but since *Today* has been making substantial losses and no non newspaper-owning bidder is in evidence no objection is expected.

The new editor and managing director of *Today* will be Mr David Montgomery, editor of the biggest Murdoch tabloid, *The News of the World.* He is expected to keep the daily in the middle-market area, endeavouring to establish it as a rival to the *Daily Mail* and *Daily Express*. The *Mail* and *Express* each sell about 1.75 million copies daily, compared with just under 340,000 for *Today*. Both, however, have been slipping in recent years.

Mr Bill O'Neill, News International's marketing specialist, said last night that the group intended to make the paper "lively and informative" and perhaps to take it a bit upmarket of the *Daily Mail.*

The Guardian,
July 1, 1987

1 **Match the definitions (A-G) to the words (1-7).**

1. mould 2. Fleet Street 3. terms 4. deal
5. clearance 6. bidder 7. endeavour

A. one who makes an offer to buy B. try hard
C. shaped cavity used to give a form to D. conditions of an agreement E. permission to go ahead
F. business transaction G. place where most papers used to have their offices

2 **Choose the appropriate endings for the following statements.**

1. The first owners of *Today*
A. kept the paper for a very long time.
B. sold the paper after a fairly long time.
C. gave up quickly.

2. When he founded *Today*, M. Eddy Shah intended
A. to follow the line of existing papers.
B. to have a new style for his paper.
C. to cooperate with existing papers.

3. Lord Young might have objected to the deal because of
A. monopoly considerations.
B. insufficient circulation.
C. a low selling price.

4. The acquisition of *Today* seems to have been
A. a very safe investment.
B. a considerable risk.
C. a very attractive prospect.

5. When bidding for *Today*, News International
A. had no definite plans.
B. had worked out a plan.
C. was looking for an editor.

6. To a foreign reader, the circulation figures for the *Daily Mail* and the *Daily Express* sound
A. really high.
B. rather low.
C. frankly disappointing.

7. Their main concern seemed to be
A. improving the quality of news coverage.
B. increasing their share of the market.
C. keeping the paper's identity and style intact.

3 **As in "newspaper", "news" is the first element in a number of words. Match the definitions (A-G) to the words (1-7).**

1. newsworthy
2. newsroom
3. newsstand
4. newsprint
5. newsagent / newsdealer (US)
6. newsreel
7. newsletter

A. paper used for newspapers
B. short film showing current events
C. circular sent to members of a group
D. place where news is received and prepared for publication or broadcasting
E. interesting enough to be reported
F. one who sells papers
G. stall in a street at which papers are sold.

"Imagine that – I didn't know that there'd been an information explosion."

PORN "RISK" IN RATINGS FIGHT

By Maggie Brown

Broadcasters will be tempted to turn to cheap, violent programmes and even soft pornography in the 1990s, Lord Rees Mogg, chairman of the Broadcasting Standards Council, warned yesterday.

He said television companies, facing financial pressures from the impact of franchise auctions and a recession in advertising revenue, would try to push up ratings in the easiest way available.

"I think there is a danger that the average, pretty tedious but pretty violent programme, which can be bought in easily and cheaply will increase in numbers because that is not a bad way of getting up ratings," Lord Rees Mogg said. "It is also obvious that there will be an increasing resort to soft porn, though hard porn is never going to be part of mainstream television".

Lord Rees Mogg, a former deputy chairman of the BBC board of governors, used his speech at the *Financial Times* cable and satellite conference to link the proposed auction of ITV franchises with lower programme standards, the key political controversy at the heart of the Broadcasting Bill (...).

He said that the chief aim of the proposed ITV auction system was to get as much money as possible for the Treasury. This was a complete switch from the old system under which ITV companies were keen to produce high quality programmes to impress the Independent Broadcasting Authority.

"The more they pay, the less money they will have for programmes, especially in the period of immediately after..."

The Independent,
March 2, 1990

1 Match the definitions (A-H) to the words (1-8).

1. warn 2. franchise 3. auction 4. tedious 5. resort 6. mainstream 7. bill 8. switch

A. sale, or attribution, to the person offering the highest price B. recourse C. proposed law D. change, transfer E. right granted to broadcast F. inform in advance, make aware of G. uninteresting, monotonous. H. dominant trend or tendency

2 **Say whether the following statements are true (T) or false (F).**

1. According to Lord Rees Mogg, television companies would be better off financially in the 1990s.
2. Viewers often like to watch cheap programmes.
3. Lord Rees Mogg was still on the BBC board of governors in March 1990.
4. He was in favour of the Broadcasting Bill.
5. He seemed to think the old system paid more attention to quality.
6. The dilemma facing TV companies is made clear in the article.

3 **Looking for words. Read the article and pick out:**

A. Two adjectives which are commonly used for drugs. Which one of them is also used for a landing and which one for a currency?
B. The word indicating the main source of revenue for ITV companies (paragraph two).
C. The word referring to programmes' levels of popularity (paragraphs two and three).
D. Two more recent means of broadcasting which are likely to play an important part in the 1990s (paragraph four).

4 **Fill in the blanks with words taken from the article.**

A. I don't really know which ____________ to watch.
B. The present slowdown in activity will probably lead to a ____________
C. He went to sleep; it was ____________ he was not interested in the show.
D. The chairman could not attend the meeting, so he asked his ____________ to represent him.

INTRODUCTION TO CHAPTERS 13,14,15,16,17,18,19,20	INTRODUCTION AUX CHAPITRES 13,14,15,16,17,18,19,20
Crime	La criminalité
Drugs	La drogue
Demonstrations	Les manifestations
Revolutions	Les révolutions
War	La guerre
Miscellaneous Topics	Centres d'intérêt divers
Accidents	Les accidents
Natural Disasters	Les catastrophes naturelles

VOCABULAIRE A HAUTE FRÉQUENCE

Physical Damage	Les dégâts matériels
to blast, to explode	exploser
a blast, an explosion	une explosion
an explosive	un explosif
to set off	déclencher
to go off	se déclencher, exploser
to damage	endommager, abîmer
damage	les dégâts
to wreck	saccager
wreckage	les débris, les décombres
to destroy	détruire
destruction	la destruction
to happen	se produire
to occur	survenir
to scatter	disperser
to devastate	ravager, dévaster
devastation	la dévastation, les ravages
devastating	dévastateur
to collapse	s'effondrer
rubble	les décombres, les gravats
debris	les débris
ruins	les ruines
to demolish	démolir
demolition	la démolition
to assess	évaluer
an assessment	une évaluation
scope, extent	l'étendue
a scale	une échelle de grandeur
the scene	les lieux
a disaster	un désastre
a catastrophe /kəˈtæstrəfi/	une catastrophe

Casualties	Les victimes
to injure, to hurt	blesser
to wound	blesser (attaque)
slight, minor /ˈmainə/	léger
serious, major	grave
an injury	une blessure
a wound	une blessure (attaque)
to bury	ensevelir
to trap	coincer, bloquer
a shock	une commotion
unhurt	indemne
to escape	s'en sortir
alive	vivant
to shelter	abriter
a shelter	un abri, un refuge
a death toll	un bilan des morts

Rescue Work	Intervention des secours
alarm	l'alarme, l'alerte
to survive	survivre
a survivor	un rescapé
to attempt	tenter
an attempt, a bid	une tentative
to rescue	secourir
a rescue operation	une opération de secours
relief	l'aide, le secours
first aid	les premiers soins
to save	sauver
an emergency	une urgence
a refugee	un réfugié
to clear	déblayer
to pull clear	dégager
a heap	un tas
a pile	un amas
to recover	retrouver, récupérer
a stretcher	une civière
to take to	transporter à
an ambulance	une ambulance
to identify	identifier
to name	nommer
to loot	piller
to demolish	démolir
demolition	la démolition
to evacuate	évacuer
evacuation	l'évacuation

Weapons	Les armes
to shoot	tirer
a shot	un coup de feu
to fire	tirer un coup de feu
a firearm	une arme à feu
to arm	armer
a pistol	un pistolet
a handgun	une arme de poing
a gun, a rifle	un fusil
gunfire	une fusillade
a shotgun	un fusil de chasse
a gunman	un homme armé
a bullet	une balle
a grenade	une grenade
automatic	automatique
a bomb	une bombe
to bomb	bombarder (avion)
a bombing	un bombardement
to machine gun	mitrailler
a machine gun	une mitrailleuse
a gun	un canon
a mortar	un mortier
a rocket	une roquette
to shell	bombarder (obus)
a shell	un obus
artillery	l'artillerie
ammunition	les munitions
to mine	miner
a mine	une mine
an armoured car	un véhicule blindé
a tank	un char d'assaut
a missile	un missile

Violent Actions	Les actions violentes
to threaten /'θretn/	menacer
a threat /θret/	une menace
to blackmail	faire du chantage
blackmail	le chantage
to kidnap, to abduct	kidnapper, enlever
an abduction, kidnapping	un enlèvement, un rapt
to attack	attaquer
an attack	une attaque
to clash with	se heurter à
a clash	un affrontement
to raid	attaquer
a bank raid	une attaque de banque
to burst into	faire irruption dans

to demand	exiger
a demand	une exigence
a ransom	une rançon
to take over	s'emparer de
to mask	masquer
a mask	un masque
to blow up	faire sauter
a target	une cible
to assassinate	assassiner
an assassination	un assassinat
a network, a ring	un réseau
to fight	lutter, combattre
a fight	un combat, une lutte
a battle	une bataille
a gunfight	un échange de coups de feu
a siege /si:dʒ/	un siège

Security — La sécurité

to crack down on sth.	réprimer qch.
a crackdown on	une répression de
to clamp down on sth.	donner un coup d'arrêt à, durcir la lutte contre
a clampdown on sth.	un durcissement de la lutte contre qch. un tour de vis
to combat sth.	mener une lutte contre qch.
to look for, to search for	rechercher
a search	une recherche, une fouille
to enquire	enquête, se renseigner
an enquiry	une enquête
to investigate	examiner, enquêter
an investigation	un examen, une enquête
a detective constable	un inspecteur de police
a detective inspector	un inspecteur principal
a detective superintendent	un commissaire de police
a detective chief superintendent	un commissaire divisionnaire
security forces	les forces de sécurité
a security guard	un vigile un convoyeur de fonds
a bodyguard	un garde du corps
to patrol	patrouiller
a patrol	une patrouille
to block	bloquer
a road block	un barrage routier

to flee	fuir, s'enfuir
to surround	cerner, entourer
to overpower	maîtriser
to arrest	arrêter
an arrest	une arrestation
to hold	interpeller
to detain	garder à vue
to outlaw	mettre hors la loi
to ban	interdire
a ban	une interdiction
a raid	une descente
to curb	juguler
to quell	étouffer, réprimer
to storm	donner l'assaut
to dismantle	démanteler
to impose	imposer
a curfew	un couvre-feu
a truce	une trêve
a ceasefire	un cessez-le-feu
a peacekeeping force	une force d'interposition
to give oneself in/up to turn oneself in	se rendre, se livrer
to surrender	se rendre, capituler
a surrender	une reddition
to prevent	empêcher, prévenir
prevention	la prévention
to free, to set free to release	relâcher, libérer
a release	une libération

EXPRESSIONS

to set fire to sth. to set sth. on fire	mettre le feu à qch.
to set sth. alight, ablaze	embraser qch.
to raise the alarm	donner l'alarme
to lift a ban	lever une interdiction
to make a getaway	prendre la fuite
to be in hiding	se cacher
to be on the run	ne pas avoir été arrêté
to be at large	être dans la nature
to take refuge	prendre refuge
to keep an open mind	ne rejeter aucune piste
to pose a threat	constituer une menace
tit for tat	la loi du talion
to be under arrest	être en état d'arrestation
to raise a ransom	réunir une rançon

at point-blank range	à bout portant
to hold sb. at gunpoint	braquer une arme sur qn.
to take up arms	prendre les armes
to be up in arms against	s'insurger contre
to lay down arms	déposer les armes
riddled with bullets	criblé de balles
to lay siege to	faire le siège de
a surface to air missile	un missile sol-air
to take one's toll	prélever son tribut
to claim 20 lives to leave 20 people dead	faire 20 morts
to lose one's life	trouver la mort
to die instantly	mourir tout de suite
to be killed outright	être tué sur le coup
to be in a coma	être dans le coma
to lose consciousness	perdre connaissance
the kiss of life, mouth to mouth resuscitation	le bouche à bouche
to recover consciousness	reprendre connaissance
to be unaccounted for	ne pas avoir été retrouvé
to be missing	être porté disparu
flags at half mast	les drapeaux en berne
to offer condolences	présenter des condoléances

VOCABULAIRE COMPLÉMENTAIRE

Physical Damage	**Les dégâts matériels**
to rip through	souffler
to shatter	fracasser
to gut	éventrer
a tangle	un enchevêtrement
remains	les restes
to cave in, to subside	s'affaisser
catastrophic	catastrophique

Casualties and Rescue work	**Les victimes et l'intervention des secours**
to dial 999 to dial 911 (US)	appeler police-secours
unscathed /ˌʌnˈskeiðd/	indemne
a cut	une coupure
to bruise /bru:z/	meurtrir, tuméfier
a bruise	une meurtrissure
to mutilate	mutiler
belongings	les possessions

to pass out	s'évanouir
to come to	revenir à soi
to resuscitate	réanimer
resuscitation	la réanimation
survival	la survie
a theory	une hypothèse
a corpse	un cadavre
a tally of deaths	un décompte des morts
a coffin	un cercueil
a shroud	un linceul
a mortuary	une morgue, une chapelle ardente
a memorial service	un service du souvenir
relatives	la famille
to shed blood	répandre le sang
bloodshed, bloodletting	l'effusion de sang
a bloodbath	un bain de sang
to mourn sb.	porter le deuil de qn.
mourning	le deuil

Violent Actions and Security — Les actions violentes et la sécurité

on the alert	en état d'alerte
to outlaw	mettre hors la loi
captive	captif
captivity	la captivité
to occupy	occuper
an occupation	une occupation
a skirmish	une escarmouche un accrochage
to ambush	tendre une embuscade tomber dans une embuscade
to erupt	se déclencher brusquement
an eruption	un déclenchement brusque
an upsurge	une recrudescence
a spate	(toute) une série
arson	l'incendie criminel
to mastermind	organiser
a mastermind	un cerveau
a scheme /ski:m/	un stratagème, un projet
a ploy	un stratagème
to avenge	venger
revenge	une revanche
to respond	répliquer
a response	une réplique

to retaliate	riposter
retaliation	la riposte
reprisals	les représailles
a carbon copy	une réplique exacte
an assumed name	un nom d'emprunt
the whereabouts	l'endroit où est qn.
to vanish	disparaître
to conceal	dissimuler
a hideaway, a hide-out	une cachette, une planque
an arms cache /kæʃ/	une cache d'armes
a haul	une prise, un butin
a hood	une cagoule
a wig	une perruque
a sniper	un tireur isolé
a ringleader	un meneur
an accomplice	un complice
complicity	la complicité
an informant, an informer	un informateur
a repentant informer	un repenti
a tip, a tip-off	un renseignement
surveillance	la surveillance
to thwart	contrecarrer
to stalk	traquer, filer
to move in	intervenir
to trap, to entrap	piéger
a trap	un piège, une souricière
a strike	un coup de main, un raid
to rage	faire rage
to bombard	bombarder
bombardment	le bombardement
headquarters	le quartier général
a deadline	une limite de temps une date butoir
to cordon off to seal off	boucler, interdire l'accès
to barricade oneself	se barricader
a police cordon	un cordon de police
to handcuff	passer les menottes à
handcuffs	les menottes
to regain (control)	reprendre (le contrôle)
to extradite	extrader
an extradition	une extradition
to besiege	assiéger
beleaguered	assiégé, investi
a shoot-out	une fusillade
a bulletproof vest	un gilet pare-balles
a marksman a sharpshooter	un tireur d'élite
a stray bullet	une balle perdue

a state of emergency	un état d'urgence
a state of siege	un état de siège
martial law	la loi martiale
to swoop	faire une descente
a swoop	un coup de filet
to round up	effectuer une rafle
a round-up	un regroupement, une rafle
to sweep	ratisser
a sweep	un ratissage
to sift through	passer au crible
to comb	fouiller, ratisser
to massacre / to slaughter	massacrer
a massacre / a slaughter	un massacre
to exterminate	exterminer
an extermination	une extermination
to execute	exécuter
a summary execution	une exécution sommaire
a mass grave	une fosse commune
genocide	le génocide

Weapons — Les armes

an arms dealer	un marchand d'armes
gun running	le trafic d'armes
a battery	une batterie
the butt	la crosse
a gun barrel	un canon de fusil
a silencer	un silencieux
the trigger	la détente
to pull the trigger	presser la détente
a sawn-off shotgun	un fusil à canon scié
a pump action shotgun	un fusil à pompe
a submachine gun	une mitraillette
an arms dump	un dépôt d'armes
ammunition	les munitions
a cartridge	une cartouche
a blank shot	un tir à blanc
a live bullet	une balle réelle
a volley	une rafale
to strafe	mitrailler, bombarder
gunshot	le plomb de chasse
a rubber bullet	une balle de caoutchouc
a limpet mine	une mine ventouse
a time bomb	une bombe à retardement
a cluster bomb	une bombe à fragmentation

13 CRIME AND PUNISHMENT — DÉLITS ET SANCTIONS

(voir *Introduction* p. 136)

VOCABULAIRE A HAUTE FRÉQUENCE

General Background	**Contexte général**
an offence	un délit, une infraction
a crime	un délit, un crime
to commit	commettre
to break	transgresser, violer
to uphold	faire respecter, maintenir
the law	la loi
an offender, a criminal	un délinquant
a law-breaker	un contrevenant
crime	la délinquance
petty crime	la petite délinquance
the crime rate	le taux de criminalité
law-abiding	respectueux de la loi
security	la sécurité
insecurity	l'insécurité

Non-Violent Crime	**Les délits sans violence**
shoplifting	le vol à l'étalage
a shoplifter	un voleur à l'étalage
to smuggle	passer en fraude
smuggling	la contrebande
to forge	contrefaire
forgery	la contrefaçon
to deceive /di'si:v/	tromper
deception	la tromperie
confidence	la confiance
to con sb.	escroquer, duper qn.
a conman	un escroc, un imposteur
to pose as	se faire passer pour
to pretend to be	affirmer être
a bogus repairman	un faux dépanneur
to trust sb.	avoir confiance en qn.

libel /ˈlaibəl/	la diffamation écrite
to steal	dérober
a thief	un voleur
a theft	un vol

Violent Crime — Les délits avec violence

to rob	voler
a robbery	un vol qualifié
an armed robbery	un vol à main armée
to hold up	braquer, neutraliser
a hold-up	un braquage
to burgle	cambrioler
a burglary	un cambriolage
a burglar	un cambrioleur
to break in	entrer par effraction
a break-in	une effraction
a hooligan	un casseur
to vandalise	vandaliser
a vandal	un vandale
vandalism	le vandalisme
a thug	un loubard
to mug, to assault	agresser
a mugging, an assault	une agression
to rape	violer
a rape	un viol
a rapist	un violeur
child abuse	les sévices aux enfants
manslaughter	homicide par imprudence
to murder	assassiner
a murder	un meurtre
attempted murder a murder attempt	tentative de meurtre
to stab	poignarder
to strangle	étrangler

Enquiries and Arrests — Enquêtes et arrestations

a constable, an officer	un agent, un gendarme
a cop, a copper	un flic
to suspect	soupçonner
a suspect	un suspect
suspicion	les soupçons
suspicious	soupçonneux, suspect
a description	un signalement

a clue	un indice
a lead /li:d/	une piste
to give away	dénoncer
evidence	témoignage, preuve
to question	interroger
to accuse	accuser
an accusation	une accusation
alleged	présumé
to charge	inculper, accuser
a charge	une inculpation, une accusation

Justice — La justice

a court	un tribunal
a magistrate	un magistrat, un juge d'instance
to judge	juger
a judge	un juge
a judgment	un jugement
a trial	un procès
a case	une affaire, un procès
to prosecute	poursuivre
prosecution	des poursuites l'accusation
a prosecutor	un procureur
to witness sth.	être témoin de qch.
a witness	un témoin
to testify	témoigner, déposer
a testimony	un témoignage
to admit, to own up	reconnaître
to confess	avouer
to deny	nier
a denial	un démenti, une dénégation
guilt	la culpabilité
guilty	coupable
not guilty	non coupable
innocent	innocent
to plead	plaider
to sentence	condamner
a sentence	une peine, une condamnation
tough, harsh, stiff	dur, rigoureux
lenient	indulgent
leniency	l'indulgence
punishment	le châtiment
to fine	donner une amende
a fine	une amende

a prison **a jail, a gaol /dʒeil/**	une prison
to jail, to gaol	emprisonner
life imprisonment	la réclusion à vie
life sentence	condamnation à perpétuité
a warder, a prison officer	un gardien, un surveillant
to escape, to break out	s'évader
an escape, a break-out	une évasion
the death penalty	la peine de mort
capital punishment	la peine capitale
to abolish	abolir
abolition	l'abolition
to restore	rétablir
restoration	le rétablissement

EXPRESSIONS

to be taken in	être dupé
to steal a car	voler une voiture
to rob a passenger	voler un passager
the mail train robbery	l'attaque du train postal
to force one's way into	s'introduire de force dans
to be set upon	se faire attaquer
to produce a weapon	sortir une arme
grievous bodily harm	coups et blessures
to appear before magistrates	être présenté au juge
to help with enquiries	être entendu par la police
to act suspiciously	avoir une attitude suspecte
to arouse suspicion	éveiller les soupçons
to be caught red-handed	être pris sur le fait
to issue a photofit picture **to release an identikit picture**	publier un portrait robot
the Serious Crime Squad	la Brigade de répression du banditisme
to be remanded on bail	être laissé en liberté sous caution, sous contrôle
to be remanded in custody	être placé en détention, être incarcéré
under house arrest	assigné à résidence
to bring to court	poursuivre en justice
to bring to trial	assigner en justice
to bring an action against **to serve a writ on sb.**	intenter une action en justice contre
to be tried in one's absence	être jugé par contumace

to settle out of court	régler à l'amiable
to be convicted of	être convaincu de, reconnu coupable de
to serve a sentence	purger une peine
to uphold a judgment	confirmer un jugement
to quash a conviction	casser une condamnation
a miscarriage of justice	une erreur judiciaire
a travesty of justice	une parodie de justice
to speak under duress	parler sous la contrainte
to take the law into one's own hands	se faire justice soi-même
to be jailed for three months	être condamné à trois mois de prison
to receive a jail sentence	être condamné à une peine d'emprisonnement
a non-custodial sentence	une peine autre que la prison
to run into trouble	avoir des ennuis
to stay out of trouble	ne plus avoir d'ennuis

VOCABULAIRE COMPLÉMENTAIRE

General Background	**Contexte général**
a wrongdoer	un malfaiteur
a misdemeanour /ˌmisdiˈmi:nə/	un méfait, un délit
lawful	légal
unlawful	illégal
illicit	illicite
an infringement	une infraction
a first offender	un délinquant primaire
a hardened criminal	un repris de justice

Non-Violent Crime	**Les délits sans violence**
misconduct	l'indélicatesse
to trespass	s'introduire sans permission
a trespasser	un intrus
trespassing	l'intrusion illégale
to poach	braconner
contraband	la contrebande
to fake	falsifier

a counterfeit note **a fake note**	un faux billet
a fence	un receleur
a breach	une violation
a breach of trust	un abus de confiance
to trick sb.	tromper qn.
a trick	un tour, une supercherie
a trickster	un filou
a confidence trick	un abus de confiance
a crook	un escroc, un filou
to swindle	escroquer, estamper
a swindle	une escroquerie
to bribe	corrompre, soudoyer
a bribe	un pot de vin
bribery	la corruption
fraud	la fraude
a fraudster	un fraudeur
to defraud	escroquer, frustrer
to defame	diffamer
defamation /defə'meiʃən/	la diffamation
defamatory /di'fæmətəri/	diffamatoire
to slander	calomnier
slander	la diffamation orale
to solicit /sə'lisit/	racoler
a prostitute	une prostituée
a pimp	un souteneur
indecent exposure	outrage public à la pudeur
gross indecency	outrage aux bonnes mœurs

Violent Crime — Les délits avec violence

a felony	un forfait, un crime
an arsonist	un incendiaire
a firebug	un pyromane
an affray	une rixe
a brawl	une bagarre
indecent assault	attentat à la pudeur
a highwayman	un bandit de grand chemin
to tie, to bind	attacher
to blindfold	bander les yeux
to gag	bâillonner
a safe	un coffre-fort
a vault	une chambre forte
to get away	se sauver
a getaway	une fuite
the mob, the mafia	la mafia
a gangster, a mobster	un truand, un gangster

a godfather	un parrain
a hired gunman	un tueur à gages
a contract	un contrat
organised crime	le crime organisé le grand banditisme
the underworld	le milieu
conspiracy	association de malfaiteurs

Enquiries and Arrests — Enquêtes et arrestations

an eye witness	un témoin oculaire
a statement	une déclaration
a reward	une récompense
a beat	une ronde, un îlot
a trail	une piste
a fingerprint	une empreinte digitale
a riddle	une énigme
an alibi /ˈælibai/	un alibi
a warrant	un mandat
a manhunt	une chasse à l'homme
to hound, to track down	traquer
a jailbreak	une évasion
to recapture	reprendre (évadé)
to be involved in	être mêlé à
a motive	un mobile
to prove	prouver
a proof	une preuve
to substantiate	fournir des preuves à l'appui de
incriminating evidence	une pièce à conviction
an inquest	une enquête après mort
a post-mortem	une autopsie
forensic evidence	expertise médico-légale
a coroner	un chargé d'enquête après mort suspecte
the culprit	l'auteur, le coupable
a put-up job a set-up	une machination un coup monté
to frame sb.	monter un coup contre qn.
an allegation	une allégation
to lock up	mettre sous les verrous

Justice — La justice

a juvenile court	un tribunal pour enfants
a criminal record	un casier judiciaire
previous convictions	condamnations antérieures

a jury	un jury
a juror	un juré
to sue /su:/	intenter une action contre
to try sb.	faire passer qn. en jugement
a lawsuit	un procès
the defendant	le prévenu
the plaintiff	le plaignant
in camera	à huis-clos
a lawyer	un homme de loi
a solicitor	un notaire un avocat-conseil
a counsel, a barrister	un avocat à la cour
a defence attorney (US)	un avocat
a district attorney (US)	un procureur
prosecution	le ministère public
the dock	le banc des accusés
a hearing	une audience, une audition
an account	une déclaration
an affidavit	une déposition
a confession	un aveu
to indict /in'dait/	mettre en accusation
an indictment	un acte d'accusation
a count	un chef d'accusation
to cross-examine	interroger un témoin de la partie adverse
a cross-examination	un contre-interrogatoire
to recant	se rétracter
a recantation	une rétractation
to sum up	conclure
summing-up	les conclusions
to rule	décider, ordonner
a ruling	une décision, un jugement
a verdict	un verdict
to acquit	acquitter
an acquittal	un acquittement
to discharge	relaxer
a discharge	une relaxe
to caution	mettre en garde
a caution	un avertissement
extenuating circumstances mitigating circumstances	circonstances atténuantes
to exonerate	disculper, innocenter
to convict	déclarer coupable
a conviction	une condamnation
a suspended sentence	une peine avec sursis
to appeal	faire appel
mercy	la clémence
to pardon	gracier, amnistier

pardon	la grâce
amnesty	l'amnistie
remission	remise de peine
on parole	en liberté conditionnelle
a bar	un barreau
a cell	une cellule
an inmate, a detainee	un détenu
solitary confinement	l'isolement carcéral
a prison governor	un directeur de prison
a remand centre **a detention centre**	un centre de détention
exercise	la promenade (en prison)
community work	les travaux d'intérêt général
alternative punishment	peine de substitution
probation	mise à l'épreuve
a probation officer	un agent de tutelle
death row /rəu/	le couloir de la mort
a stay of execution	un sursis à exécution
an executioner	un bourreau
to deter	dissuader
deterrent	dissuasif
to prevent	prévenir, empêcher
prevention	la prévention
a neighbourhood watch scheme	un comité de vigilance de quartier

Practise your vocabulary.

1. What forms of crime are those which make people feel unsafe in large cities?
2. Do you know of anyone among your neighbours or your relations who has been the victim of a crime?
3. What are the causes of the rise in the crime rate according to conservative-minded people?
4. What are the views of liberal-minded people?
5. Why do a number of people sometimes take the law into their own hands?
6. Are there any dangers in this attitude?
7. What are some of the reasons why prisons are often in the news?
8. What are some of the arguments used by those who favour the restoration of the death penalty?

Youth attacks woman

A woman was recovering in hospital at Okehampton last night after being brutally attacked by a youth armed with a stick. She suffered a fractured nose, severe bruising and possible internal injuries in what police described as "a vicious and unprovoked assault."

The 37-year-old woman's torment began just before 1 p.m. as she was walking her dog along the tramlines between Fatherford and Okehampton station. The youth, aged between 14 and 16, suddenly sprang at her, hit her repeatedly with a stick and punched her in the face.

He demanded money and when she said she had none told her "to bring some along next time". He ran off and the woman staggered to the road where residents helped her to hospital.

Police said last night that she was being detained for observation and her husband was at her bedside.

The youth was described as being about 5ft. 6in. tall of slim build and with short brown hair. He was wearing a dark blue parka with a fur-trimmed hood, dark trousers and trainers. Anyone with information is asked to telephone police on Okehampton 2201 or their nearest police station.

The Western Morning News,
April 4, 1986

1 Match the definitions (A-F) to the words (1-6).

1. stick
2. bruise
3. vicious
4. stagger
5. hood
6. trainers

A. part of a garment which can cover the head and neck
B. walk unsteadily as if ready to fall
C. running shoes
D. mark left on the skin after receiving a blow
E. piece of wood
F. wicked or cruel

2 Say whether the following statements are true (T) or false (F).

1. The first sentence is a good summary of the passage.
2. The attack happened in a busy place.
3. The woman had no time to react.
4. The youth implied that he would attack her again in the future.
5. The woman ran for help.

6. We know right from the first paragraph that her being detained for observation was fully justified.
7. The youth was tall.
8. The police are relying solely on local residents for information.
9. Such an incident would be reported differently in a national newspaper.

3 **Fill in the blanks with words taken from the article.**

1. Several arrests were made when demonstrators clashed with the police and it is reported that several people are still ____________
2. A lot of damage was caused by the gale, specially in the western area, which was severely ______________ .
3. After being punched repeatedly by the defending champion, the challenger ____________ back to his corner.
4. He was not feeling well last week but now he has fully ____________ .
5. When he fell off his bike, he bumped into a tree and was badly ____________ on the forehead.
6. They ____________ big losses because a lot of customers stayed away during the railway strike.

4 **One sentence has been cut into parts and the parts scrambled. Put them back into the right order. (Punctuation and the capital letter at the beginning of the sentence have been removed.)**

Man's body found

beside a country lane / Oxfordshire / was found with stab wounds / at Hampton Gay / police launched a murder inquiry / near Kidlington / after the body of a 70-year-old taxi driver

Nurse foils mugger

A Clifton nurse fought back when a mugger snatched her handbag.

The nurse, aged 25, was in Cotham Hill Bristol, when a scruffy man grabbed her bag.

She chased him and kicked him, forcing him to drop the bag. Then the man hit her in the face before running off.

The nurse was not badly hurt and gave the police a full description of her attacker.

He is aged about 25 with unkempt dark collar-length hair and was wearing a leather jacket and jeans.

The Evening Post, Bristol

TWO SHOT IN SECURITY VAN RAID

By Terry Kirby

A security guard and a motorcyclist were injured when two men fired several shots during an armed raid on a security van in Surrey yesterday.

The raiders, both armed with handguns, fired at least six shots during the raid on a Group 4 van delivering to the National Westminster Bank in Coulsdon. They escaped empty-handed.

Neither man was seriously injured but both were detained in hospital last night.

Scotland Yard said the raid began as the van stopped outside the bank. The two gunmen confronted the driver and a second guard who had got out. They then knocked on the side of the van and demanded that a third guard inside pass out the money. One of the robbers then fired two shots into the ground.

The robbers ran off but a passing motorcyclist stopped and tackled the men. He was shot in the thigh. The two guards chased the gunmen up an alley, where three shots were fired, one of which hit a guard in the foot.

Police said both gunmen were white. One was in his 30s, about 5ft 8in to 5ft 10in tall, and wearing a trilby hat and dark-rimmed glasses. The other man was younger, 5ft 4in to 5ft 6in tall, and had dark, shoulder-length hair.

The Independent, August 26, 1987

1 **Match the definitions (A-F) to the words (1-6).**

1. van
2. deliver
3. tackle
4. thigh
5. alley
6. trilby

A. upper part of the leg, above the knee
B. make an attempt to stop
C. narrow lane or passage
D. a man's soft felt hat
E. carry goods to a destination
F. covered motor vehicle for transporting goods

2 **Say whether the following statements are true (T) or false (F).**

1. The injured security guard was there all day to protect the bank and its customers.
2. The van had come to take away the money deposited by the bank's customers.

3. The raiders escaped empty-handed because they had dropped their guns.
4. They threatened the guard who was inside the van.
5. The motorcyclist was both courageous and reckless.
6. It is obvious that the security guards also fired several shots.
7. One detail is reminiscent of Al Capone's days.
8. The raiders' behaviour leads one to believe that they were part of an organised crime ring.

3 **The word "shot" can take on different meanings according to the context. Find the appropriate definitions (A-G) corresponding to the phrases (1-7).**

1. a shot in the arm
2. like a shot
3. a shot in the dark
4. a big shot, a hotshot
5. have a shot at
6. a good shot
7. shot put

A. try to, attempt to
B. an important person
C. one who shoots well
D. athletics event with a heavy metal ball
E. something that revives or restores
F. a wild guess
G. very quickly

4 **Choose the appropriate endings (A-F) for the following sentences (1-6).**

1. One of two murderers who broke out of Perth prison on Monday night
2. Police launched a murder inquiry yesterday after the body of a boy, aged 12,
3. Mr Wilson, 58, who was standing at the side of his pool, was shot once in the head in what appeared to be a professional assassination
4. Sir James Hennessy, the Chief Inspector of prisons, wrote in his report that poor conditions and overcrowding
5. A Conservative peer has launched a campaign for the reintroduction of the death penalty – by lethal injection –
6. The four suspects were convicted solely on confessions, which they said had been beaten out of them

A. had been major causes of last year's serious prison riots.
B. for certain types of murder, including that of police and prison officers.
C. by the police and which they retracted at their trial.

D. was recaptured yesterday hiding in the attic of a doctor's surgery.
E. was found partially buried yesterday.
F. by a young, grey-tracksuited man who had arrived at the house on a yellow bicycle.

Meter conman steals jewels

Money and two gold rings have been stolen from an elderly woman in St Werburghs, Bristol, by a man claiming to be an electricity meter reader.

The man called at her house in James Street. He was allowed in although he had no identification and was not wearing a uniform.

The pensioner later discovered he had stolen £28 and two gold rings set with rubies.

The man was white, in his mid 20s, 5ft 3ins tall, thin, had neatly-cut black hair and was wearing dark trousers and a grey and dark red jumper.

He had an Irish accent.

The Evening Post,
Bristol

14

DRUGS LA DROGUE

(voir *Introduction* p. 136)

VOCABULAIRE A HAUTE FRÉQUENCE

Drugs	**La drogue**
dope	la drogue
narcotics /nɑːˈkɔtiks/	les stupéfiants
glue	la colle
glue sniffing	l'inhalation de solvants
a solvent	un solvant
hemp	le chanvre
marijuana /ˌmæriˈhwɑːnə/	la marijuana
cannabis	le cannabis
hashish	le haschish
LSD	le LSD
cocaine /kəˈkein/	la cocaïne
crack	le crack
opium	l'opium
heroin	l'héroïne
powder	la poudre
a soft drug	une drogue douce
a hard drug	une drogue dure

Addiction	**La dépendance**
a joint	un joint
to inhale, to sniff	inhaler, respirer
to swallow	avaler
to inject	injecter
an injection	une injection
a syringe /ˈsirindʒ/	une seringue
a needle	une aiguille
a fix	une piqûre, une injection
a dose	une dose
an overdose	une overdose
high	défoncé
a kick	une sensation
a trip	un trip
to take to	se mettre à
to use	utiliser

a user	un usager
an abuser, an addict	un toxicomane
a habit	habitude, accoutumance
abuse, addiction	la toxicomanie
dependence	la dépendance

Drug Traffic	**Le trafic de drogue**
to consume	consommer
consumption	la consommation
a smuggler	un passeur
to traffic	faire le trafic de
a trafficker]	[un trafiquant
a dealer]	[un pourvoyeur
to deal in	faire le trafic de
trafficking	le trafic
a pusher	un revendeur
a connection	une filière
to supply	fournir
supply	l'approvisionnement
available	disponible
to launder money	blanchir l'argent
laundering	le blanchiment

Processing	**La fabrication**
poppy	le pavot
raw	brut
to refine	raffiner
a refinery	une raffinerie
a laboratory	un laboratoire
a chemist	un chimiste
to process	traiter
a process	un traitement
powder	la poudre

The Fight against Drugs	**La lutte contre la drogue**
to possess	détenir
possession	la détention
to seize	saisir
a seizure /ˈsiːʒə/	une saisie
a street value	une valeur marchande
customs	la douane
a customs officer	un douanier
a drugs test	un contrôle anti-dopage
to detoxify	désintoxiquer
detoxification	la désintoxication

to rehabilitate	réadapter, réhabiliter
rehabilitation	la réhabilitation
to wean	sevrer
to wean oneself off	se détacher de
to get off drugs	abandonner la drogue
to give up sth.	renoncer à qch.
to relapse	rechuter
a relapse	une rechute

EXPRESSIONS

to be on drugs	se droguer
to experiment with drugs / to dabble with drugs	toucher à la drogue / tâter de la drogue
to stay clear of drugs	ne pas toucher à la drogue
to fail a drugs test	subir un contrôle positif
to get high / to get stoned	s'éclater / se défoncer
to be hooked on / to be dependent on	être intoxiqué / être en état de dépendance
to develop a habit	contracter une habitude
to kick drugs	renoncer à la drogue
to go back on drugs	se remettre à la drogue

VOCABULAIRE COMPLÉMENTAIRE

Drugs	**La drogue**
acid	le LSD
pot, grass	l'herbe, la marijuana
hash	le hasch
a reefer	un joint
coke	la came
amphetamines	les amphétamines
barbiturates	les barbituriques
mescaline	la mescaline
hallucinogen /həˈlu:sinəˌdʒən/	hallucinogène

paste	la pâte
resin	la résine
base	la base

Addiction — La dépendance

hypodermic	hypodermique
a disposable syringe	une seringue jetable
a jab, a shot	une piqûre
intravenous	intraveineux
to hype up	se shooter, se piquer
to snort	renifler
withdrawal symptoms	des symptômes de manque
a junkie	un drogué

Drug Traffic — Le trafic de drogue

a lord, a warlord	un seigneur de la guerre
a baron	un baron
a runner	un passeur
a peddler	un revendeur
to ship, to consign	expédier
a shipment, a consignment	une expédition

Processing — La fabrication

coca	la coca
a substitute	un produit de remplacement
a by-product	un sous-produit
a chemical	un produit chimique
a lab	un labo

The Fight against Drugs — La lutte contre la drogue

to legalise	légaliser
legalisation	la légalisation
to confiscate	confisquer
confiscation	la confiscation
the bigwigs / the top brass	les gros bonnets
small fry	le menu fretin
a drugs clinic	un centre de soins aux toxicomanes
a drugs squad	une brigade des stupéfiants

Practise your vocabulary.

1. Which drugs are said to be soft and which ones are said to be hard?
2. Why do a lot of people consider soft drugs as dangerous?
3. Why is it often said that drugs increase the crime rate?
4. Can drug addicts receive any help?

Addicts' syringes pose risk to children

The Dutch border town of Venlo has launched a campaign to sweep it clean of syringes discarded by German heroin addicts, after a five-year-old was injured by a needle in a playground and had to undergo an Aids test.

Venlo is also starting a syringe distribution programme, an information campaign and a telephone hotline for reporting the whereabouts of discarded hypodermics.

"Our estimate is that in one year, some 20,000 used needles are left behind by intravenous drug users in public places, causing a possible risk for everyone, children and adults," a town hall spokesman Jan van Haperen said.

The campaign comes at a time when the Dutch public is becoming increasingly aware of the threat of Aids which can be transmitted via hypodermic syringes carrying blood infected with the virus.

The needle clean-up campaign highlights the continuing illicit drug problem afflicting Dutch border towns like Venlo, which draw large numbers of German addicts.

April 17, 1987

1 Match the definitions (A-D) to the words (1-4).

1. border	A. give prominence to
2. discard	B. direct line
3. hotline	C. frontier
4. highlight	D. throw away

2 **Say whether the following statements are true (T) or false (F).**

1. It was essential to mention that Venlo was a border town.
2. Townspeople feared for their children's health.
3. They planned to take drastic measures against drug addicts.
4. One adjective, in the third paragraph, explains why the risk existed.
5. The Dutch public paid little attention to the threat.
6. The conditions seemed to be the same in the Netherlands and in Germany for drug addicts.

3 **Test your knowledge. Only one statement is correct in each pair. Which one?**

A. An *acid test* usually means a drugs test.
B. The usual meaning of an *acid test* is a rigorous test that gives conclusive proof.

C. The sole meaning of a *sweeper* is one whose job is to clean up.
D. A *sweeper* can also be one of the defenders in a football team.

4 **As in "hotline", the word "line" can often have a special meaning. Match the definitions (A-H) to the phrases (1-5).**

1. to toe the line	A. to set a limit
2. to drop a line	B. not to put down the phone receiver
3. to cross the line	C. to write to somebody
4. to draw the line	D. to submit to discipline, to conform
5. to hold the line	E. to change hemisphere

5 **One sentence has been cut into parts and the parts scrambled. Put them back into the right order. (The capital letter at the beginning of the sentence has been removed.)**

Cocaine seized

from Chile and Peru / at Liverpool docks / from a ship which had arrived / customs officers seized / worth £5m / 50 kg of cocaine

US MAKES BIGGEST COCAINE SEIZURE

Jane Rosen in New York and agencies in Los Angeles

Within hours of a Washington meeting between President Bush and Colombia's President Virgilio Barco, US authorities in California made the biggest seizure of cocaine on record.

They found at least 18 tons of the drug valued at £7 billion.

One of the issues raised at the presidents' meeting was US drug consumption, which President Barco has long criticised as the fuel supporting the violent drug traffickers who plague his country.

About $10 million in cash was seized with the cocaine haul at a warehouse in the suburbs of Los Angeles, according to Mr Ralph Lochridge, a spokesman for the Drug Enforcement Administration.

"This seizure should put to rest any further speculation that Los Angeles is in fact the major pathway for cocaine entering the country and has become a major distribution centre in the United States," Mr Lochridge said.

It was the biggest cocaine seizure in history, easily topping the previous US record of 7,200 lbs in Tampa, Florida, last year, and a 12-ton seizure in Colombia, Mr Lochridge said.

The cocaine was seized in a light industrial area of Sylmar, a section of Los Angeles, in the north San Fernando Valley.

Three men whose names were not immediately released were arrested for investigation of conspiring to distribute cocaine.

The DEA had been investigating and conducting "intense surveillance" for a year before moving in about midnight, Mr Lochridge said...

The Guardian,
September 30, 1989

Match the definitions (A-H) to the words (1-8).

1. on record 2. plague 3. haul 4. lbs 5. warehouse 6. put to rest 7. pathway 8. move in

A. a measure of weight (pound), originally *libra* B. bury (a dead person) C. place where goods are stored D. amount caught at one go E. a road or a track for people walking F. interfere, take action G. publicly known, that has left a trace H. afflict, annoy

2 Choose the appropriate endings for the following sentences.

1. With regard to the meeting, the seizure happened
A. at the wrong time.
B. at the right time.
C. at an irrelevant time.

2. President Barco blamed US drug users for
A. not consuming enough.
B. creating a profitable market.
C. setting up trade barriers.

3. According to Mr Lochridge, this seizure would
A. damage the reputation of Los Angeles.
B. improve the reputation of Los Angeles.
C. leave the reputation of Los Angeles unchanged.

4. The 12-ton seizure was made
A. in the capital of South Carolina.
B. in the federal district where Washington is.
C. in a South American country.

5. Reading that the cocaine was found in a industrial area
A. is no surprise for the attentive reader.
B. is totally unexpected for the reader.
C. is in contradiction with the fourth paragraph.

6. We may suppose that the names were not released because
A. they did not know the names.
B. they wanted to contact relatives first.
C. they hoped to arrest other people in the ring.

7. The special precautions taken by the DEA are shown in the last paragraph by
A. three words.
B. two words.
C. one word.

3 What words in the article could be replaced by those in the following list?

A. to carry out B. to estimate C. a storehouse
D. to break E. to make known

15 DEMONSTRATIONS AND RIOTS — LES MANIFESTATIONS ET LES ÉMEUTES

(voir *Introduction* p. 136)

VOCABULAIRE A HAUTE FRÉQUENCE

Gatherings	**Les rassemblements**
to campaign for	faire campagne pour
a campaign	une campagne
a campaigner, an activist	un militant
to gather	(se) rassembler
a crowd	une foule
to organise	organiser
to stage, to hold	tenir, organiser
a meeting	une réunion
to demonstrate	manifester
a demonstration	une manifestation
to protest /prəˈtest/	protester
a protest /ˈprəutest/	une protestation une manifestation
to march	défiler
a march	une marche, un défilé
to shout	crier
a shout	un cri
a slogan	un slogan
a placard /ˈplækɑ:d/	une pancarte
a banner	une banderole
a mob	une foule agitée
to pass off peacefully	se dérouler sans incident

Security	**La sécurité**
a precaution	une précaution
a measure	une mesure
security forces	les forces de sécurité
riot police	la police anti-émeutes
to call in	faire appel à
to contain	contenir

to maintain, to keep	maintenir
order	l'ordre
to restore	rétablir
calm	le calme
a helmet	un casque
a shield	un bouclier
a baton	une courte matraque
to wield	brandir, manier

Tension and Clashes — La tension et les affrontements

an incident	un incident
trouble	des ennuis, des incidents
unrest	l'agitation
to disturb	troubler
a disturbance	des troubles
to surge	déferler
a surge	un déferlement
to trigger	déclencher
to flare up	se déclencher brusquement
a flare-up	une flambée
to erupt	faire éruption
to degenerate	dégénérer
to clash with	se heurter à, affronter
a clash	un affrontement
a scuffle	une échauffourée
fierce /fiəs/	farouche
to drive back, to drive off	repousser
to break up, to disperse	(se) disperser

Riots — Les émeutes

to riot	manifester avec violence
to throw	jeter
to pelt	bombarder (projectiles)
to hurl	balancer
a missile	un projectile
a petrol bomb	un cocktail Molotov
to overturn	retourner
chaos /keiɔs/	la pagaille
to use force	utiliser la force
tear gas	les gaz lacrymogènes
a water cannon	un canon à eau
to charge	charger
a charge	une charge
to ransack	saccager

EXPRESSIONS

a peaceful demonstration	une manifestation dans le calme
to call a demonstration	appeler à manifester
to take to the street	descendre dans la rue
law and order	l'ordre public
to keep in hand	maîtriser, contrôler
to get out of hand	dégénérer
to be marred by	être gâché par
to force one's way	se frayer un passage
a breach of the peace / a public order offence	une atteinte à la tranquillité publique
violence erupted again	la violence a de nouveau éclaté
an outbreak of violence	une explosion de violence
an outburst of violence	une éruption de violence
fighting broke out	des bagarres ont éclaté
to go on the rampage	se déchaîner
to bring to a standstill	paralyser
to bring chaos	semer la confusion
to open fire	ouvrir le feu
to condone violence	admettre la violence

VOCABULAIRE COMPLÉMENTAIRE

Gatherings	**Les rassemblements**
a sit-in	un sit-in
a demo	une manif
a counter demonstration	une contre-manifestation
to parade	défiler
a parade	un défilé, une parade
a route	un parcours, un itinéraire
a steward, a marshal	un membre du service d'ordre des manifestants
a loud hailer	un mégaphone
to chant	scander
to muster	rassembler
to hand out	distribuer
a leaflet	un tract

Security	La sécurité
a set-up	un dispositif
a police cordon	un cordon de police
to don	revêtir
gear	une tenue
clad in	revêtu de
a visor /ˈvaizə/	une visière
a truncheon /ˈtrʌntʃən/ a club	une longue matraque
to stem	endiguer
to hold off	tenir à distance
to restrain	maîtriser, contenir

Tension and Clashes	La tension et les affrontements
a troublemaker	un perturbateur
an agitator	un agitateur
to provoke	provoquer
unprovoked	sans provocation
provocative	provocateur
provocation	la provocation
an agent provocateur	un agent provocateur
to daub	barbouiller
to dent	cabosser
to prohibit	interdire
unlawful assembly illegal gathering	rassemblement interdit
public disorder	trouble de l'ordre public
criminal damage	dégradations volontaires
assault	violences (délit)
to outnumber	déborder
to obstruct	entraver
an obstruction	une entrave
a smoke grenade	une grenade fumigène
a teargas canister	une grenade lacrymogène
a bystander, an onlooker	un badaud

Riots	Les émeutes
to defy	braver
in defiance of	sans tenir compte de
a catapult	un lance-pierres
to stone	lapider
a hail	une grêle
a Balaclava helmet	un passe-montagne
a pitched battle	une bataille rangée
a warning shot	un coup de semonce

birdshot	du petit plomb
to block	bloquer
to tear up	arracher, desceller
to set up	dresser
to erect /iˈrekt/	ériger
a barricade /ˌbæriˈkeid/	une barricade

Practise your vocabulary.

1. Describe what is meant by a peaceful demonstration?
2. What can clashes with security forces be caused by?
3. How do security forces try to keep order?
4. Describe the scene when clashes occur.
5. How do the organisers of the demonstration and security officials usually explain incidents to the media afterwards?
6. Can you think of a few examples showing that demonstrations can lead to overwhelming changes?

Pro-Iraqi marchers parade in Morocco

An estimated 300,000 people marched through Rabat yesterday in a pro-Iraqi parade organised by five opposition parties and Islamic fundamentalists. The well-organised parade was the first officially authorised street demonstration in Morocco since the Gulf crisis erupted, and the largest seen in the country since independence in 1956.

No incidents were reported and security forces kept a low profile. The marchers carried banners denouncing the US, Israel and their allies, and burned American, French, British and Israeli flags in the centre of the city. The three-hour-long parade was organised by five opposition parties led by the old-guard Istiqlal party and the Socialist Union of People's Forces, trade unions, lawyers, human rights and student groups.

Reuter,
February 4, 1991

PROTESTERS RETURN TO BUCHAREST SQUARE

Ian Traynor in Bucharest

The uneasy calm that prevailed over the weekend broke last night when demonstrators returned to Bucharest's University Square, the scene of last week's rioting and violence.

A small but swelling group of protesters chanting "Down with communism", "Down with the criminals" and "Down with Iliescu" took the square four days after pro-front miners perpetrated acts of wanton brutality against antigovernment protesters who had squatted there for seven weeks.

An army officer turned up to bargain with the demonstrators while police sought to keep traffic moving. Some participants called on the demonstrators not to block the traffic.

A larger crowd of curious onlookers assembled, mingling with soldiers who took over patrolling of the square from miners on Friday.

The renewal of the anti-government protests precedes the expected inauguration today of Ion Iliescu, the leader of the ruling National Salvation Front, as President at a session of the new Parliament.

The climate of fear generated by last week's violence was exemplified yesterday by the cancellation of an opposition rally scheduled to take place in the western city of Timisoara where last December's revolution started. Suspicions that provocateurs might seek to cause further trouble were cited as the reason for the cancellation.

Despite the severe intimidation of the opposition parties last week, when miners supporting Mr Iliescu ransacked their offices and attacked the homes of their leaders, opposition MPs insisted they would attend the session...

The Guardian, June 18, 1990

1 Match the definitions (A-F) to the words (1-6).

1. prevail
2. swell
3. wanton
4. turn up

A. be present at
B. arrive, appear
C. arranged, due to take place
D. grow in size
E. without provocation, unchecked

5. scheduled

6. attend

F. appear as the most important, be widespread

2 **Say whether the following statements are true (T) or false (F).**

1. The calm was short-lived.
2. The miners did not support the government.
3. Both the army and the demonstrators seemed to show some moderation.
4. There seemed to be no obvious link between the army and the miners.
5. The demonstration was timed right to attract more attention.
6. People in Timisoara took no account of the events in Bucharest.
7. The miners had received some detailed information.

3 **The first meaning of the word "square" is a geometric figure with four equal sides and corners at right angles. But it can also take on other meanings. Match the definitions (A-E) to the various uses (1-5).**

1. square deal
2. square peg (in a round hole)
3. square meal
4. square-shouldered
5. square

B. strong in appearance
E. conventional, old-fashioned
C. fair and honest arrangement
D. substantial, plentiful food
E. misfit, unsuited

4 **Looking for words. Read the article and pick out:**

1. Two words showing that people did not feel safe (paragraphs one and six).
2. One verb which is often associated with the wind.
3. A synonym for "bystander".
4. The name of the political party in office.
5. The noun showing the aim of the miners' action (last paragraph).

5 **Fill in the blanks with words from the following list. Use each word once only. Verbs are given in the infinitive.**

procession peaceful to stage to address flags

Bristol Sikhs will __________ a march to the city centre on Sunday.
Five leaders in full traditional dress and carrying _____ will head the __________ from the Sikh Temple in Fishponds Road to Castle Green, where speakers will __________ the crowd.
The organisers say the march will be __________ .

The Evening Post, Bristol

Fifty injured as South Korean police push back rioters

At least 10,000 students and workers demanding the overthrow of President Roh Tae-woo staged violent protests in Kwangju for more than six hours yesterday.

Police said about 50 police and protesters were injured, including a student hit in the eyes by stones. Doctors said the student may lose his sight. About 200 people were arrested, news reports said.

Combat-clad police, armed with shields, helmets and clubs, fired hundreds of teargas shells to drive back protesters who charged in groups of 300 to 1,000. Protesters tore up pavements and built fires at a dozen intersections to light firebombs.

Citizens in doorways and alleys cheered the protesters and shouted insults at the police but most did not join in the violence as pitched battles raged around them.

At one point, dozens of students throwing firebombs at police accidentally started a fire in a shop, and then used the firetruck called to extinguish the flames to shield them from police.

Several students chased by police dashed into a Catholic church to avoid arrest, and parishioners rushed outside to guard the gate.

About 40 taxis with headlights on drove through the streets honking their horns to support the protesters.

The battles covered an area stretching 1.2 miles from the provincial government headquarters in the city centre...

Associated Press,
May 21, 1990

1 **Match the definitions (A-E) to the words (1-5).**

1. overthrow
2. alley
3. pitched battle
4. honk
5. headquarters

A. sound loudly
B. centre from which operations are controlled
C. downfall, departure
D. organised fighting with large numbers
E. narrow passage between houses

2 **Choose the appropriate endings for the following sentences.**

1. The motives behind the protest were apparently
A. religious.
B. political.
C. economic.

2. What the police said implied the student had been hit by
A. the police.
B. other protesters.
C. the firemen.

3. Protesters were
A. determined to fight.
B. non-violent.
C. easily dispersed.

4. Students tried
A. to set a shop on fire.
B. to stop the firemen.
C. to shelter behind the firemen.

5. The protest took place
A. in the capital.
B. away from the capital.
C. in the suburbs of the capital.

6. Support for the protesters is mentioned, directly or indirectly,
A. once.
B. twice.
C. three times.

3 **Looking for words.**

1.*Associated Press* is an American news agency. Find the words a British news agency would probably have used instead of:
A. (teargas) shells B. firebombs C. firetruck

2. Pick out two words in the fourth paragraph showing the intensity of the fighting.
3. In which paragraph is an idea of hasty movement expressed three times in close succession?

4 **"Head" is often used to build other words, as in "headlights" and "headquarters". Find the appropriate definition (A-G) for each of the words constructed in the same way (1-7).**

1. headline	A. forward motion
2. head butt	B. any head covering
3. headway	C. phrase at the top of an article
4. headache	D. height above the ground, under a bridge for example
5. headroom	E. striking the ball with the head (soccer)
6. headgear	F. hitting an opponent with the head
7. header	G. pain in the head

16

TERRORISM AND REVOLUTIONS | LE TERRORISME ET LES RÉVOLUTIONS

(voir *Introduction* p. 136)

VOCABULAIRE A HAUTE FRÉQUENCE

Terrorism	**Le terrorisme**
a terrorist	un terroriste
a target	une cible
to plant	poser, déposer
to booby trap	piéger à l'explosif
a booby trap	un piège
a car bomb	une voiture piégée
a letter bomb	une lettre piégée
an explosive device	un engin explosif
a bombing	un attentat à la bombe
a bomber	un poseur de bombe

Hijackings	**Les détournements**
to hijack	détourner un véhicule
to skyjack	détourner un avion
a hijacker	un pirate
a skyjacker	un pirate de l'air
to divert	dérouter
to refuel	refaire le plein

Revolutionary Movements	**Les mouvements révolutionnaires**
a faction	une faction, une fraction
to rise	se soulever
an uprising	un soulèvement
to rebel /ri'bel/	se rebeller
a rebellion	une rébellion
a rebel /'rebl/	un rebelle

underground	clandestin
an insurrection	une insurrection
a guerrilla	un guérillero
to revolt	se révolter
a revolt	une révolte
to struggle	lutter
an armed struggle	une lutte armée
a civil war	une guerre civile
a homeland	une patrie

Seizing Power	**La prise du pouvoir**
to plot	comploter
a plot	un complot
to foment	fomenter
a conspiracy	une conspiration
a separatist	un séparatiste
a coup	un coup d'État, un putsch
to topple	faire tomber
to overthrow	renverser
to set up, to establish	établir

EXPRESSIONS

to resort to violence	avoir recours à la violence
to prime a bomb	amorcer une bombe
to carry out a bombing	perpétrer un attentat
to admit responsibility to claim responsibility	reconnaître, revendiquer la responsabilité
it was the work of...	c'était l'œuvre de...
to be behind sth.	être l'auteur de qch.
to make safe	rendre inoffensif
to meet a demand	satisfaire une exigence
to deal with terrorists	négocier avec les terroristes
to do a deal	passer un marché
to have dealings with	avoir des tractations avec
to condone terrorism	admettre le terrorisme
to sponsor terrorism	cautionner le terrorisme
to keep tabs on sb.	surveiller étroitement qn.
to nip in the bud	étouffer dans l'œuf
to be in league with	être de mèche avec
a show of strength	une démonstration de force
a test of strength	une épreuve de force
to mount an operation	monter une opération

VOCABULAIRE COMPLÉMENTAIRE

Terrorism	Le terrorisme
a commando	un commando
a prime target	une cible de choix
a hit man	un homme de main
a hostage taker	un preneur d'otages
a captor	un ravisseur
a reunion	des retrouvailles
debriefing	un entretien après libération
to harbour	abriter
a sanctuary	un sanctuaire
a haven	un havre, un refuge
to sabotage	saboter
a saboteur	un saboteur
a sabotage	un sabotage
an atrocity	une exaction
the necklace	le supplice du collier
a death squad	un escadron de la mort
an anti-terrorist squad	une brigade anti-terroriste
to break away from	se séparer de
a breakaway group a splinter group	un groupe dissident
a fringe movement	un groupuscule
an offshoot	une ramification
the Red Brigades	les Brigades rouges

Bombings	Les attentats à la bombe
to perpetrate	perpétrer
an outrage	un attentat
a home-made bomb	une bombe artisanale
a primer, a detonator	un détonateur
a hoax	un canular
remote control	le contrôle à distance
indiscriminate	aveugle
at random	au hasard
to defuse	désamorcer
to detonate	faire exploser
a bomb disposal expert	un artificier

Revolutionary Movements	Les mouvements révolutionnaires
to stand up	se dresser
an upheaval /ʌpˈhi:vəl/	un bouleversement
an insurgent	un insurgé
insurgent	insurrectionnel
turmoil	les turbulences
a feud	une lutte interne
the hard core	les irréductibles
intercommunal clashes	les affrontements entre communautés
a mutiny	une mutinerie
a mutineer /mju:tiˈniə/	un mutin
guerrilla warfare	la lutte de guérilla
a militia /miˈliʃə/	une milice
a militiaman	un militien
a vigilante	une barbouze, un membre d'une milice privée
to secede	faire sécession
secession	la sécession
partition	la partition
motherland	la mère-patrie
self-determination	l'auto-détermination
to disband	renvoyer dans les foyers
to grant	accorder
a status	un statut
independent	indépendant
independence	l'indépendance
sovereignty /ˈsɔvrənti/	la souveraineté

Combating Rebellion and Terrorism	La lutte contre la rébellion et le terrorisme
to frisk	fouiller corporellement
repression	la répression
a supergrass	un inculpé indicateur (Ulster)
covert	en sous-main, clandestin
undercover	clandestin, occulte
a no-go area	une zone interdite
to quash, to put down	réprimer, étouffer
to foil	déjouer
to crush	écraser
a firing squad	un peloton d'exécution
bloodless	sans effusion de sang
bloody	sanglant

Seizing Power	La prise du pouvoir
to depose	déposer
to oust	évincer
an attempted coup / a coup attempt	une tentative de coup d'État
to destabilise	déstabiliser
destabilisation	la déstabilisation
to undermine	saper

Practise your vocabulary.

1. Can you explain how bombings are carried out?
2. What happens if an explosive device is discovered before it explodes?
3. What are the usual consequences of a bombing?
4. How do skyjackers operate most of the time?
5. What sort of demands do they make?
6. What are the different positions authorities may decide to adopt when faced with terrorism?

Colombia hijack

Medellin – An armed man hijacked a Colombian Boeing 727 airliner with more than 100 people on board soon after it took off from Medellin airport on an internal flight. The 135 passengers were released before the plane took off again from Medellin for Panama, whence it departed for the Caribbean island of Aruba. The hijacker expected to pick up $100,000 there before continuing to Cuba. He had told passengers he was terminally ill, and wanted to spend his last few days happily.

Associated Press,
May 24, 1988

Coup toll rises

Five people were killed and 20 wounded in the failed weekend coup in Madagascar during which rebels held the state radio station. Journalists and technicians taken hostage escaped unhurt.

Reuter,
April 2, 1990

IRISHMAN ARRESTED WITH RIFLES

By Phil Reeves

Detectives from Scotland Yard were scouring London last night for the lodgings of a young Irishman arrested in a car with two loaded Kalashnikov rifles.

In an unusual move, Commander George Churchill-Coleman, head of the Anti-Terrorist branch, released a photograph and detailed description of the man, and said: "It is absolutely essential we find out where this man was living and quickly."

The urgency of the appeal suggests that detectives believe the address will lead them to a cache of arms and ammunition, possible clues to the whereabouts of an IRA unit.

Police did not identify the man, arrested after a high-speed car chase through north London, but reliable sources named him as Kevin Barry O'Donnell, aged 19, from Linastrain, Coalisland, Co Tyrone. The police refused to reveal if they were connecting the incident with the IRA, although it came after last week's two IRA bombings in London, in which an army sergeant died and eight people were injured.

The arrest happened after a police traffic patrol car attempted to pull in a green Ford Cortina for a routine check as it was driving through Wood Green, north London, at 3am yesterday. There was a short chase before the car was stopped in Lordship Lane. Two loaded AK47s were found on the vehicle's back seat. No explosives were recovered, although the area was evacuated for several hours...

The Independent,
May 23, 1990

1 **Match the explanations (A-D) to the words (1-4).**

1. scour
2. lodgings
3. whereabouts
4. pull in

A. stop at the side of the road
B. place where somebody is
C. rented accommodation
D. make a thorough search

2 **Say whether the following statements are true (T) or false (F).**

1. Detectives were trying to find the young Irishman.
2. The Anti-Terrorist branch hoped that some neighbour or landlady would come forward.

3. It is obvious why it was essential to act quickly.
4. There was no leak of information.
5. The IRA had probably claimed responsibility for the two bombings.
6. The traffic patrol were looking for a particular car.
7. The arrest happened in mid-afternoon.
8. The two rifles were ready for use.
9. The police feared the car might be booby-trapped.

3 Fill in the blanks with a preposition.

1. The injured driver was immediately taken __________ hospital by ambulance.
2. The raiders shot twice __________ the security guard.
3. A masked gunman burst __________ the shop.
4. Two hijackers took __________ the airliner shortly after take-off.
5. They blew __________ the device after evacuating the area.
6. A group of demonstrators set fire __________ a parked car.
7. The building was set __________ fire by the explosion.
8. Police have not found him yet, he is still __________ the run.

Loyalist killed in his shop

Police in Northern Ireland continued their inquiries today into the murder of 51-year-old Mr John McKeague, a prominent loyalist who was shot by a youth who burst into his tobacconist shop in East Belfast yesterday evening.

The Irish National Liberation Army claimed responsibility in a call to a local radio station using a special code word.

But police investigating the killing said they were keeping an open mind.

Mr McKeague was shot twice in the head at point blank range.

His killer is understood to have run off in the direction of the Short Strand area, the only Catholic district in East Belfast.

The Evening Post, Bristol

SRI LANKAN TRUCE AT RISK

Christopher Morris and agencies in Colombo

A ceasefire agreed after six days of fighting between Sri Lankan government forces and Tamil Tiger guerrillas on Saturday night appeared to be in danger of collapsing late yesterday, as attacks on army bases in the east continued.

The government said rebels shot and killed a soldier in the Tiger-controlled northern town of Vavuniya, 135 miles north-east of Colombo. Another soldier, wounded by sniper fire on Saturday night near the port of Trincomanlee, died yesterday.

The rebels fired on an air force helicopter when it tried to land at Mankulam, 25 miles west of Vavunyia, and blew up a bridge in the district on Saturday night, preventing army reinforcements from reaching the area.

Residents of Batticaloa said a university lecturer was killed when air force helicopters strafed rebel positions near the town.

Batticaloa, a rebel-held coastal town 136 miles north-east of Colombo, was the first casualty in the collapse of the previous ceasefire, which had held for 13 months. The Batticaloa police station was the first to be captured by the Tigers and is still in rebel hands.

The government and the rebels said the present ceasefire appeared to be holding, but a security official said: "It is likely that the ceasefire may be called off on Monday if rebel attacks continue"...

The Guardian, June 18, 1990

1 **Match the definitions (A-D) to the words (1-4).**

1. collapse
2. sniper
3. strafe
4. call off

A. bombard from the air or fire at with a machine gun
B. give orders to stop something
C. fall down suddenly, disintegrate
D. one who fire shots from a hiding-place

2 **Say whether the statements are true (T) or false (F).**

1. Right from the beginning we know that both sides were to blame for the collapse of the ceasefire.
2. If we are to judge by the first two casualties, it may have been a bit early to draw any conclusions.
3. The rebels might have feared the government would take unfair advantage of the truce.

4. There were no civilian casualties.
5. The rebellion had been going on for a long time.
6. Both sides tried to play down the incidents.
7. It is easy for rebels to know when a ceasefire has been agreed.

3 **"Fire" is the second element in "ceasefire", but it often appears as a first element in a number of words. Match the definitions (A-H) to the words (1-8) in the following list.**

1. fire drill	A. building that would burn easily and allow no escape
2. firefly	B. small bird with a brightly-coloured head
3. firedamp	C. one who sets something on fire intentionally
4. firetrap	D. procedure to follow in case of fire
5. firebug	E. explosive gas in coal-mines
6. fireproof	F. device used for making a display at night with coloured smoke, sparks and flames
7. firecrest	G. flying insect which glows with phosphorescent light
8. firework	H. that does not burn

4 **One sentence has been cut into parts and the parts scrambled. Put them back into the right order. (Punctuation and the capital letter at the beginning have been removed.)**

Bomber sentenced

of twenty years in a French prison yesterday / a pro-Iranian / 13 people in bomb attacks in Paris / Muslim fundamentalist / accused of killing / Fouad Ali Saleh / was sentenced to a maximum

US airmen attacked

Snipers fired automatic weapons at a bus carrying 28 US airmen along a mountain road in Honduras at the weekend. Seven soldiers were wounded, two seriously, US officials said.

AP, April 2, 1990

17 WAR AND ESPIONAGE / LA GUERRE ET L'ESPIONNAGE

(voir *Introduction* p. 136)

VOCABULAIRE A HAUTE FRÉQUENCE

General background	Contexte général
military	militaire
a serviceman	un militaire
a civilian	un civil
a soldier /ˈsəuldʒə/	un soldat
a sailor	un marin
an airman	un aviateur
the army	l'armée
the navy	la Marine nationale
the air force	l'armée de l'air
the armed forces	les forces armées
an officer	un officier
a captain	un capitaine
a veteran	un ancien combattant
a base	une base

Weapons	Les armes
conventional	conventionnel, classique
nuclear	nucléaire
the atom bomb	la bombe atomique
the H-bomb	la bombe H
deadly	mortel, meurtrier
to test	essayer
a test	un essai
proliferation	la prolifération
to deter	dissuader
a deterrent	une force de dissuasion
deterrence	la dissuasion
a ballistic missile	un missile balistique
intercontinental	intercontinental

strategic	stratégique
range	la portée
medium range	de moyenne portée
intermediate range	de portée intermédiaire
a warhead	une ogive
to site, to install	installer
a site, an installation	un site, une installation
to deploy	déployer
deployment	le déploiement
to launch	lancer
Star Wars	la guerre des étoiles
offensive	offensif
defensive	défensif
an arsenal	un arsenal
an arms race	une course aux armements
to build up	renforcer, accumuler
arms build-up	accumulation des armements / le surarmement
to stockpile	constituer des stocks
a stockpile	un stock
a vessel	un vaisseau
a submarine	un sous-marin
a torpedo /tɔːˈpiːdəu/	une torpille
chemical /ˈkemikəl/	chimique
nerve gas	gaz neuro-toxique
germ warfare	la guerre bactériologique

Espionage — L'espionnage

to spy	espionner
a spy	un espion
intelligence	les renseignements
secret	secret
covert	en sous-main, clandestin
undercover	clandestin, occulte
an agent	un agent
to infiltrate	infiltrer
an infiltration	une infiltration
to defect	passer dans l'autre camp
a defector	un transfuge
to pass	transmettre, divulguer
classified	classé secret
a file	un dossier
to uncover	mettre à jour, révéler
to expose	démasquer
to betray	trahir

a betrayal	une trahison
a traitor	un traitre
treason	la trahison

Starting a War	**L'entrée en guerre**
an ally	un allié
to ally with	allier à
a coalition	une coalition
an enemy	un ennemi
a conflict	un conflit
an embargo	un embargo
to break out	éclater
to invade	envahir
an invasion	une invasion
a border, a frontier	une frontière
to land	débarquer
a landing	un débarquement
an offensive	une offensive

Combat	**Les combats**
to drop a bomb	jeter une bombe
to shoot down, to down	abattre (un avion)
to sink	couler
to torpedo	torpiller
to intercept	intercepter
a battle	une bataille
a battlefield	un champ de bataille
a front	un front
to repel	repousser
to overwhelm	submerger
to inflict	infliger
a loss	une perte
a prisoner	un prisonnier
to defeat	vaincre
a defeat	une défaite
a victory	une victoire
to liberate	libérer (un territoire)
liberation	la libération
to pull out, to withdraw	se retirer
a withdrawal, a pull-out	un retrait
to sign	signer
an armistice	un armistice
a treaty	un traité
peace	la paix

EXPRESSIONS

to join the army	s'engager dans l'armée
a chief of staff	un chef d'état-major
to be in command of	avoir le commandement de
the Star Spangled Banner	la Bannière étoilée
the Union Flag	le drapeau britannique
a shot across the bows	un coup de semonce
to declare war on	déclarer la guerre à
to be at war with	être en guerre avec
a weapon of last resort	une arme de dernier recours
Strategic Defense Initiative	l'Initiative de défense stratégique
to stick to one's guns	ne pas en démordre
to put up a good fight	bien se battre
to inflict heavy losses	infliger de lourdes pertes
to sustain heavy losses	subir de lourdes pertes
to strike a mine	heurter une mine
to die in action	mourir au combat
to put out of action	mettre hors de combat
a war of attrition	une guerre d'usure
a scorched earth policy	une politique de la terre brûlée
incompatible with their status	incompatible avec leur statut
to have access to	avoir accès

VOCABULAIRE COMPLÉMENTAIRE

General background	**Contexte général**
the Admiralty	le ministère de la Marine
a battalion	un bataillon
a platoon	une section
a squadron	un escadron, une escadrille
a seaman	un marin
a convoy	un convoi
a paratrooper	un parachutiste
airborne	aéroporté
marines	l'infanterie de marine
conscription	la conscription
a conscript	un conscrit

to draft (US)	appeler
draft (US)	la conscription
a draftee (US)	un appelé
a draft dodger (US)	un insoumis
a pacifist	un pacifiste
a peace movement	un mouvement pacifiste
cannon fodder	la chair à canon
a conscientious objector	un objecteur de conscience
a reservist	un réserviste
to enlist	s'engager
the barracks	la caserne
a garrison	une garnison
a war memorial	un monument aux morts
the national anthem	l'hymne national
a patriot /ˈpætriət/	un patriote
patriotic /pætriˈɔtik/	patriotique
patriotism	le patriotisme
jingoism	le chauvinisme national
jingoistic	chauvin
a flexible response	une riposte graduée
a task force	une force d'intervention
a buffer zone	une zone tampon
a peacekeeping force	une force d'interposition
combat troops	les troupes de combat
crack troops, elite troops	les troupes d'élite
logistics	la logistique
a prisoner of war	un prisonnier de guerre

Military Personnel — Le personnel militaire

an admiral	un amiral
a commander	un chef militaire
a commander-in-chief	un commandant en chef
a general	un général
a brigadier-general	un général de brigade
a major-general	un général de division
a lieutenant-general	un général de corps d'armée
a colonel /ˈkə:nl/	un colonel
a major	un commandant
a lieutenant /lefˈtenənt/	un lieutenant
a non-commissioned officer	un sous-officier
a sergeant /ˈsɑ:dʒənt/	un sergent
a private	un simple soldat
a chaplain	un aumônier
a standard bearer	un porte-drapeau

Weapons	**Les armes**
a fleet	une flotte
a destroyer	un contre-torpilleur
a frigate	une frégate
an aircraft carrier	un porte-avions
a minesweeper	un dragueur de mines
a flagship	un navire amiral
amphibious	amphibie
anti-aircraft	anti-aérien
a chopper	un hélico
a fighter	un chasseur
a bomber	un bombardier
a stealth bomber	un bombardier furtif
a strike helicopter a helicopter gunship	un hélicoptère d'attaque
a personnel carrier	un transport de troupes
a first-strike weapon	arme de première frappe
to escalate	(s') intensifier
escalation	l'escalade
to wipe out	anéantir
a neutron bomb	une bombe à neutrons
a fuel air bomb	bombe à effet de souffle
to train on	orienter sur
to home in	se diriger vers
incoming	assaillant
anti-ballistic anti-missile	anti-missile
a shield	un bouclier
a laser	un laser
a beam	un rayon
a sensor	un capteur
a decoy	un leurre
smart weapons	les armes intelligentes
bacteriological	bactériologique
mustard	la moutarde
binary	binaire
a sealed room	une pièce étanche
to scrap	mettre au rebut
armament, weaponry	l'armement
overkill	la surcapacité de destruction
a balance	un équilibre
to disarm	désarmer
disarmament	le désarmement
unilateral	unilatéral
multilateral	multilatéral
a moratorium	un moratoire

Espionage	L'espionnage
counter espionage counter intelligence	le contre-espionnage
hush-hush	archi-secret
a mole	une taupe
a cipher	un chiffre, un code
to decipher	déchiffrer
to tap	mettre sur écoute
to bug	installer un micro
to lure	persuader par la ruse
a bait	un appât
to expel	expulser
an expulsion	une expulsion
to swap	échanger
a swap	un échange

Starting a War	L'entrée en guerre
to manœuvre /məˈnuːvə/	manœuvrer
a manœuvre	une manœuvre
to concentrate	concentrer
a concentration	une concentration
to reinforce, to beef up	renforcer
a reinforcement	un renforcement
to call up	appeler, rappeler
a call-up	un appel, un rappel
an alliance	une alliance
neutral	neutre
neutrality	la neutralité
a warrior	un guerrier
a warmonger	un va-t-en guerre
a hawk	un faucon
a dove	une colombe
to blockade	faire le blocus de
a blockade	un blocus
to intervene /ˌintəˈviːn/	intervenir
an intervention	une intervention
an aggression	une agression
an aggressor	un agresseur
a pre-emptive strike	une attaque préventive

Combat	Les combats
a ground or land offensive	une offensive terrestre
to overrun	envahir
a counterattack	une contre-attaque
to strike back	répliquer
an onslaught, an assault	un assaut

a stronghold	un bastion
to pound	pilonner
to airdrop	parachuter
an airdrop	un parachutage
a dogfight	un combat aérien
to bail out, to eject	s'éjecter
to withstand sth.	résister à qch.
to hold out	tenir bon
to fight off, to repulse	repousser
a trench	une tranchée
to entrench	retrancher
to dig in	se retrancher
a foxhole	un abri individuel
to close in	cerner
to encircle	encercler
to advance	avancer
an advance	une avancée
to scuttle	saborder
to retreat	battre en retraite
a retreat	une retraite
to fall back	se replier
a setback	un revers
to rout /raut/	mettre en déroute
a rout	une déroute
to desert	déserter
to capture	capturer
a capture	une capture
unconditional	sans condition
to capitulate	capituler
a capitulation	une capitulation
an armistice	un armistice
peace talks	des pourparlers de paix
a safe haven	une enclave
a security zone	une zone de protection

Practise your vocabulary.

1. What different sorts of weapons do countries have?
2. What were the special features of the Cold War situation between East and West?
3. How did various detente agreements change the situation?
4. What are the main arguments for and against nuclear weapons?
5. What preparations are made when a country decides to put itself in a state of readiness for war?

MYSTERY MAN WHO PLAYED OUT A CLASSIC ESPIONAGE ROLE

By Michael Evans, Defence Correspondent

Erwin Van Haarlem played the classic role of an undercover agent sent to a foreign country as a long term "illegal" with orders to settle into the community as an innocent citizen, having a legitimate background and respectable job.

He arrived in Britain in 1975 with a false identity, created for him by the STB, the Czech secret intelligence service which is recognized as one of Eastern Europe's most active and efficient espionage organizations.

His true mission in Britain was never discovered by MI5, Britain's domestic counter-intelligence service also known as the Security Service. He remained a mystery man. He was not caught trying to steal military secrets or bribe or blackmail British officials. Nor had he been exposed as the mastermind of a spy network.

Although he put a lot of effort into getting to know groups trying to help Soviet Jewish dissidents, the STB would not have spent so much time and money creating an undercover agent, only to use him for infiltrating pressure groups. Nor would they have "tasked" him to spend his waking hours drawing up lists of British companies with American Star Wars contracts, although, according to notes he had made in his flat, this was one of his commissions.

As a highly intelligent and fully trained agent, his mission must have had higher goals. After Van Haarlem was recruited, probably during his military service, he would have undergone at least three years of training, learning how to live a double life...

The Times,
March 4, 1989

1 **Match the definitions (A-E) to the words (1-5).**

1. background
2. bribe
3. blackmail
4. mastermind
5. waking

A. plan and direct (a scheme)
B. while awake or active
C. give something in order to influence
D. a person's experience, education or social class
E. threaten to disclose something discreditable

2 **Test your knowledge. Only one statement is correct in the following pair. Which one?**

A. The espionage agency of the British Government is MI4.
B. MI6 is the espionage agency of the British Government.

3 **Choose the appropriate endings for the following sentences.**

1. The desire of secret agents to go unnoticed is shown in the first paragraph
A. by one adjective.
B. by two adjectives.
C. by three adjectives.

2. The fact that Erwin Van Haarlem was sent by a communist regime can be inferred, in the second paragraph, from
A. one reference.
B. two references.
C. three references.

3. "I" in MI5 is pronounced like
A. the letter "i".
B. the figure "1".
C. the letter "e".

4. Secret agents can obtain the services of people because of
A. blackmail.
B. greed and blackmail.
C. greed but not blackmail.

5. In paragraph four, the journalist points out
A. one of the secret agent's activities.
B. two of the secret agent's activities.
C. three of the secret agent's activities.

6. MI5 probably knew about some of his activities because
A. he confessed.
B. they searched the place where he lived.
C. someone betrayed him.

7. In the end, MI5 felt
A. all his activities had been discovered.
B. there was still some doubt about his activities.
C. he must have had only minor activities.

4 **Looking for words. Read the article and pick out:**

A. Two words used in sharp contrast in the first paragraph.
B. Two verbs implying opposite roles for the person at the receiving end (third paragraph).
C. The way near certainty and uncertainty are expressed in close succession (fifth paragraph).
D. One adjective which is particularly suited to the lives of secret agents (fifth paragraph).

Saddam makes peace with Iran

Saddam Hussein, the Iraqi President, yesterday offered Iran a peace treaty on Iranian terms, bringing a formal end to the war fought between Iraq and Iran between 1980 and 1988.

The Iraqi leader made no secret in his letter to President Ali Abkar Hashemi Rafsanjani of Iran that he wants to sign a peace treaty with Iran in order to devote all Iraq's resources to the present crisis in the Gulf which followed Iraq's annexation of Kuwait.

The Iraqi offer makes major concessions to Iran. President Saddam now says he will accept the 1975 Algiers agreement with Iran, which divided the Shatt al-Arab waterway between the two countries.

Iran said it was "optimistic" about the Iraqi move. Speaking on Tehran radio, the foreign ministry spokesman Morteza Sarmadi said: "We are happy that Iraq finally accepted the views of the Islamic Republic of Iran which will bring lasting and just peace to the countries and the region."

Iraq's move yesterday is the first significant effort by Baghdad since the invasion of Kuwait to respond to its growing diplomatic and economic isolation. The most immediate benefit to Iraq of a treaty with Iran would be to free most of the 24 Iraqi divisions – half Iraq's army – on the Iranian border for deployment farther south to face the American forces building up in Saudi Arabia...

The Independent,
August 16, 1990

1 **Match the definitions (A-C) to the words (1-3).**

1. formal
2. move
3. build up

A. decision, initiative
B. accumulate, reinforce
C. following established conventions, official

2 **Say whether the following statements are true (T) or false (F).**

1. We know right from the beginning that Iran was likely to accept the offer.
2. The Iraqi leader did not reveal the motives behind the move.
3. The Iraqi President played a major part in creating tension in the Gulf.
4. Saddam Hussein made an about-turn as regards the Algiers agreement.
5. In his statement, the foreign ministry spokesman implied that only Iran and Iraq would be affected by the peace treaty.
6. Iran is a theocracy.
7. There was no tension between Iran and Iraq once the fighting had stopped.
8. American forces posed a growing threat to Iraq.
9. In the article, the masculine gender is used for the names of countries.

"I now start thee, World War III! Boom! Bam! Crash! Bang! Kerflooie! Pow! Voom! Ka-boom! Ka-bang! Ka-pow! Ka-putz! BIG silence. The end! Amen! If you heard that, Major, just kidding. Just kidding!"

3 **Looking for words. Read the article and pick out:**

A. Three town names with a different spelling in English and in French.
B. Two country names with the same sort of difference.
C. One noun, in paragraph two, showing the seriousness of the situation.
D. Two words, in paragraph three, revealing that Saddam Hussein had gone a long way to please Iran.

4 **Fill in the blanks with the appropriate words from the following list. Use each word once only. Verbs are given in the infinitive.**
danger intelligence secret knowledge network
hackers to discover to break into research

Youths hacked into secret Nasa network

By Gareth Parry

Young west German computer ____________ have successfully ________ a top secret worldwide computer ____________ which connects the North American Space Agency's scientific ____________ centres with its counterparts in Britain, France, Germany, Switzerland and Japan.

The attack has been kept ____________ by the ____________ services, although the scandal was ____________ months ago, because it is feared that the ____________ the youths may have gained puts them, and the integrity of various American and European space development programmes, in extreme ____________ from Eastern bloc agents.

The Guardian, September 15, 1987

RESISTANCE CRUMBLES AS COALITION FORCES PUSH INTO IRAQ AND KUWAIT

By Michael Smith, Defence Staff

Allied forces were racing across the deserts of Iraq and Kuwait as part of a four-pronged attack on a 300-mile front last night, meeting only limited resistance from retreating enemy troops. Amid reports that Iraq's army was crumbling in the face of the onslaught, Gen Norman Schwarzkopf, the allied commander, said 5,500 enemy soldiers had given themselves up within the first ten hours and many hundreds more were waving white flags of surrender. French and Saudi forces said they had captured an additional 3,000 prisoners.

Inside Kuwait long lines of captured Iraqis were being marched across the desert. Contradicting claims came from many sides on a day of confusion, which allied planners had previously said was just what they intended – to keep the Iraqis guessing.

Gen Schwarzkopf said he was delighted with the way the operation was going. "The offensive is proceeding with dramatic success."

Coalition troops were doing a great job, he said, but added: "The war is not over yet."

Gen Schwarzkopf said he had no reports of Iraqi chemical weapons being used, but correspondents with the US Marines said one chemical mine was triggered by an armoured bulldozer.

Allied casualties so far in the offensive had been "extremely light", according to Gen Schwarzkopf. Pentagon sources put the number of American servicemen killed at 11.

In London, the Defence Secretary, Mr King, said the offensive had got to a "good start", but he added: "The first Iraqi forces that have been encountered are arguably their least capable, and some with the lowest morale."

"It would be a mistake to assume that in the rest of the campaign the Iraqi forces will show as little resistance as the allies have encountered."

Gen Schwarzkopf said US Marines, airborne troops and special forces, with French and Arab forces, had achieved their first day objectives within the first 10 hours.

British, American and Arab armour and infantry, making what appeared to be the main thrust into Iraq to cut off the occupying forces, were "moving north with great speed", he said.

Nevertheless, the allied progress was being hampered by poor weather and a heavy shroud of black smoke from the more than 200 Kuwaiti oil wells set on fire as part of the Iraqi scorched earth policy...

The Daily Telegraph,
February 25, 1991

18 MISCELLANEOUS TOPICS — SUJETS DIVERS

(voir *Introduction* p. 136)

VOCABULAIRE A HAUTE FRÉQUENCE

Sexuality	La sexualité
morals	la moralité
sex	le sexe
sexual intercourse	rapport sexuel
an affair	une liaison
permissive	permissif
permissiveness	la permissivité
contraception	la contraception
contraceptive	contraceptif
a pill	une pilule
a condom	un préservatif
family planning	le planning familial
birth control	la régulation des naissances
a homosexual, a gay	un homosexuel
a lesbian	une lesbienne
heterosexual, straight	hétérosexuel

Abortion	L'avortement
pregnant	enceinte
a pregnancy	une grossesse
a single mother	une mère célibataire
unborn	pas encore né
to terminate	interrompre
a termination	une interruption
to abort	avorter
an abortion	un avortement
an embryo /ˈembriəu/	un embryon

a fœtus /ˈfi:təs/	un fœtus
a human being	un être humain
to legalise	légaliser
legalisation	la légalisation

Women's Liberation — La libération de la femme

male	masculin
female	féminin
to dominate	dominer
dominance	la dominance
an object	un objet
sexism	le sexisme
a sexist	un sexiste
a male chauvinist	un phallocrate
male chauvinism	la phallocratie
equality	l'égalité
an opportunity	une chance
to liberate	libérer
to emancipate	émanciper
emancipation	l'émancipation
to stereotype /ˈsteriətaip/	stéréotyper
a stereotype	un stéréotype
housekeeping	les travaux du ménage

Immigration — L'immigration

a foreigner an alien /ˈeiliən/	un étranger
foreign, alien	étranger
to emigrate	émigrer
emigration	l'émigration
an emigrant	un émigrant
immigration	l'immigration
an immigrant	un immigrant
to migrate /maiˈgreit/	migrer
a migration	une migration
a migrant	un migrant
to settle	s'installer
a settlement	une installation une colonie
a permit	un permis
legal	en situation régulière
illegal	clandestin
a citizen	un citoyen

citizenship	la citoyenneté
to naturalise	naturaliser
naturalisation	la naturalisation
to melt	fondre
a melting-pot	un creuset
to adapt	s'adapter
adaptation	l'adaptation
to integrate	(s')intégrer
integration	l'intégration
a quota /ˈkwəutə/	un contingent
ethnic	ethnique
a minority	un minorité
to resent sth.	être hostile à qch.
resentment	l'animosité
a prejudice	un préjugé
racial	racial
tension	la tension
a racist, a racialist	un raciste
racism, racialism	le racisme
to discriminate	faire de la discrimination
discrimination	la discrimination
to segregate	faire de la ségrégation
segregation	la ségrégation

Human Rights — Les droits de l'homme

to oppress	opprimer
oppression	l'oppression
free	libre
freedom	la liberté
to move	se déplacer
movement	le déplacement
to banish	exiler, bannir
to deport	déporter
deportation	la déportation
a right	un droit
a charter	une charte
a convention	une convention
to abuse sth. /əˈbju:z/	attenter à qch
an abuse /əˈbju:s/	une atteinte un non-respect
to violate	violer
a violation	une violation
a case	un cas
to persecute	persécuter
persecution	la persecution
to harass	harceler
harassment	le harcèlement

to pick on sb.	harceler qn.
a dissident	un dissident
to torture	torturer
an ordeal /ɔːˈdiːl/	une épreuve, un calvaire
to disappear, to vanish	disparaître
a disappearance	une disparition
missing	disparu
to grant	accorder
to deny	refuser
an exist visa	un visa de sortie
political asylum	l'asile politique
a gulag /ˈguːlæg/	un goulag
a concentration camp	un camp de concentration
a labour camp	un camp de travail

Electronics and Computers — L'électronique et les ordinateurs

a component	un composant
a transistor	le transistor
silicon	le silicium
a chip	une puce
data /ˈdeitə/	les données
a data base	une base de données
to process	traiter
processing	le traitement
a processor	un processeur
word processing	le traitement de textes
computing	l'informatique
to computerise	informatiser
computerisation	l'informatisation
a disk	une disquette
a floppy disk	une disquette souple
a key	une touche
a keyboard	un clavier
a monitor	un moniteur
a central processing unit	une unité centrale
to store	mettre en mémoire
storage capacity	la capacité de mémoire
a memory	une mémoire
to erase /iˈreiz/ to delete /diˈliːt/	effacer
a program	un programme
software	le logiciel
hardware	le matériel
to hack	pirater
a hacker	un pirate informatique

EXPRESSIONS

to have sex	avoir des rapports sexuels
a red-light district	un quartier réservé/chaud
to have an abortion	se faire avorter
to be born out of wedlock	être né hors mariage
a single parent family	une famille monoparentale
to go out to work	prendre un emploi
the right of abode	le droit de s'établir
to be prejudiced against	avoir des préjugés contre
to be detained without trial	être détenu sans jugement
a prisoner of conscience	un prisonnier d'opinion
the Data Protection Registrar	la Commission informatique et liberté
computer aided design	la conception assistée par ordinateur
computer aided manufacture	la fabrication assistée par ordinateur

VOCABULAIRE COMPLÉMENTAIRE

Sexuality	La sexualité
promiscuous	de mœurs légères
promiscuity	la promiscuité sexuelle
casual sex	les rapports sexuels de rencontre
sexual harassment	le harcèlement sexuel
a brothel	une maison close
a clinic	un centre médico-social
a French letter	une capote anglaise
a sheath	un préservatif
a diaphragm	un diaphragme
a coil	un stérilet
a jelly	une gelée
to sterilise	stériliser
sterilisation	la stérilisation

Abortion	L'avortement
unwanted	non souhaité
legitimate	légitime
illegitimate	illégitime
a bastard	un bâtard
a right-to-lifer	un opposant à l'avortement
pro-choice	partisan de l'avortement

Women's Liberation	La libération de la femme
motherhood	la maternité
to bring up children	élever des enfants
a day-care centre (US) / a creche / a day nursery	une halte-garderie / une crèche
a chore	une besogne, une corvée
domestic appliances	les appareils ménagers
to break up	se briser (mariage)
to divorce	divorcer
a divorce	un divorce
alimony	une pension alimentaire

Immigration	L'immigration
a native	un autochtone
a resident	un habitant
a national	un ressortissant
to adjust	(s')adapter
an adjustment	une adaptation
to assimilate	assimiler
an assimilation	une assimilation
a root	une racine
to uproot	déraciner
a way of life	un mode de vie
a lifestyle	un style de vie
an inner city area	un quartier urbain défavorisé
a menial job	un emploi subalterne
to exploit	exploiter
exploitation	l'exploitation
a sweatshop	un atelier clandestin
xenophobia /zenəˈfəubiə/	la xénophobie
to repatriate	rapatrier
repatriation	le rapatriement

Human Rights	Les droits de l'homme
a resolution	une résolution
to comply with sth.	se conformer à qch.
to guarantee /ˌgærənˈti:/	garantir
a guarantee	une garantie
to safeguard	sauvegarder
a safeguard	une sauvegarde
a breach	une infraction / un manquement
to flout	bafouer

to intimidate	intimider
intimidation	l'intimidation
to muzzle	museler
a witch hunt	une chasse aux sorcières
a pass	un laisser-passer
a hunger strike	une grève de la faim
to forcefeed	alimenter de force
to exile /ˈeksail/	exiler
exile	l'exil
an exile	un exilé
an exodus	un exode
an influx	un afflux

Electronics and Computers — L'électronique et les ordinateurs

a circuit /ˈsəːkit/	un circuit
input	l'entrée
output	la sortie
a sensor	un capteur
to display	afficher
a display	un affichage
to print	imprimer
a printer	une imprimante
a daisywheel	une marguerite
a dot matrix	une matrice à aiguilles
to transmit	transmettre
transmission	la transmission
to connect	relier
connection	la liaison
a network	un réseau
compatible	compatible
a spreadsheet	un tableur
a mainframe computer	un ordinateur de réseau
a prodigal whiz	un petit génie
a whiz kid	un enfant prodige

Practise your vocabulary.

1. What are some of the changes that have affected sexual behaviour in the second half of the twentieth century?
2. Why are a lot of people in favour of abortion?
3. Why do others strongly oppose it?
4. What can you say about the position of women today?
5. Why are immigrants often in the news in developed countries?
6. Are human rights abuses still common today?
7. Is it difficult to use a personal computer?

IDAHO SET TO BAN MOST ABORTIONS

Simon Tisdall in Washington

The long-running, nationwide battle over abortion rights intensified yesterday as legislators in Idaho prepared to vote on a bill which would in effect render illegal 95 per cent of all abortions performed in the state. For the first time, the proposed new law also sets out stiff criminal penalties for doctors who fail to comply.

The Idaho bill, which both pro and anti-abortion groups expect will be approved, is being viewed as a precedent of national importance. It follows last July's landmark Supreme Court "Webster v. Reproductive Services" ruling that gave states freedom to shape their own abortion laws. Attempts in Alabama and Utah to pass similarly restrictive legislation were thwarted earlier this year.

An official at the National Abortion Rights Action League bureau in Washington said yesterday: "It is dangerous for the women of Idaho and for all American women."

The Idaho legislation outlaws abortion except in certain, tightly defined cases. Rape victims qualify only if the crime has been reported within seven days of its occurrence.

Victims of incest qualify only if they are under 18 and the crime has been reported. Two other exceptions are if the fœtus is judged to be "profoundly" deformed; or if the pregnancy threatens the mother's life.

Of approximately 1,650 abortions performed each year in Idaho, it is estimated that only 5 per cent would be legal under the new law...

The Guardian,
March 23, 1990

1 Match the definitions (A-G) to the words (1-7).

1. comply
2. landmark
3. v. (versus)
4. ruling
5. thwart
6. rape
7. occurrence

A. obstruct, oppose successfully
B. sexual intercourse without consent
C. happening, event
D. against, in opposition to
E. act in accordance
F. decision made by a judge
G. change that marks a turning-point

2 **Say whether the following statements are true (T) or false (F).**

1. Idaho was only an episode.
2. No explanation is given for the meaning of the word "bill".
3. Only women would be affected by the proposed new law.
4. The Supreme Court gave its ruling in 1989.
5. Idaho was likely to be the first state to adopt new legislation on abortion.
6. Four exceptions were mentioned.
7. We already knew that only 5 per cent of abortions would be legal.

3 **Looking for words. Read the article and pick out:**

A. Equivalents for "to escalate" "to carry out", "harsh", "to consider" and "to ban".
B. One word which would be spelt differently in American English (paragraph five).
C. One state with a well-known religious background.
D. Two adverbs showing that the proposed new legislation would be very restrictive.

4 **Test your knowledge. Only one statement is correct in the following pair. Which one?**

A. In 1954, the Supreme Court ruled that segregated public schools were illegal.
B. Integration in public schools was made compulsory by Congress in 1954.

"The committee on women's rights will now come to order."

Chad's torture

London (Reuter) – Amnesty International accused Chad of torturing and secretly executing political prisoners, saying hundreds of detainees had disappeared. "In response to armed opposition and insurgencies, the authorities have condoned or permitted arbitrary arrest, secret detention, torture and extrajudicial execution," it said, adding the government of President Hissène Habré had given no information about hundreds arrested in the past eight years.

March 7, 1990

RECRUITMENT AND RACISM

Francis Beckett

An Asian graduate arrived at the reception desk of a big company for a job interview. "You're not on my list," said the receptionist. "But I haven't told you my name yet," replied the graduate.

I heard this story from Marie Stewart, an Afro-Caribbean woman with a PhD, who has "lost count of the number of times I turned up for interviews and got looks which said: No, you can't be Dr Stewart".

She now works for Project Fullemploy, advising companies on how to avoid discriminating against ethnic minorities in recruitment. Research published this year by the Commission for Racial Equality shows that graduates who are members of ethnic minorities have a harder time getting job than their white counterparts, and often settle for inferior posts.

The CRE researchers matched an ethnic-minority sample of students with a white sample. Nearly three-quarters of the former received no job offers in their final year; only half of white graduates did not. Soon after graduation, only one in three of the ethnic minority graduates still had no job offers: the figure for whites was less than one in four.

Graduates from ethnic minorities are much more likely than other graduates to be employed in the often denigrated public sector. Graduates of Caribbean and African origin are much less likely to work in industry, while Afro-Asians and Asians are more likely to be self-employed...

The Independent,
June 14, 1990

1 **Match the definitions (A-F) to the words (1-6).**

1. graduate	A. a person closely corresponding to another
2. Ph. D.	B. specimen showing what the rest is like
3. lose count	C. accept in spite of dissatisfaction
4. counterpart	D. one who holds a university degree
5. settle for	E. be unable to give the number of times
6. sample	F. Doctor of Philosophy (the highest university degree)

2 **Say whether the following statements are true (T) or false (F).**

1. The article deals with racial discrimination in the US.
2. The receptionist said "You're not on my list" to Marie Stewart.
3. It was an example of segregation.
4. Marie Stewart was very sensitive to what she could read on people's faces.
5. Graduates from ethnic minorities were doubly penalised.
6. 25 per cent of the ethnic minority sample received no job offer in their final year.
7. It was only a minor difference when compared to the white sample.
8. On the whole, higher education seemed to be a good passport for a job.
9. In a way, it could be said that ethnic minority graduates get what white graduates don't want.
10. All ethnic minority groups fall into the same category.

3 **As in "self-employed", the first element in many words is "self". Match the definitions (A-I) to the words (1-9).**

1. self-catering	A. putting one's own interest first
2. self-conscious	B. needing no help from others
3. self-contained	C. calm, having control over one's emotions

4. self-evident	D. convinced that one is better than others
5. self-indulgent	E. needing no further demonstration
6. self-possessed	F. having its own kitchen, bathroom and lavatory
7. self-righteous	G. giving way too easily to desires
8. self-seeking	H. accommodation in which you prepare your own food
9. self-sufficient	I. shy, embarrassed

Tass goes public on exit visa

Moscow: A dissident psychiatrist, Mr Anatoly Koryagin has been granted permission to emigrate to Switzerland, Tass news agency confirmed yesterday. It was believed to be the first such announcement by the Soviet media regarding the departure of a dissident.

Mr Koryagin, who is 48, was released from a labour camp in February after being pardoned by the Supreme Soviet in a review of dissident cases.

He was sentenced to seven years in prison and five years in exile in 1981 on charges of anti Soviet agitation and propaganda, after accusing Soviet authorities of confining dissidents to mental hospitals...

Associated Press,
April 24, 1987

19

ACCIDENTS — LES ACCIDENTS

(voir *Introduction* p. 136)

VOCABULAIRE A HAUTE FRÉQUENCE

Road Crashes	**Les accidents de la route**
a moped	un cyclomoteur
a vehicle	un véhicule
a lorry, a truck (US)	un camion
a tanker (lorry)	un camion-citerne
a coach	un car
a caravan	une caravane
a seat belt	une ceinture de sécurité
a pedestrian	un piéton
a motorist	un automobiliste
a crash helmet	un casque
a bend, a corner	un virage, un tournant
to overtake	doubler
to brake	freiner
a brake	un frein
to slow down	ralentir
to pull up	s'arrêter
to pull out	déboîter
a pile-up	un carambolage
to skid	déraper

Rail Crashes	**Les accidents de chemin de fer**
a station	une gare
the railway the railroad (US)	le chemin de fer
the locomotive the engine	la locomotive

a carriage	un wagon
a passenger train	un train de voyageurs
a goods train a freight train	un train de marchandises
a commuter train	un train de banlieue
a level crossing	un passage à niveau
a track	une voie
a line	une ligne
a rail	un rail
to derail	dérailler

Plane Crashes — Les accidents d'avion

an aircraft	un appareil
an airliner	un avion de ligne
a jumbo jet	un gros porteur
a jet engine	un réacteur
a flight	un vol
to land	atterrir
to take off	décoller
take-off	le décollage
an airport	un aéroport
a runway	une piste
a control tower	une tour de contrôle
a pilot	un pilote
a hostess, a stewardess	une hôtesse
to crash	s'abîmer, s'écraser
the flight recorder	l'enregistreur de vol

Shipwrecks — Les naufrages

a vessel	un vaisseau
a trawler	un chalutier
a cargo ship, a freighter	un cargo
a merchant vessel	un navire marchand
an oil tanker	un pétrolier
a captain	un commandant
to sail	naviguer
a sailor	un marin
a fisherman	un marin-pêcheur
shipping	la navigation
to register	immatriculer
to run aground	s'échouer
a hull	une coque
a hold	une soute
to sink	sombrer
to abandon	évacuer

to drift	dériver
a lifeboat	un canot de sauvetage
to pick up	recueillir
a tug	un remorqueur
to tow	remorquer
a wreck	une épave
to drown	se noyer

Mining Accidents — Les accidents de mine

a coal-mine, a coal-pit a colliery	une mine de charbon
a miner	un mineur
a pitman, a collier	un mineur de charbon
a shaft	un puits
a gallery	une galerie
fire damp	le grisou
dust	la poussière
to drill, to bore	creuser, forer

Fires — Les incendies

a blaze	un incendie, un brasier
ablaze	en flammes
to catch fire	prendre feu
to burn, to blaze	brûler
a burn	une brûlure
overcome	intoxiqué
to inhale	respirer, aspirer
a fireman	un pompier
a fire engine a firetruck (US)	une pompe à incendie
to pour	déverser
a ladder	une échelle
to put out, to extinguish	éteindre
to char	calciner
ashes	les cendres

Climbing Accidents — Les accidents de montagne

a peak	un pic
to climb, to scale	grimper, escalader
ascent	l'ascension
a rope	une corde
a cliff	une falaise

Common Vocabulary	Vocabulaire commun
safety	la sécurité
a passenger	un passager
a crew	un équipage
to carry, to transport	transporter
on board, aboard	à bord
an engine failure	une panne de moteur
to overturn	se retourner
to hit	heurter
to bump into, to run into to crash into	percuter
to knock down	renverser
to run over	écraser
to collide with	entrer en collision avec
a collision	une collision
a head-on collision	une collision de front
to involve	impliquer, comprendre
a shock	un choc, une commotion
to bruise /bru:z/	meurtrir
a bruise	une meurtrissure
a stitch	un point de suture
a distress signal	un signal de détresse
May Day, an SOS message	un SOS
to locate	localiser

EXPRESSIONS

in the opposite direction	en sens inverse
a hit-and-run driver	un chauffard (avec délit de fuite)
to ride pillion	être le passager d'un deux roues
to come off the rails	quitter les rails
an unmanned level crossing	un passage à niveau non gardé
to be bound for	être à destination de
to be on one's way to to be en route to	faire route vers
to be due to land at	dont l'atterrissage est prévu à
to ditch in the sea	faire un amerrissage forcé
to lose control	perdre le contrôle
to bring under control	maîtriser
to go out of control	échapper au contrôle
to winch to safety	hélitreuiller
to be detained in hospital	être hospitalisé

VOCABULAIRE COMPLÉMENTAIRE

Road Crashes	Les accidents de la route
an estate car / a station wagon (US)	un break
to slew round	faire un tête à queue
a roadworthy car	une voiture en bon état
an articulated lorry	un semi-remorque
a trailer	une remorque
to jacknife	se mettre en travers
a juggernaut	un mastodonte
winding	sinueux
to swerve	faire un écart
a high-sided vehicle	un véhicule à haute carrosserie

Rail Crashes	Les accidents de chemin de fer
rolling stock	le matériel roulant
a truck, a wagon	un wagon de marchandises
a derailment	un déraillement
an embankment	une levée de terre
a driver	un mécanicien
a guard	un chef de train
a buffer	un butoir
points	un aiguillage

Air crashes	Les accidents aériens
a freight plane	un avion cargo
a wide-body jet	un avion gros-porteur
the body	la carlingue
to pressurise	pressuriser
pressurisation	la pressurisation
the fuselage	le fuselage
the landing gear / the undercarriage	le train d'atterrissage
an escape chute	un toboggan
an airstrip	une piste sommaire
airworthy	en état de vol
to ground	clouer au sol
a balloon /bə'lu:n/	un ballon

an airship	un dirigeable
an ultra light	un ultra léger
a glider	un planeur
a hang glider	un deltaplane
a paraglider	un parapente
a descent	une descente
to disintegrate	se désintégrer
disintegration	la désintégration
to scatter	disperser
a mid-air collision	une collision en vol

Shipwrecks / Les naufrages

a flag of convenience	un pavillon de complaisance
a trawl net	un chalut
a shipping lane	un couloir de navigation
a sailing ship	un voilier
a sailing dinghy	un dériveur
a bulk carrier	un vraquier
a container vessel	un porte-conteneurs
crippled	désemparé
stricken	en détresse
the bridge	la passerelle
the deck	le pont
a rudder	un gouvernail
a line	un câble
to list	gîter
to capsize	chavirer
to bail out	écoper
a beacon	une balise
a flare	une fusée de détresse
a coastguard	un garde-côte
a life-raft	un radeau de survie
adrift	à la dérive
to refloat	renflouer

Fires / Les incendies

a fire brigade	un corps de pompiers
a breathing apparatus	un appareil respiratoire
an inferno	une fournaise
a conflagration	un sinistre
a seat of fire	un foyer d'incendie
to ignite	(s')allumer
embers	des braises
a short-circuit	un court-circuit
fumes	les émanations
to smoulder	couver

to douse	noyer en arrosant
foam	la mousse
to spray	pulvériser
to smother	étouffer
remains	les restes
a brushfire	un feu de broussailles

Climbing Accidents — Les accidents de montagne

a mountaineer /ˌmauntiˈniə/	un alpiniste
a potholer	un spéléologue
an expedition	une expédition
a ledge	une corniche
a crevasse /krəˈvæs/	une crevasse
exposure	le refroidissement
frostbite	des gelures

Common Vocabulary — Vocabulaire commun

to career	aller à toute vitesse
hypothermia /ˌhaipəuˈθɔːmiə/	l'hypothermie
to ram	emboutir
to plough into	s'encastrer dans
concussion	commotion
to hamper	gêner
a near miss	un risque sérieux de collision
to maintain, to service	entretenir
maintenance, servicing	l'entretien
to overhaul	réviser
an overhaul	une révision
negligence, carelessness	la négligence

Practise your vocabulary.

1. What decisions may a motorist have to take when driving along in his vehicle?
2. How can rail crashes occur?
3. What are the main items to be found in newspaper reports of a plane crash?
4. What happens when a ship is in difficulty?
5. How do firemen tackle a fire?
6. Why do rescue services often find it difficult to reach the victims in a mine accident?
7. What part can the weather play in the various types of accidents?

167 FEARED DEAD IN JET

From Peter Chapman in Mexico City

A Mexican airliner en route from Mexico City to Los Angeles crashed in flames about 170 miles northwest of here yesterday, with 167 passengers and crew on board.

The Boeing 727 belonging to the state airline, Mexicana de Aviacion, crashed in fog and rain in a mountainous area known as Marabitio.

Six military helicopters sent to search for survivors were hampered by bad weather.

Initial indications were that, given the nature of the terrain in which the airliner crashed, hopes of finding survivors were slim.

A spokesman at Mexico City airport said contact with the flight was lost 14 minutes after take-off. The crash came at the end of the Easter holiday period, but there was no immediate information on whether foreigners were aboard.

The plane had been in contact with the Mexico City control tower and apparently the pilot was making an emergency descent at the time of the crash, the airport source said.

The Guardian, April 1, 1986

MEXICAN AIR CRASH INQUIRY

From Peter Chapman in Mexico City

The Mexican Government has ordered an "exhaustive" inquiry into Monday's air crash in a remote mountain region 150 miles north-west of the capital. All 166 people reported to have been on board were killed.

More than 24 hours after the crash, the flight box recorder of the Boeing 727 operated by the state owned Mexicana airline had still not been recovered, and the cause of the disaster remains a mystery.

The last word heard of the aircraft came only a little over 10 minutes into its flight when the pilot reported the plane had pressurisation problems and was losing altitude. The disaster is believed to have occurred when it exploded in midair about 15 minutes later.

Mexicana, like all Mexico's state-run enterprises, has been subject to rigorous cost-cutting in the past three years of deep economic crisis, but its maintenance and safety record is considered good.

The Guardian, April 2, 1986

1 **Match the definitions (A-F) to the words (1-6).**

1. hamper
2. slim
3. exhaustive
4. remote
5. state-run
6. record

A. facts known about the past
B. nationalised
C. get in the way of, obstruct
D. small, insufficient
E. far away, distant
F. thorough, complete

2 **Say whether the following statements are true (T) or false (F).**

1. It was an intercontinental flight.
2. Fog and rain were not the only hazards in the area.
3. Foreigners were more likely to be aboard because of the time of year.
4. The pilot had reported some trouble.
5. It was essential for the Government to order an inquiry.
6. There were 166 passengers on board.
7. Sabotage could not be ruled out.
8. It is easy to spot the argument that could be used by trade unions or opposition parties.
9. The two articles conflict over certain details.

3 **Looking for words.**

1. Find the other spelling for the word "inquiry".
2. The crash happened north-west of Mexico City. In the same way, where are the following towns or cities in relation to London:
A. Bristol B. Cambridge C. Brighton.

Subway deaths

At least three people were killed and a dozen trapped when a subway train derailed in a tunnel in Philadelphia yesterday, police said.

Reuter, March 8, 1990

MOTORWAY U-TURN LEAVES FOUR DEAD, 74 INJURED

By Ruth Gledhill, Stewart Tendler and Rodney Cowton

Four people were killed and 74 injured when a van tried to do a U-turn on the M4 motorway near Heathrow airport, London, yesterday afternoon [...]

The accident happened just after 2 pm when a medium-sized blue van, loaded with bottles of beer, pulled out from the hard shoulder on the westbound carriageway, and tried to make a U-turn through an emergency crossing-point in the central barrier, onto the eastbound carriageway. As it did so, it struck a coach which was carrying a party of tourists westward on an afternoon trip to Windsor; the impact forced the coach through the gap in the barrier onto the eastbound carriageway.

Part of the van was demolished on the westbound carriageway, but some of it was carried onto the eastbound carriageway where it was struck by a National Express coach carrying 46 passengers from Penzance to London.

The coach then slewed across the motorway trapping a blue Ford Granada, travelling east, and crushing it against the Windsor-bound coach. Both coaches ended up facing in the same direction diagonally onto the hard shoulder of the eastbound carriageway.

The four dead people were said to be the driver and his mate in the van, a woman coach passenger, and an elderly man from the National Express coach...

The Times,
September 10, 1987

1 **Match the explanations (A-E) to the words (1-5).**

1. U-turn
2. hard shoulder
3. carriageway
4. slew
5. mate

A. twist sideways, rotate
B. companion, fellow-worker
C. lane along motorways for emergency stops
D. going back in the opposite direction
E. part of a road used by vehicles

2 **Say whether the following statements are true (T) or false (F).**

1. U-turns are prohibited on motorways.
2. It must have been a busy stretch of the motorway.
3. The van was parked on the right-hand side.
4. Emergency crossing points are used, for example, when there are road works on one of the carriageways.
5. The coach swerved to the right when it was struck by the van.
6. The van was in collision with two coaches.
7. The National Express coach was travelling east.
8. At least 1 person was killed in each of the vehicles involved in the crash.
9. Regular coach services operate over long distances in Britain.

3 **Looking for words.**

Pick out two phrases showing that "to do" and "to make" can sometimes be interchangeable.

4 **Which of the following explanations are correct?**

Bridges are often traffic black spots because

1. they are high over the water.
2. side winds can cause trouble.
3. cars are parked on either side.
4. fishermen reduce visibility.
5. the road surface is often slippery.
6. the bridge may be narrower than the road leading up to it.

5 **Fill in the blanks in the following article with words from the list below. Use each word once only. Put the verbs into the past tense.**

minor down to die to release to hit to happen to leave to take

A man __________ today after a car __________ the road, __________ a telegraph pole and plunged _____ a 14-foot embankment at Staple Fitzpaine, near Taunton. Another man, who was in the car, was __________ to East Reach hospital. The accidents __________ early this morning on a __________ road. Police have not yet __________ the names of the two men.

The Evening Post, Bristol

Fire ravages Spanish forests

Some 300 Spanish firemen and volunteers fought a forest fire in mountains in the southern province of Granada yesterday and evacuated 50 children from a summer camp threatened by the blaze.

Emergency services said the fire had already charred more than 1,700 acres of forest and forced the closure of four miles of highway between the city of Granada and the beach resort of Almunecar.

A fire in the eastern region of Valencia was still burning after two days and had destroyed 3,700 acres of woodland.

Reuter,
August 8, 1990

Britons' message

A boat used by two Britons who disappeared nearly a month ago on a fishing trip has been found drifting empty off the Seychelles Islands in the Indian Ocean, a port official reported yesterday. Philip Beadle of Durham and Norman Roberts of Cheltenham had left messages scrawled inside the boat. One of them said; "Beadle, Roberts, July 1990, Mahe Seychelles, engine problems."

Reuter,
July 31, 1990

20 NATURAL DISASTERS / LES CATASTROPHES NATURELLES

(voir *Introduction* p. 136)

VOCABULAIRE A HAUTE FRÉQUENCE

Earthquakes	**Les tremblements de terre**
a tremor	une secousse (tellurique)
a shock wave	une onde de choc
a quake / an earthquake	un séisme / un tremblement de terre
to measure	mesurer
to register	atteindre
a scale	une échelle
magnitude	l'amplitude, la magnitude
an aftershock	une secousse résiduelle
to rock	ébranler
a crack	une fissure
a fault	une faille
a landslide, a landslip	un glissement de terrain

Wind and Rain	**Le vent et la pluie**
a gale	un coup de vent / une tempête
a storm	une tempête
a hurricane /ˈhʌrikən/	un ouragan
a tornado /tɔːˈneidəu/	une tornade
a cyclone /ˈsaikləun/	un cyclone
the path	le trajet, la trajectoire
a typhoon /taiˈfuːn/	un typhon
torrential	diluvien
to rip off	arracher
to blow down	abattre
to sweep across	balayer

Volcanoes	Les volcans
a volcano /vɔl'keinəu/	un volcan
a crater /'kreitə/	un cratère
to erupt	entrer en éruption
an eruption	une éruption
to steam	dégager de la vapeur
steam	la vapeur
to spew out	vomir
lava /'lɑːvə/	la lave
ash	la cendre

Miscellaneous Disasters	Les catastrophes diverses
an avalanche	une avalanche
a flood	une inondation
to flood	inonder
to swell	gonfler
swell	la houle
the tide	la marée
a tidal wave	un raz de marée
to overflow	déborder
waterlogged	détrempé, gorgé d'eau
a bank	une rive
a sandbag	un sac de sable
to sandbag	protéger avec des sacs de sable
a dyke	une digue
mud	la boue
a dam	un barrage
to burst	se rompre
to wash away	emporter
to drown	submerger, noyer
drought /draut/	la sécheresse

Common Vocabulary	Vocabulaire commun
physical damage	les dégâts matériels
to hit, to strike	frapper, atteindre
to affect	toucher
to disrupt	perturber
a disruption	une perturbation
to be cut off	être coupé du reste
to be stranded, marooned	être bloqué, coincé
chaos /'keiɔs/	le chaos, la pagaille
havoc	les ravages, les dégâts

the aftermath	les conséquences, la suite
homeless	sans abri
makeshift	de fortune
a stricken area	une zone sinistrée
to warn	avertir
a warning	un avertissement, un avis
power lines	les lignes électriques
power supply	l'alimentation en courant
a power failure	une panne de courant
a power cut	une coupure de courant
to wipe out	anéantir

EXPRESSIONS

to overflow its banks / to burst its bank	déborder / sortir de son lit
to bring chaos	semer la confusion
to bring havoc	provoquer de gros dégâts
to leave a trail of damage / to cut a path of destruction	tout détruire sur son passage
to take shelter	s'abriter
overhead power lines	les lignes électriques aériennes
a stricken area	une zone sinistrée

VOCABULAIRE COMPLÉMENTAIRE

Earthquakes	**Les tremblements de terre**
to sway	osciller
a foundation	une fondation
concrete	le béton
to slip off	glisser
to crumble	s'effriter
an epicentre /ˈepisentə/	un épicentre
seismological /ˌsaizməˈlɔdʒikəl/	sismologique
a seismologist /saizˈmɔlədʒist/	un sismologue
to raze	raser

Wind and Rain	**Le vent et la pluie**
a whirlwind	un tourbillon
to roar	rugir
to batter	battre, assaillir
to lash	fouetter
a groundswell	une lame de fond
to whip up	soulever, faire monter
to flatten	aplatir
to toss	ballotter
to board up	obstruer avec des planches

Volcanoes	**Les volcans**
volcanic	volcanique
to rumble	gronder
a rumble	un grondement
to spit	cracher
a plume	un panache
a slope	une pente
a flow, an outflow	une coulée
a layer	une couche

Common Vocabulary	**Vocabulaire commun**
structural damage	dégâts aux installations
a swathe /sweið/	un sillage, une traînée
to engulf	engloutir
matchwood	des fétus de bois
to uproot	déraciner
to seal	colmater
a chasm /ˈkæzəm/	un gouffre
to wipe off	effacer de la carte

Practise your vocabulary.

1. Can you describe an earthquake?
2. What can make rescue work especially difficult?
3. What can the effects of a strong gale be?
4. Why are volcanic eruptions often easy to predict?
5. When do floods happen?
6. What are some of the consequences when an area has been flooded?

Hurricane warning

Tropical Storm Diana became Hurricane Diana yesterday after picking up strength in the Gulf of Mexico. Warnings went out along a 400-mile stretch of the Gulf of Mexico.

Associated Press

14 KILLED AS GALES BRING NEW HAVOC

Andrew Culf and Martin Wainwright

At least 14 people died as severe gales swept across Britain yesterday causing structural damage, widespread flooding and transport chaos.

The storm also caused havoc in Germany, where nine were reported to have been killed; in France, where five died; in Belgium, where four were killed; and in the Irish Republic, where one person died.

The London Weather Centre warned that the 80mph gales, coming a month after the storms of January 25 which killed 46 people in Britain, would continue today in the South and South-west.

Six of yesterday's victims were motorists, and another six died when trees, chimneys or walls were brought down.

Flooding affected large parts of North Wales and the West Country as mountainous seas breached coastal defences. At Towyn, in Clwyd, where waves smashed a 200-yard hole in the sea wall, sending five-foot floods through the town, four RAF helicopters were used to evacuate more than 100 people. Thirty others were taken to hospital suffering from shock and hypothermia.

Elsewhere in North Wales, children at several schools had to stand on desks and chairs to escape water cascading through their classrooms.

Last night thousands of homes were without electricity, and many roads were blocked by fallen trees and overturned vehicles. Damage to overhead cables also severely disrupted rail services, while ferry sailings were suspended and flights delayed.

Police and motoring organisations advised drivers to stay at home unless their journeys were absolutely necessary.

The Guardian,
February 27, 1990

1 Choose the appropriate endings for the sentences.

1. When reporting about the gale, in the first paragraph, the journalists mentioned
A. two consequences.
B. three consequences.
C. four consequences.

2. In the second paragraph, they mentioned
A. one consequence.
B. two consequences.
C. three consequences.

3. The wind blew at about
A. 130 kilometres an hour.
B. 150 kilometres an hour.
C. 110 kilometres an hour.

4. Apparently, the wind blew from
A. the west.
B. the north.
C. the east.

5. It is obvious that the tide
A. played no part in the disaster.
B. played only a small part in the disaster.
C. played a major part in the disaster.

6. During such a gale
A. it is dangerous to be outside.
B. it is safe to be outside if you take shelter.
C. it is dangerous both outside and inside.

7. If we read the article carefully, we realise that
A. all major means of long-distance transport were affected.
B. air transport was not affected.
C. rail services had completely stopped.

8. We know that the situation was worse in January because
A. the number of victims was higher.
B. the number of victims was higher and also a different word is used.
C. the number of victims was higher but the word used is strictly a synonym for "gale".

2 **Fill in the blanks with the appropriate words from the following list. Use each word once only. Verbs are given in the infinitive.**

to engulf missing to die unknown Swiss to pull disaster bus

Eight people have _____ in Switzerland's worst avalanche ___________ in 15 years and three more were still _____ last night.

The bodies were ______ from a car and a small __ buried under tons of snow after the avalanche ______ a road between Zermatt and Taesch in the south west of the country. Five of the dead were ______ , two were West Germans but the nationality of the eighth victim is _______ .

THOUSANDS DIE IN IRAN EARTHQUAKE

By Elizabeth Nash

An earthquake devastated north-west Iran early yesterday, killing up to 10,000 people and injuring nearly 8,000, according to Iranian reports. Many were trapped beneath fallen buildings and rescue workers were unable to reach stricken areas because entire mountainsides had collapsed on to the roads.

The quake affected an area 100 miles wide and caused mudslides which wiped out entire towns and villages. It is the most devastating earthquake to hit Iran since 1978 when 25,000 people died around the eastern desert town of Tabas.

President Ali Akbar Hashemi Rafsanjani declared three days of mourning. He set up a relief headquarters in the presidential palace in Tehran and called on the Iranian people to mobilise for relief and rescue work. The government immediately mobilised a huge rescue operation, sending special flights to the area with emergency supplies and airlifting the injured from over-stretched hospitals.

The epicentre of yesterday's earthquake was in the alluvial depression of the Caspian Sea, near the Soviet town of Lenkoran. The US Geological Survey in Colorado said it reached 7.7 on the open-ended Richter scale. Another strong aftershock measuring 6.5 hit the area almost 12 hours after the first.

At least 1,660 died and 3,000 were injured in Zanjan, Iranian radio said, and more than 300 bodies were pulled from the rubble in Gilan on the Caspian coast. Three C-130 aircraft shuttled between Tehran and the north-western city of Rasht near the Caspian Sea to airlift the injured to hospital, and the national carrier, Iran Air, arranged special flights. Helicopters were flying victims to Tehran to relieve the region's overcrowded hospitals...

The Independent,
June 22, 1990

1 **Match the definitions (A-E) to the words (1-5).**

1. beneath	A. period of sorrow after a death
2. mourning	B. place from which operations are controlled
3. headquarters	C. below, under
4. over-stretch	D. move from one point to another and back on a regular service
5. shuttle	E. exceed the limit of capacity

2 **Say whether the following statements are true (T) or false (F).**

1. The exact death toll was known.
2. It was the most devastating earthquake in Iran's history.
3. The same part of the country was affected in 1978.
4. The government played a leading role in rescue operations.
5. It was not essential to mention the aftershock.
6. We can easily understand why they relied so much on air transport.
7. The journalist probably did not visit the scene of the disaster.

3 **Choose the appropriate endings (A-D) for the sentences (1-4).**

1. The most devastating tornado on record on the Canadian prairies ripped through the city of Edmonton, Alberta, at the weekend,
2. Rescue teams dug into a 36ft mound of earth and rocks yesterday in a search for people
3. Thousands of early morning workers were ordered to evacuate downtown office buildings,
4. Electricity and water engineers reinforced by troops were battling last night to restore supplies

A. and power failures trapped scores of them in stalled elevators.
B. to more than a million people cut off by some of the worst snowstorms for a decade.
C. flattening 300 homes, killing at least 25 people injuring another 250 and causing £25 million of damage.
D. buried by a landslide that crashed down on a Colombian shanty town, killing at least 95.

4 **Two different sentences have been cut into parts and the parts scrambled. Put them back into the right order. (Punctuation and the capital letters at the beginning of the sentences have been removed.)**

during the morning rush hour / and forcing the closure of three freeways / and a dozen aftershocks / killing at least 5 persons / a strong earthquake / and severely damaging dozens of buildings / struck the Los Angeles area / injuring more than 100

in a strong tremor / when 64 people died / to hit Southern California / the worst earthquake / measured at 6.4 on the Richter scale / since 1971 / it appeared to be

21

THE WEATHER LE TEMPS

VOCABULAIRE A HAUTE FRÉQUENCE

Common features	Traits communs
fine, fair	beau
unsettled	instable
changeable	variable
dull	maussade
clear	clair
sunny, bright	ensoleillé
to brighten up	s'éclaircir, se dégager
sunshine	l'ensoleillement
mist	la brume
fog	le brouillard
slight, light	léger
thick	épais
dense	dense
to form	se former
to lift	se lever
a patch	une nappe
patchy	en nappes
an anticyclone	un anticyclone
a depression	une dépression
pressure	la pression
a ridge	une dorsale
a trough	une zone (basse pression)
a front	un front
widespread	répandu, général
a spell a period /ˈpiəriəd/	une période
to range from... to	aller de... à (températures)
a range	une gamme
a prospect	une perspective
an outlook	une prévision
a weather forecast	un bulletin météorologique
Celsius	Celsius, centigrade
bad weather	les intempéries
an area /ˈɛəriə/	une zone

Wind	**Le vent**
calm	calme
windy	avec du vent
windswept	balayé par le vent
moderate	modéré
fresh	frais
to freshen	fraîchir
strong, high, heavy	fort, violent
a breeze	une brise
to gust	souffler en rafales
a gust	une rafale
to turn	tourner
to veer	remonter (sens des aiguilles)
to back	descendre (sens inverse)
prevailing	dominant
a gale	un coup de vent une tempête
severe /si'viə/	fort
a storm	une forte tempête
stormy	très agité, orageux
to let up	se calmer
a let-up, a lull	une accalmie, un répit
to blow over	se calmer, s'apaiser
to die down	tomber
southerly	du sud
southwards	vers le sud

Rain	**La pluie**
rainfall	les précipitations
rainy	pluvieux
wet, damp	humide
cloudy	nuageux
to cloud over	se couvrir
drizzle	la bruine
light rain	le crachin
a shower	une averse
an outbreak of rain	une ondée
to pour	tomber à flots
to dry up	devenir plus sec
to clear away	se dégager
a thunderstorm	un orage
thunder	le tonnerre
thundery	orageux
to brew	couver
to break out	éclater
lightning	la foudre

hail	la grêle
a rainbow	un arc-en-ciel

Heat — La chaleur

mild	doux
warm	chaud
warmth	la chaleur modérée
hot	très chaud
a heat wave	la canicule
dry	sec
drought /draut/	la sécheresse

Cold — Le froid

cool	frais
chilly	très frais
to freeze	geler
freeze	le gel
a frost	une gelée
a sharp frost	une forte gelée
freezing-point	zéro degré centigrade
minus 6	moins 6
hoar frost, white frost	la gelée blanche
ice	la glace
icy	glacé, glacial
sleet	le grésil
to snow	neiger
snowy	neigeux
to melt	fondre

EXPRESSIONS

a trough of low pressure	une zone dépressionnaire
a ridge of high pressure	une ligne de hautes pressions
a breath of wind	un souffle de vent
it's pouring with rain	il pleut à verse
a clap of thunder	un coup de tonnerre
a flash of lightning / a bolt of lightning	un éclair
a bolt out of the blue	un coup de tonnerre dans un ciel bleu
to ride out the storm	laisser passer l'orage
it's a mixed bag	il y a un peu de tout
to bear the brunt of	être touché de plein fouet
the thaw sets in	le dégel s'installe
to cut no ice	ne pas impressionner
to bask in the sun.	se dorer au soleil

VOCABULAIRE COMPLÉMENTAIRE

Common Features	Traits communs
settled	stable
set fair	beau fixe
to break through	percer
a mixture	un mélange
haze	la brume légère
smog	le smog
to thicken (up)	s'épaissir
to hang around, to linger	traîner
to persist	persister
to prevail	l'emporter
to extend	s'étendre
to establish	s'établir
prolonged	prolongé
to wear off, to weaken	s'affaiblir
a disturbance	une perturbation
to fill	se combler
the met office	les services de la météo
a weatherman	un météorologue
a meteorologist	un météorologiste
a synopsis	un résumé de la situation
to predict	prévoir
overnight	pendant la nuit
coastal	côtier
inland	à l'intérieur (du pays)

Wind	Le vent
brisk	vif
an airflow, an airstream	un flux d'air
breezy	avec de la brise
to whip up	activer
to strengthen, to pick up	se renforcer
a squall	une bourrasque
to ease off	s'atténuer, mollir
to abate, to subside	s'apaiser, se calmer
a shift	une saute
south-westerly	du sud-ouest

Rain	La pluie
the damp, moisture	l'humidité
overcast	couvert
to edge into	se glisser, s'introduire

a belt	une frange
a blustery shower / **a squally shower**	une giboulée / une averse avec rafales
torrential	torrentiel, diluvien
a downpour, a deluge	un déluge
odd	épars
isolated	isolé
persistent	persistant
to break up	se disperser
a bright interval	une éclaircie
to peter out	s'effilocher
to die away	s'affaiblir, cesser
a hailstone	un grêlon

Heat — La chaleur

sultry	étouffant
close	lourd
to pick up	remonter (températures)
sun-tanned	bronzé
sun-stroke	une insolation

Cold — Le froid

wintry	hivernal
frosty	glacial
groundfrost	gelée au sol
raw	rigoureux
the ice cap	la calotte glaciaire
the tip of the iceberg	la partie visible de l'iceberg
a flurry	une rafale (neige)
to thaw	dégeler
a thaw	un dégel
slush	la neige fondante
a cold snap	un coup de froid

Practise your vocabulary.

1. What are the main changes that can occur in the appearance of the sky?
2. Why do a lot of people pay attention to the weather forecast?
3. How can the wind affect the weather?
4. What further details do weathermen often give when announcing fog?
5. Does talking about the weather play any part in social life?

Snow surprises California and damages crops

LOS ANGELES – A rare snowstorm in Southern California and elsewhere in the state threatened crops, created havoc on freeways and stranded motorists despite the arrival Thursday of warmer weather and rain.

The storm blew snow and ice across Southern California on Wednesday after breaking low-temperature records throughout the northern and central parts of the state and around the United States.

The cold killed citrus, vegetables and floral crops in some areas. Many growers and packers said lemon groves were hard hit by the cold wave, with some early estimates saying that up to 35 per cent of the crop may have been damaged.

California is the nation's top producer of lemons, a crop valued at $152 million in 1987.

Asparagus growers in the Sacramento and San Joaquim valleys reported frost damage. Small farmers who grow leaf lettuce also were hurt.

Temperatures rose moderately in most parts of the United States, but the Alaskan front refused to die. Strong wind and cold weather poured into the Great Lakes, leaving snow drifts 10 feet (3 meters) high in northern Michigan.

Associated Press,
February 10, 1989

1 Match the definitions (A-F) to the words (1-6).

1. havoc
2. freeway
3. strand
4. citrus
5. grove
6. (snow) drift

A. leave helpless
B. heaped up by the wind
C. fruit such as orange, lemon, grapefruit, etc.
D. confusion, chaos
E. a major road with no intersections
F. small wooded area

2 Say whether the following statements are true (T) or false (F).

1. Damage and disruption are accounted for by one adjective in the first paragraph.
2. It is quite apparent that California is a very large state.
3. Estimates given of the damage were the definitive ones.

4. Most of the damage to the crops was caused by snow.
5. Most fruit seems to be grown by small farmers.
6. Airflow plays an essential part in weather changes.
7. They would have coped better with such a situation in Minnesota.

3 **As in "snowstorms" and "snow drifts", "snow" is the first part in a number of words. Match the definitions (A-G) to the words (1-7).**

1. snowgoose
2. snowmobile
3. snowball
4. snowplough
5. snowdrop
6. snowshoe
7. snowflake

A. early spring flower
B. vehicle for clearing away snow
C. frame for walking on snow
D. vehicle for travelling on snow
E. North American bird
F. small feather-like crystal
G. snow pressed between the hands

4 **Looking for words.**

Pick out three characteristics of American English:
A. One word relating to traffic (first paragraph).
B. A sentence pattern (absence of a preposition in the first paragraph).
C. A different spelling for one word (last paragraph).

5 **Choose the correct endings (A-D) for the following sentences (1-4).**

1. Scotland will have a mixture of showers
2. South-east England will have a much brighter day though
3. It will be windy everywhere as heavy rain
4. Over Britain there will be a very strong westerly airflow

A. there may be quite a bit of cloud at times.
B. giving gales in places and a lot of showers.
C. and sunny intervals though many southern counties will remain dry.
D. with sleet and snow on the hills pushes rapidly north-east into Scotland.

Rain on the way

After a fine, warm and sunny spell of weather in central Europe the unsettled weather over Iberia looks set to move north-east.

The area of high pressure that led to the settled weather is declining quickly and drifting south-east to be near Greece by the middle of the week.

An area of low pressure will move from northern Spain across northern France and then towards western Russia. Unsettled weather over Spain and Portugal will move across France and southern Britain today, with some heavy rain in places.

Outbreaks of rain will also affect southern Scandinavia and snow is likely as colder air spreads from the north. Outbreaks of rain will then spread to central and eastern Europe on Tuesday as the cold air now flowing into Britain and Scandinavia continues pushing south to give central Europe and Scandinavia a much colder spell of weather with sharp overnight frosts and snow showers in places.

The weather further south is expected to be fairly unsettled over the central and western Mediterranean, with showers and some sunshine.

BRITAIN: a front will be lying across central Britain.

After a misty start in parts of the south, the day is expected to be fairly cloudy across England and Wales. Outbreaks of rain already in some areas will spread to many other parts of England and Wales during the day. Some of the rain could be heavy. Northern England, central and southern Scotland and Northern Ireland are also expected to begin cloudy with some rain at times, but it will become drier and brighter later.

Northern Scotland will be bright with wintry showers, which are also likely in central and eastern Scotland.

The Guardian, April 2, 1990

1 Choose the appropriate endings for the following sentences.

1. The weather was about to
A. improve.
B. get worse.
C. stay unchanged.

2. Iberia means
A. Spain.
B. Portugal.
C. Spain and Portugal.

3. The area of low pressure would move
A. north.
B. north-west.
C. north-east.

4. Scandinavia means
A. Norway.
B. Norway and Sweden.
C. Norway, Sweden, Denmark and Iceland.

5. The adjective "northern", because of its meaning and not because of its position, is written with a capital "N"
A. once.
B. twice.
C. three times.

6. The weather in Britain
A. could be entirely defined with the elements used before in the first part of the article.
B. was completely different from what it was in the rest of Europe.
C. had a special mention that would please those who like stereotypes.

2 Test your knowledge. Only one statement is correct in each pair. Which one?

A. Depressions move clockwise.
B. Depressions move anticlockwise.

C. Anticyclones move clockwise.
D. Anticyclones move anticlockwise.

3 One sentence has been cut into parts and the parts scrambled. Put them back into the right order. (Punctuation and the capital letter at the beginning of the sentence have been removed.)

in fresh to strong winds / further moderate snowfalls / it seems no let-up is in sight / the forecast is for / which could turn into drifts

Celsius and Fahrenheit (C: Celsius; F: Fahrenheit)
O °C = 32 °F
100 °C = 212 °F

F temperature = 9/5 C temperature plus 32.
C temperature = 5/9 F temperature minus 32.

22 TRAVEL AND TRAFFIC — LES VOYAGES ET LA CIRCULATION

VOCABULAIRE A HAUTE FRÉQUENCE

The Weather	Le temps
poor visibility	mauvaise visibilité
(black) ice	le verglas
icy	verglacé
a patch	une plaque
treacherous /ˈtretʃərəs/	plein d'embûches, traître
hazardous	dangereux, risqué
slippery	glissant
a snowdrift	une congère
snowbound	enneigé
flooded	inondé
to be stranded	être bloqué
to close	barrer
a closure	une fermeture
to block	bloquer
to abandon	abandonner
to re-open	ouvrir de nouveau
care	la prudence
a crossing	une traversée
smooth	calme
choppy	légèrement agitée
rough	agitée

Incidents	Les incidents
to disrupt	perturber
a disruption	une perturbation
chaos /ˈkeiɔs/	la confusion, le chaos
chaotic	chaotique
road works	les travaux routiers
to break down	tomber en panne
a breakdown	une panne

Traffic Flow	La circulation
a trip, a journey	un voyage
to travel	voyager
busy	animé
heavy	dense
crowded	chargé
congested	encombré
congestion	encombrement
a tailback	une retenue
a jam	un embouteillage
to crawl	avancer au pas
eastbound	vers l'est
southbound	vers le sud
speed	la vitesse
a limit	une limitation
a restriction	une restriction
to avoid	éviter
to divert	dévier
a diversion	une déviation
an alternative route	un itinéraire de remplacement
rush hours, peak hours	les heures de pointe
to commute	faire la navette entre son domicile et son travail
a commuter	un banlieusard

Road Traffic	La circulation routière
the Highway Code	le code de la route
a driving licence	un permis de conduire
a driving test	un examen d'obtention du permis
a built-up area	une agglomération
a thoroughfare	une artère
main	principal
a carriageway	une chaussée
a dual carriageway	une quatre-voies
a motorway a freeway (US)	une autoroute
a lane	un couloir
the hard shoulder	la bande d'arrêt d'urgence
a junction	une bretelle d'accès et/ou de sortie, un échangeur
a turn-off	une sortie
a bypass	une route de contournement

a ring road a beltway (US)	une rocade un périphérique
a rest area	une aire de repos
a service area	une aire de services
a filling station	une station-service
petrol gasoline, gas (US)	l'essence
diesel (oil)	le gazole
a roundabout	un rond-point
clockwise	dans le sens des aiguilles
anticlockwise	dans les sens inverse des aiguilles
a toll	un péage
to park	garer, stationner
a car park a parking lot (US)	un parking
drink driving	la conduite en état d'alcoolémie
careless	imprudent
reckless	dangereux
to speed	commettre un excès de vitesse

Public Transport — Les transports publics

the underground the tube the subway (US)	le métro
a ferry	un ferry
a ferry terminal	une gare maritime
to board, to get on board	monter à bord
to sail	naviguer, partir
a sailing	un départ de bateau
a harbour, a port	un port
to run	fonctionner
to delay	retarder
a delay	un retard
a schedule /'ʃedju:l/	un horaire
on schedule	à l'heure
a scheduled flight	un vol régulier
nonstop	sans escale
to charter	affréter
a charter plane	un avion charter
an air traffic controller	un contrôleur de la navigation aérienne
to depart	partir
a departure	un départ
an arrival	une arrivée
incoming traffic	le trafic à l'arrivée

outgoing traffic	le trafic au départ
to cancel	annuler
a cancellation	une annulation
to check	vérifier
to enquire /inˈkwaiə/	se renseigner
an enquiry	une demande de renseignements
information	des renseignements

Holidays — Les vacances

a vacation (US)	un congé
a bank holiday	un jour férié
a holidaymaker	un vacancier
a package holiday	un séjour à forfait
a holiday resort	une station de vacances
to rent	louer
to book, to reserve	réserver
a reservation	une réservation
a berth	une couchette
a travel agent	un agent de voyages
a travel agency	une agence de voyages
a tour operator	un voyagiste, un organisateur de voyages
accommodation	le logement
a boarding-house / a guest-house	une pension de famille
board and lodging	la pension
to put sb. up	loger qn.
self-catering accommodation	une location meublée
an en suite bedroom	une chambre avec w.c. et salle d'eau privés
no vacancies	complet

EXPRESSIONS

visibility down to 20 yards	visibilité réduite à 20 mètres
closed to traffic	interdit à la circulation
to drive with extra care	conduire avec une extrême prudence
to set out on a journey	se mettre en route
to go dead slow / to go at a crawl	avancer au pas

bumper to bumper	pare-chocs contre pare-chocs
a one-way street	une rue à sens unique
to do, to make a U-turn	faire demi-tour
to ban sb. from driving	suspendre le permis de qn.
fully booked up	complet (à la réservation)
back to normal	retour à la normale
to enquire with somebody	se renseigner auprès de qn.
a high-speed train	un train à grande vitesse
a roll-on roll-off ship	un navire roulier
to be a good sailor	avoir le pied marin
to stagger holidays	étaler les vacances
to blow in the bag	souffler dans le ballon

VOCABULAIRE COMPLÉMENTAIRE

The Weather	**Le temps**
fogbound	noyé dans le brouillard
to grit	sabler
grit	le gravier, le sable
to drift	accumuler
impassable	impraticable
unusable	inutilisable, impraticable
marooned	bloqué, isolé

Incidents	**Les incidents**
to shed	répandre
a load	un chargement
to leak	s'échapper (liquide, gaz)
a leak, a leakage	une fuite
to burst	éclater, se rompre
a burst	une rupture (canalisation)
a main	une canalisation
maintenance	l'entretien
a repair	une réparation
re-surfacing	la réfection du revêtement
a recovery vehicle	une dépanneuse

Traffic Flow	**La circulation**
packed	comble, bondé
to slow down	ralentir
a slow-down	un ralentissement

a bumper	un pare-chocs
a traffic warden	un contractuel
a ticket	un ticket
a fine	une amende
a clamp / **a Denver boot**	un sabot de blocage
a contraflow system	une mise en deux sens d'une voie à sens unique
a weekend motorist	un chauffeur du dimanche
a major road	une route principale
a minor road	une route secondaire
a country lane	un chemin rural
an access	un accès
a stretch	une portion, une section
a lay-by	une bande de stationnement
an interchange	un échangeur
a turnpike (US)	une autoroute à péage
a breathaliser / **a drunkometer (US)**	un éthylomètre
a breath test	un passage à l'éthylomètre
intoxicated	en état d'ébriété
to disqualify	frapper d'une suspension
a disqualification	une suspension, un retrait
to take away	retirer
an endorsement	une mention sur le permis

Public Transport — Les transports publics

a wharf, a quay /ki:/	un quai
to dock	accoster
a hovercraft	un aéroglisseur
a taxiway	une piste de dégagement
jet lag	l'effet du décalage horaire

Practise your vocabulary.

1. How do the main hazards affect road traffic in winter?
2. What sort of warnings are given on the radio to motorists about various incidents?
3. What is often typical of road traffic during the holiday period?
4. What has been done in most European countries over the past decades to make road traffic easier?
5. How can people set about preparing the holidays they want to spend away from home?

AIRPORTS PREPARE FOR CHAOS AS STRIKE TALKS BREAK DOWN

By Phil Reeves and Tim McGirk

Thousands of holidaymakers face a Bank Holiday weekend of chaos and delays at airports after Spanish air traffic controllers decided to go ahead with a 24-hour strike for the second week running.

Authorities at Gatwick Airport, from which depart the majority of flights to Spain, said that disruption could be worse than last weekend.

Delays of between six and eight hours will begin when the strike takes effect at 7am tomorrow, and are expected to continue until Tuesday.

Some passengers may have to wait far longer. Last weekend several thousand holidaymakers were held up for more than 14 hours, and one party of Spaniards waited 30 hours before boarding a flight home.

Talks between the Barcelona air traffic controllers and the aviation authorities broke down yesterday. Afterwards the strike committee at Barcelona airport said it was "highly improbable" that the strike would be called off.

Britain's 16 airports with flights to Spain are again bracing themselves for a chaotic few days, and in Spain's popular package tour resorts British holidaymakers will spend a frustrating weekend awaiting flights home.

At Gatwick, entertainers, extra caterers, and 1,000 extra seats will be brought in to cope with stranded passengers. Three marquees will again be used to ease the crowding within the terminal...

The Independent,
August 28, 1987

1 **Match the definitions (A-F) to the words (1-6).**

1. go ahead
2. break down
3. call off
4. brace
5. caterer
6. marquee

A. provider of food and drink
B. prepare to face
C. start, continue
D. large tent
E. stop, not start
F. collapse, fail

2 **Say whether the following statements are true (T) or false (F).**

1. The strike had been on for one week.
2. French people also have a bank holiday at the same time of the year.
3. It was natural that the disruption should be worse that weekend than the previous one.
4. It takes some time for flights to get back to normal after a strike.
5. The reason for the dispute is not stated in the extract.
6. Spain seems to be one of the favourite destinations for British holidaymakers.
7. It is pleasant for those flying home to have some extra time abroad during a strike.
8. Authorities at Gatwick took great pains to make things easier for passengers.

3 **Looking for words. Read the article and find:**

A. Two reasons for travellers to lose their tempers (first paragraph).
B. A popular way of taking a holiday abroad (sixth paragraph).

4 **Fill in the blanks with the appropriate words from the following list. Use each word once only. Verbs are given in the infinitive.**

to cancel to abandon to paralyse to hit deep to trap

1. The snowstorms ____________ road and rail links and left motorists ________ in snowdrifts up to 12 ft ________
2. ____________ vehicles littered roads and hundreds of trains were ____________ as severe snowfalls __________ most areas.

5 **Test your knowledge. Only one statement is right in each pair. Which one?**

A. Motorists have to pay a toll to drive along British motorways.
B. Access to British motorways is free for motorists.

C. In Britain, motorists go clockwise round roundabouts.
D. British motorists drive anticlockwise round roundabounts

COFFEE STOP FOR DRIVERS

By Lin Jenkins

Police on the major holiday routes to the West Country are again supplying drivers with free black coffee in a campaign to prevent accidents caused by fatigue behind the wheel.

After eight-mile tailbacks on the M5 and numerous accidents they have set up coffee stops to urge drivers to take a break during the busy holiday rush. This is the third year the campaign has been operated...

The Daily Telegraph

Freeze hits roads

Gritting lorries went into action at 4am in Bristol today as freezing temperatures left the city's roads icy and treacherous.

The overnight frost was harsh and widespread, with temperatures falling to minus 5C in Yeovil. But most main roads kept dry.

A Bristol city council team of nine lorries began gritting in the early hours of the morning, paying particular attention to the Cumberland Basin, bridges and other accident blackspots.

The police say that drivers were careful and there were no reports of accidents caused by the icy roads.

Today will be another cold day, dry, but with some sunshine and temperatures around 4C.

The Evening Post,
Bristol

1 **Choose the appropriate endings for the following sentences.**

1. When hazardous driving conditions developed in Bristol, the traffic officials

A. were taken by surprise.
B. were expecting them.
C. were looking forward to them.

2. When compared to the city's roads, the main roads around Bristol were

A. less treacherous.
B. more treacherous.
C. just as tracherous.

3. Once roads have been gritted, vehicles
A. have to slow down.
B. are less likely to skid.
C. have poor visibility.

4. Given the temperatures predicted for the day,
A. it was likely to freeze again overnight.
B. ice would form again during the day.
C. there was no risk of frost overnight.

Say whether the following statements are true (T) or false (F).

1. Such winter conditions are unusual in the Bristol area.
2. The authorities know where trouble is likely to occur.
3. The police were angered by motorists' behaviour.

Trains disrupted

Train services were disrupted across Italy yesterday by a 24-hour wildcat strike of station masters. Scores of trains were cancelled or delayed, leaving hundreds of passengers stranded.

Associated Press,
April 2, 1990

23

SPORT — LE SPORT

VOCABULAIRE A HAUTE FRÉQUENCE

Sports and Sportsmen	Les sports et les sportifs
football, soccer /ˈsɔkə/	le football
cycling	le cyclisme
motor-racing	la course automobile
athletics /æθˈletiks/	l'athlétisme
an athlete /ˈæθliːt/	un athlète
a runner	un coureur
boxing	la boxe
a team	une équipe
a champion	un champion
a substitute	un remplaçant
a manager	un directeur technique
a manager (soccer) a coach	un entraîneur
to train	s'entraîner
to practise	pratiquer
practice	la pratique
a referee /ˌrefəˈriː/	un arbitre
a ball	un ballon
shape, fitness	la forme
fit	en forme

Sporting Events	Les événements sportifs
to play	jouer, disputer
an event	un événement
a game	une partie
a tie	une rencontre éliminatoire
away	à l'extérieur
at home	à domicile
a visitor	un visiteur
to race	participer à une course

a race	une course
horse racing	les courses de chevaux
a tournament	un tournoi
a Grand Prix	un grand prix
Olympic	olympique
to attempt	tenter
a bid, an attempt	une tentative
to compete (in)	participer (à)
a competition	une compétition
a competitor	un concurrent
an opponent	un adversaire
a stage	une étape
a friendly match	une rencontre amicale
a championship	un championnat
a cup	une coupe
a round	un tour, une reprise
a final	une finale

Sports Results — Les résultats sportifs

to score	marquer
a goal	un but
a try	un essai
a point	un point
to serve	servir
a serve	un service
to lead	mener
a lead	une avance
a penalty	une pénalité
to win	gagner
a win, a victory	une victoire
to defeat	vaincre
a defeat	une défaite
to lose	perdre
to draw, to tie	faire match nul
a draw	un match nul
to qualify to be through	se qualifier
to knock out to eliminate	éliminer
elimination	l'élimination
to retain	conserver
a title	un titre
to set up	établir
a record	un record
a performance	une performance
to finish	terminer

Spectators and Facilities	**Les spectateurs et les installations**
a stadium	un stade
a ground	un terrain
the pitch	l'aire de jeu, le terrain
a stand	une tribune
the terraces	les gradins
a spectator	un spectateur
to watch	regarder
to attend sth.	assister à qch.
attendance	l'assistance
a track	une piste
a lap	un tour (de piste)
to support	encourager
support	le soutien
a supporter, a fan	un supporter
to behave	se conduire
behaviour	la conduite
to cheer	acclamer
to hiss at sb.	siffler qn.
to jeer at sb.	railler, huer
to boo	conspuer, huer
a hooligan	un casseur, un voyou
hooliganism	le vandalisme

EXPRESSIONS

short of practice	à court d'entraînement
in fine form	en bonne forme
to turn professional	devenir professionnel
Arsenal versus Chelsea	Arsenal contre Chelsea
the first round of the Cup	le premier tour de la Coupe
with one game in hand	avec un match de retard
to be held to a draw	être contraint au match nul
to clinch a title	décrocher un titre
to take a battering	subir une déroute
to drop one's serve	perdre son service
to break sb.'s serve	prendre le service de qn.
against all odds	contre toute attente
to be the odds-on favourite	être le grand favori
to cross the finishing line	franchir la ligne d'arrivée
to carry shoulder high	porter en triomphe
to play for time	jouer la montre

to score an own goal	marquer contre son camp
to disallow a goal	refuser un but
to lower one's guard	baisser sa garde
to throw in the towel	jeter l'éponge
to clock under 4 minutes	être chronométré à moins de 4 minutes
top of the table	en tête du classement
bottom of the table	en queue de classement
to fail a drugs test	subir un contrôle positif

VOCABULAIRE COMPLÉMENTAIRE

Sports and Sportsmen	**Les sports et les sportifs**
a tracksuit	un survêtement
swimming	la natation
freestyle	(nage) libre
breaststroke	la brasse classique
diving	le plongeon
fencing	l'escrime
wrestling	la lutte, le catch
skiing	le ski
skating	le patinage
sailing	la voile
sailboarding, windsurfing	la planche à voile
a sailboard	une planche à voile
rowing	l'aviron
hiking, rambling	la randonnée
judo	le judo
a judoist	un judoka
a racing car	une voiture de course
a racing driver	un pilote de course
Formula One	la formule 1
practice	les essais
the pits	les stands
show jumping	le saut d'obstacles
a side	une formation
a squad	un groupe
a team mate	un coéquipier
a runner-up	un deuxième (classement)
a skipper	un capitaine
a fitness test	un dernier essai pour voir si le joueur peut jouer
to substitute for sb.	remplacer qn.

a substitute	un remplaçant
an umpire	un juge, un arbitre
a linesman	un juge de touche
a post	un poteau
the crossbar	la barre transversale
amateur	amateur
professional	professionnel
to select	sélectionner
a selector	un sélectionneur
to cap (soccer, rugby)	sélectionner
a cap (soccer, rugby)	une sélection
a foul	une irrégularité
a free kick	un coup franc
a penalty kick	un pénalty
to book	avertir
a booking	un avertissement
a yellow card	un carton jaune
to send off	expulser
a send-off	une expulsion
to suspend	suspendre
a suspension	une suspension
to transfer	transférer
a transfer	un transfert
a transfer fee	le montant d'un transfert

Sporting Events — Les événements sportifs

a single-handed race	une course en solitaire (voile)
a fixture	une épreuve
to contest, to contend	disputer
a contest	une rencontre
a contestant, a contender	un concurrent
a heat	une éliminatoire
a dead-heat	un résultat ex-æquo
to field	aligner (un joueur)
a field	l'ensemble des concurrents
kick-off	le coup d'envoi
to shoot	tirer
a shot	un tir
to wrongfoot	prendre à contrepied
to volley	reprendre de volée
a volley	une volée
half-time	la mi-temps
injury time	les arrêts de jeu
extra time	les prolongations

a quarter-final	un quart de finale
a semi-final	une demi-finale
play-off	la finale des premiers
on aggregate	sur l'ensemble des deux rencontres
the Grand Slam	le Grand Chelem

Soccer	**Le football**
a midfielder	un milieu de terrain
a striker	un avant de pointe
a sweeper	un libéro
the penalty area / **the box**	la surface de réparation
to save	parer, sauver
a save	une parade
a cross	un centre
a header	une tête
to clear	dégager
a clearance	un dégagement
a throw-in	une remise de la touche
a penalty shootout	la séance de tirs au but
the football pools	le loto sportif

Rugby Football	**Le rugby**
a scrum	une mêlée
a loose scrum	une mêlée ouverte
a scrum half	un demi de mêlée
a fly half	un demi d'ouverture
a prop	un pilier
a hooker	un talonneur
a ruck	un regroupement
a line-out	une remise à la touche
a drop kick	un coup de pied tombé

Tennis	**Le tennis**
lawn	le gazon
clay	la terre battue
a singles match	un simple
a doubles match	un double
a forehand drive	un coup droit
a backhand drive	un revers
a net	un filet
a net approach	une montée au filet
a seeded player	une tête de série
the seeds	les têtes de série
30-love	30-zéro

deuce	égalité
advantage	avantage
a tie-break	un jeu décisif
in straight sets	sans concéder un set

Athletics	**L'athlétisme**
high jump	le saut en hauteur
long jump	le saut en longueur
pole vault	le saut à la perche
triple jump	le triple saut
discus	le disque
shot put	le lancer de poids
javelin	le javelot
hammer	le marteau
a hurdle	une haie
the finishing straight	la dernière ligne droite

Miscellaneous Sports	**Sports divers**
multihull	multicoque
a trimaran /ˈtraiməˌræn/	un trimaran
a catamaran /ˌkætəməˈræn/	un catamaran
a single-handed race	une course en solitaire
an instructor	un moniteur
downhill	la descente (ski)
the yellow jersey	le maillot jaune
an overall leader	un leader au classement général

Sports Results	**Les résultats sportifs**
to outplay	surclasser
to overwhelm, to crush	écraser
to thrash	battre à plate couture
to trounce	rosser
a rout	une déroute
to outpoint	surclasser (boxe)
on points	aux points
to abandon	abandonner
to triumph	triompher
a triumph	un triomphe
a success	un succès
a showing	une prestation
a goalless draw	un match nul 0 à 0
two-nil	deux à zéro

the final whistle	le coup de sifflet final
a trophy	un trophée
a medal	une médaille
a podium	un podium
to dethrone	détrôner
to celebrate	fêter
celebrations	les réjouissances
to congratulate	féliciter
congratulations	les félicitations
to draw	tirer au sort
a draw	un tirage au sort
to relegate	reléguer
relegation	la relégation
a table	un classement
a division	une division
to cheat	tricher
a drugs test	un contrôle anti-dopage
anabolic steroids	les stéroïdes anabolisants

Spectators and Facilities — Les spectateurs et les installations

a gate	une grille, une porte une assistance, une foule
a capacity crowd	un stade, une salle combles
a turnstile	un tourniquet
a grandstand	une tribune d'honneur
a dressing-room	un vestiaire
the venue /ˈvenju:/	le lieu de déroulement
a ticket tout	un revendeur de billets
to gamble	jouer de l'argent
to bet	parier
a punter	un parieur

Practise your vocabulary.

1. What should boys and girls do if their ambition is to take part in high-level competition?
2. What may clubs expect when they take part in an international competition – a European cup for example?
3. What are the different elements involved in a soccer or rugby match?
4. What are the various reactions spectators may have during a match?
5. Why do people play sport?

YOUNG SAMPRAS HAS HIS SIGHTS ON WIMBLEDON

Mike Dickson on the 18-year-old American who wants to be a right-handed Laver

Pete Sampras awoke yesterday morning ranked 17th in the world and a marked man. Until Sunday night he had successfully glided along in the slipstream of the American wunderkinde Chang and Agassi, but after his victory at the Ebel Pro Indoor Championship he will reluctantly have to share the weight of expectation.

His 7-6, 7-5, 6-2 triumph over Andres Gomez further supported the claim of those who feel he has the brightest future of the young American quartet which also includes Jim Courier.

Unlike those other three players Sampras has an elegant cultured serve-and-volley game which hardly befits someone whose family originates from Sparta in Greece. He is also blessed with a sense of proportion and refreshing ordinariness, neither descriptions applicable to Agassi or Chang in their different ways.

This may be due to a complete lack of tennis heritage within the Sampras family. His father Sam is an aircraft engineer and mother Georgia a housewife. "They don't play tennis, and mom doesn't even know the rules." (...)

Given the dearth of emerging serve-and-volleyers, his billing as a potential Wimbledon champion – by other people, not himself – may not be so far fetched. In addition to the Americans, the best of his contemporaries in Europe, such as Goran Ivanisevic and Sergi Bruguera, are a long way from becoming so accomplished on the faster surfaces...

The Guardian, February 27, 1990

1 Match the definitions (A-H) to the words (1-8).

1. have one's sights on
2. slipstream
3. reluctant
4. befit
5. blessed
6. dearth
7. billing
8. far-fetched

A. inadequate supply, scarcity
B. being put on a list
C. fortunate in having
D. improbable, unlikely
E. be appropriate to, suitable for
F. aim at, have as a goal
G. air behind a moving object
H. unwilling, not eager

2 **Say whether the following statements are true (T) or false (F).**

1. Until that Sunday night, Sampras had drawn less attention than Chang and Agassi.
2. He seemed very anxious to get to the top.
3. Sampras won in straight sets against Gomez.
4. The reputation of a city in classical times is hinted at.
5. Pete Sampras sounds popular with journalists.
6. It may be inferred that tennis players are often influenced by their families or relatives.
7. Sampras' style of play would be an asset at Wimbledon.

3 **As in "housewife", "house" is the first element in a number of words. Match the definitions (A-E) to the words (1-5).**

1. household	A. a teacher with special responsibilities, usually in a boarding-school.
2. housebreaking	B. party given after moving into a new home
3. house-warming	C. entering a building (by force) to steal
4. house arrest	D. people living together in one house
5. housemaster	E. forbidden by law to leave one's house

4 **Fill in the blanks with words from the following list. Use each word once only. Verbs are given in the infinitive.**

pitch to watch home to use fans to urge

Plymouth police ____ dogs yesterday to prevent a repeat of last year's soccer violence when Bristol City ______ arrived in the city to ____ their team play Argyle.

About 100 Bristol fans were met at Plymouth station by police dog-handlers, who ____ them to take the next train ____ . The match was postponed because the ____ was waterlogged.

The Western Morning News,
April 1, 1986

5 **Test your knowledge. Only one statement is correct in the pair below. Which one?**

A. Rod Laver was Wimbledon singles champion once but he never won the Grand Slam.
B. Rod Laver won Wimbledon four times and the Grand Slam once.

PROST HAS THE FINAL WORD IN SENNA'S BACK YARD

By Tim Collings in Sao Paulo

Alain Prost won one of the most satisfying and spectacular victories of his Formula One career when he took full advantage of the misfortunes of his great rival, Ayrton Senna, to claim his first victory for Ferrari by winning the Brazilian Grand Prix at Interlagos yesterday.

Having trailed behind the Brazilian's Honda Marlboro McLaren in the pack for much of the 71-lap race, Prost was virtually handed the 40th victory of his career when Japan's Satoru Nakajima baulked Senna as he attempted to pass him on the 40th lap.

The incident left Senna's car with a damaged nose cone and front which required a long pit stop to be replaced before he could continue.

"I knew I could not catch up so I just settled for third place", said Senna, whose ill luck left a 70,000 crowd at the Autodromo Carlos Jose Pace disappointed in their hopes of seeing a victory by the home-town hero.

The celebrations took place instead in the delighted Ferrari garages where Prost and Nigel Mansell, who finished fourth, were feted like heroes following the team's dismal showing in Phoenix two weeks ago when both cars failed to finish.

Prost, after inheriting the lead, had pulled away to win by a clear 13.564 seconds ahead of Austrian Gerhard Berger who claimed his first points since moving to McLaren by finishing second...

March 26, 1990

1 Match the definitions (A-E) to the words (1-5).

1. baulk	A. accept in spite of dissatisfaction
2. pits	B. appearance, performance
3. settle for	C. get in the way of
4. dismal	D. place where racing cars can stop for fuel, tyres, etc.
5. showing	E. miserable, disastrous

2 **Say whether the following statements are true (T) or false (F).**

1. It could be said that Alain Prost was doubly satisfied, at least.
2. The French racing driver was very active in the first part of the race.
3. Satoru Nakajima was in the lead when the incident happened.
4. When he started again, Senna had resigned himself to the fact that he couldn't win.
5. The Ferrari team were both overjoyed and relieved.
6. It is possible to name the first four in the Brazilian Grand Prix.

3 **Looking for words. Read the article and pick out:**

1. A verb phrase and two verbs showing that Alain Prost was lucky (first, second and last paragraphs).
2. A noun and a noun phrase showing it was the opposite for Senna (first and fourth paragraphs).
3. A verb phrase meaning that, up to the 40th lap, Alain Prost's performance had been modest (second paragraph).

4 **Fill in the blanks with the appropriate words. (All three sentences describe easy wins.)**

1. In the end, victory was handed to him on a ______ .
2. He constantly increased his lead and finally won __________ down.
3. When the leading horse came to the finishing straight, there was no pressure by the rest of the contenders and the winner could __________ home.

5 **Test your knowledge. Only one statement is correct in each pair. Which one?**

A. Only the first five racing drivers in a Grand Prix score points for the World Championship.
B. The racing driver ending up in sixth place at a Grand Prix scores one point for the World Championship.

C. In 1990, Alain Prost was the record holder for the number of World Championship titles in motor racing.
D. In 1990, the record for the number of World Championship titles in motor racing was still held by Juan Manuel Fangio.

24

COUNTRIES AND PEOPLE — LES PAYS ET LES GENS

L'anglais utilise parfois un nom différent de l'adjectif pour désigner les habitants. Dans ce cas, il est précédé de l'article indéfini.

A-C

Afghanistan	l'Afghanistan
Afghan	afghan
an Afghanistani	un Afghan
Albania	l'Albanie
Albanian	albanais
Algeria	l'Algérie
Algerian	algérien
Angola	l'Angola
Angolan	angolais
Argentina	l'Argentine
Argentinian	argentin
Australia	l'Australie
Australian	australien
Austria	l'Autriche
Austrian	autrichien
Bangladesh	le Bangladesh
Bangladeshi	bengalais
Belgium	la Belgique
Belgian	belge
Benin	le Bénin
Beninese	béninois
Bolivia	la Bolivie
Bolivian	bolivien
Brazil	le Brésil
Brazilian	brésilien
Burma	la Birmanie
Burmese	birman
Cambodia	le Cambodge
Cambodian	cambodgien
Cameroon	le Cameroun
Cameroonian	camerounais

Canada	le Canada
Canadian	canadien
Chad	le Tchad
Chadian	tchadien
Chile	le Chili
Chilean	chilien
China	la Chine
Chinese	chinois
Colombia	la Colombie
Colombian	colombien
the Congo	le Congo
Congolese	congolais
Cuba	Cuba
Cuban	cubain
Cyprus	Chypre
Cyprian	chypriote
a Cypriot	un Chypriote
Czechoslovakia	la Tchécoslovaquie
Czech	tchèque
Czechoslovakian	un Tchécoslovaque

D-I

Denmark	le Danemark
Danish	danois
a Dane	un Danois
Ecuador	l'Équateur
Ecuadorian	équatorien
Egypt	l'Égypte
Egyptian	égyptien
El Salvador	le Salvador
Salvadorian	salvadorien
England	l'Angleterre
English	anglais
an Englishman	un Anglais
Eritrea	l'Érythrée
Eritrean	érythréen
Estonia	l'Estonie
Estonian	estonien
Ethiopia	l'Éthiopie
Ethiopian	éthiopien

Finland	la Finlande
Finnish	finlandais
a Finn	un Finlandais
France	la France
French	français
the Gambia	la Gambie
Gambian	gambien
Germany	l'Allemagne
German	allemand
Ghana	le Ghana
Ghanaian	ghanéen
Great Britain	la Grande-Bretagne
British	britannique
a Briton	un Britannique
Greece	la Grèce
Greek	grec
Grenada	la Grenade
Grenadian	grenadien
Guatemala	le Guatemala
Guatemaltan	guatemaltèque
Guinea	la Guinée
Guinean	guinéen
Guyana	la Guyane
Guyanese	guyanais
Haiti	Haïti
Haitian	haïtien
Holland	la Hollande
Dutch	hollandais
a Dutchman	un Hollandais
Hungary	la Hongrie
Hungarian	hongrois
Iceland	l'Islande
Icelandic	islandais
an Icelander	un Islandais
India	l'Inde
Indian	indien
Indonesia	l'Indonésie
Indonesian	indonésien
Iran	l'Iran
Iranian	iranien
Iraq	l'Irak
Iraqi	irakien
Ireland	l'Irlande
Irish	irlandais
an Irishman	un Irlandais
Israel	Israël
Israeli	israélien
Italy	l'Italie
Italian	italien

Jamaica	la Jamaïque
Jamaican	jamaïcain
Japan	le Japon
Japanese	japonais
Java	Java
Javanese	javanais
Jordan	la Jordanie
Jordanian	jordanien
Kampuchea	le Kampuchéa
Kampuchean	kampuchéen
Kenya	le Kenya
Kenyan	kenyan
Korea	la Corée
Korean	coréen
Kuwait	le Koweït
Kuwaiti	koweïtien, koweïti
Laos	le Laos
Laotian	laotien
Latvia	la Lettonie
Latvian	letton
Lebanon	le Liban
Lebanese	libanais
Liberia	le Libéria
Liberian	libérien
Libya	la Libye
Libyan	libyen
Lithuania	la Lituanie
Lithuanian	lituanien
Luxembourg, Luxemburg	le Luxembourg
Luxemburger	luxembourgeois
Malaysia	la Malaisie
Malaysian	malais
Malta	Malte
Maltese	maltais
Mexico	le Mexique
Mexican	mexicain
Morocco	le Maroc
Moroccan	marocain
Namibia	la Namibie
Namibian	namibien
the Netherlands	les Pays-Bas
New Zealand	la Nouvelle-Zélande
a New Zealander	un Néo-zélandais
Nicaragua	le Nicaragua
Nicaraguan	nicaraguayen
Niger	le Niger

Nigeria	le Nigéria
Nigerian	nigérian
Norway	la Norvège
Norwegian	norvégien

P-Z

Pakistan	le Pakistan
Pakistani	pakistanais
Palestine	la Palestine
Palestinian	palestinien
Paraguay	le Paraguay
Paraguayan	paraguayen
Peru	le Pérou
Peruvian	péruvien
the Philippines	les Philippines
Phillipine, Filipino	philippin
a Filipino	un Philippin
Poland	la Pologne
Polish	polonais
Portugal	le Portugal
Portuguese	portugais
Romania, Roumania	la Roumanie
Romanian, Roumanian	roumain
Russia	la Russie
Russian	russe
Saudi Arabia	l'Arabie saoudite
Saudi	saoudien
Scotland	l'Écosse
Scottish, Scots	écossais
a Scot, a Scotsman	un Écossais
Senegal	le Sénégal
Senegalese	sénégalais
Somalia	la Somalie
Somalian, Somali	somalien
a Somali	un Somalien
South Africa	l'Afrique du Sud
South African	sud-africain
Spain	l'Espagne
Spanish	espagnol
a Spaniard	un Espagnol
Sri Lanka	le Sri Lanka
Sri Lankan	sri lankais

Sudan	le Soudan
Sudanese	soudanais
Sweden	la Suède
Swedish	suédois
a Swede	un Suédois
Switzerland	la Suisse
Swiss	suisse
Syria	la Syrie
Syrian	syrien
Taiwan	Taiwan
Taiwanese	taiwanais
Tanzania	la Tanzanie
Tanzanian	tanzanien
Thailand	la Thaïlande
Thai	thaïlandais
Tibet	le Tibet
Tibetan	tibétain
Togo	le Togo
Togolese	togolais
Tunisia	la Tunisie
Tunisian	tunisien
Turkey	la Turquie
Turkish	turc
a Turk	un Turc
Uganda	l'Ouganda
Ugandan	ougandais
Uruguay	l'Uruguay
Uruguayan	uruguayen
Venezuela	le Venezuela
Venezuelan	vénézuélien
Vietnam	le Vietnam
Vietnamese	vietnamien
Wales	le Pays de Galles
Welsh	gallois
a Welshman	un Gallois
the West Indies	les Antilles
West Indian	antillais
Yugoslavia	la Yougoslavie
Yugoslavian	yougoslave
a Yugoslav	un Yougoslave
Zaire	le Zaïre
Zairean	Zaïrois
Zambia	la Zambie
Zambian	zambien
Zimbabwe	le Zimbabwe
Zimbabwean	du Zimbabwe

CORRIGÉ

Les références de page correspondent aux pages où vous trouverez les articles sur lesquels portent les exercices.

POLLUTION

page 14

1. 1/C, 2/D, 3/A, 4/E, 5/B.
2. 1/F, 2/T, 3/T, 4/F, 5/F, 6/T, 7/T, 8/F, 9/T.
3. still, to rise, to increase.
4. a) to contaminate, b) to multiply, c) to destine, d) to participate, e) to examine, f) to privatise, g) to demonstrate, h) to organise, i) to consider, j) to frustrate, k) to preserve, l) to discriminate, m) to educate, n) to exaggerate, o) to provoke.
5. are to get, would fall, could be expected.
6. A/T, C/T.

page 16

1. 1/E, 2/F, 3/D, 4/C, 5/A, 6/B.
2. 1/B, 2/A, 3/C, 4/B, 5/A, 6/C, 7/C.
3. 1a) the nineteen forties, b) the nineteen fifties, c) the nineteen sixties ; 2a) the seventies, b) the eighties, c) the nineties ; 3. had managed to, had succeeded in.

THE ECONOMY I

page 27

1. 1/C, 2/H, 3/B, 4/G, 5/D, 6/A, 7/J, 8/E, 9/I, 10/F.
2. 1/B, 2/C, 3/C, 4/A, 5/B, 6/B, 7/A.
3. a) one twentieth, b) one tenth, c) one fifth, d) one third, e) two fifths, f) one half, g) three fifths, h) two thirds.

page 29

1. 1/T, 2/T, 3/T, 4/F, 5/F, 6/F, 7/T.
2. 1/D, 2/F, 3/B, 4/E, 5/A, 6/C.
3. 1. to blacken, 2. to darken, 3. to weaken, 4. to shorten, 5. to widen, 6. to heighten, 7. to lengthen, 8. to worsen, 9. to lessen.
4. A/T.

THE ECONOMY II

page 38

1. 1/B, 2/E, 3/A, 4/C, 5/D.
2. 1/T, 2/T, 3/F, 4/T, 5/T, 6/F, 7/F.
3. A/T, C/T.
4. 1/C, 2/D, 3/E, 4/B, 5/A, 6/H, 7/F, 8/J, 9/G, 10/I.

page 40

1. 1/F, 2/T, 3/F, 4/F, 5/F, 6/T, 7/T.
2. 1. worries, fears, concerns, 2. squeeze, recession, losses, fall, decline 3. drive, lead.
3. 1. overpaid, 2. overcharged, 3. overdrawn, 4. overflowed, 5. overjoyed, 6. overslept, 7. overwhelmed/overpowered, 8. oversubscribed.
4. 1/C, 2/D, 3/E, 4/A, 5/B.
5. slump, reported, currencies, nearly, further, early, down.

THE THIRD WORLD

page 47

1. 1/C, 2/A, 3/B.
2. 1/B, 2/C, 3/A, 4/B, 5/C, 6/A.
3. 1. to supply, home, migration, 2. fuel, chopped down, sale, 3. relief, starvation.
4. 1/T.

page 49

1. 1/E, 2/D, 3/A, 4/F, 5/B, 6/C.
2. 1/T, 2/T, 3/F, 4/F, 5/F, 6/T, 7/T, 8/T.
3. 1. commodity, 2. productivity, efficient, 3. supply and demand.

EMPLOYMENT

page 56

1. 1/T, 2/T, 3/F, 4/F, 5/T, 6/F, 7/T, 8/F, 9/T.
2. 1. to axe, to cut, 2. workforce, 3. cuts, 4. to improve, 5. once, 6. output, 7. plant.
3. 1/H, 2/C, 3/A, 4/F, 5/G, 6/I, 7/D, 8/E, 9/B.
4. 1. to computerise, staff, quarter, 2. executives, overwork, pace, 3. unemployment, labour, seasonally-adjusted.

page 58

1. 1/B, 2/D, 3/A, 4/C.
2. 1/B, 2/A, 3/C, 4/B, 5/C.
3. 2. successful, 4. heartless, 5. ruthless, 7. plentiful, 9. dutiful, 10. eventful, 11. jobless, 12. spotless, 14. defenceless, 16. countless.

DISPUTES AND TENSION

page 67

1. 1/C, 2/G, 3/A, 4/F, 5/B, 6/D, 7/E.
2. 1/C, 2/A, 3/A, 4/C, 5/B, 6/A, 7/B.
3. Production of Rolls Royce cars stopped at Crewe yesterday after 40 workers walked out when told to stop eating fish and chips in working time. The men had been given time off to attend the funeral of a colleague. They brought fish and chips back to the factory because they didn't have time for lunch.

page 69

1. 1/B, 2/H, 3/E, 4/A, 5/G, 6/C, 7/F, 8/D.
2. 1/F, 2/T, 3/F, 4/T, 5/F, 6/T.
3. 1. limited, restrained, 2. blockade, 3. continued, built up, tightening, to prevent, 4. (the US) has ;
5a) to undercut/to undersell, b) to undergo,
c) to underlie, d) to underline/to underscore,
e) to undertake, f) to underwrite.

MEDICINE

page 78

1. 1/B, 2/A, 3/D, 4/C.
2. 1/F, 2/F, 3/T, 4/F, 5/T, 6/T.
3. a) clear, likely, b) cross-checking, c) was not admitted, d) campaign, provide, implemented, project, e) combat, infants, confirmation, limited, believed.
4. 1. develop, tested, volunteers, 2. treated, cells, marrow, 3. screening, elderly, breast, illness.
5. Elizabeth Taylor, who is suffering from serious pneumonia, is improving, and doctors are optimistic about her recovery. The seven-times married, 58-year-old actress is in the intensive care unit in Santa Monica, California.

page 80

1. 1/D, 2/F, 3/E, 4/B, 5/A, 6/C.
2. 1/C, 2/A, 3/B, 4/B, 5/A, 6/B, 7/A.
3. 1/C, 2/D, 3/E, 4/A, 5/B.

SPACE

page 86

1. 1/C, 2/F, 3/A, 4/E, 5/D, 6/B.
2. 1/C, 2/A, 3/C, 4/B, 5/A, 6/C.
3. 1. mechanical, 2. civil, 3. chemical, 4. aeronautical, 5. genetic.
4. a) space station, b) complete technological departure.

page 88

1. 1/B, 2/E, 3/D, 4/C, 5/A.
2. 1/T, 2/F, 3/T, 4/T, 5/T, 6/F, 7/T, 8/T, 9/F.
3. a) cargo bay, aboard, meteorologists, b) back-up.
4. A/T, D/T, E/T.

POLITICS I

page 95

1. 1/E, 2/D, 3/F, 4/A, 5/G, 6/C, 7/B.
2. 1/T, 2/F, 3/T, 4/T, 5/F, 6/T, 7/T.
3. 1. overall, hung, 2. coalition, 3. join, 4. former.
4. A/T.

page 97

1. 1/D, 2/E, 3/A, 4/F, 5/B, 6/C.
2. 1/F, 2/T, 3/T, 4/T, 5/F, 6/T, 7/T.
3. 1. forecast, 2. prompted, 3. drop, 4. constituencies, 5. look forward, 6. investment, 7. rewarded.
4. Nepal, where at least 50 people were killed during pro-democracy demonstrations on Friday, is lifting a 30-year-old ban on political parties. The move was announced from the palace of King Birendra who had earlier met opposition leaders.

POLITICS II

page 107 (before the article)

2. A/T, D/T.

page 107

1. 1/E, 2/D, 3/A, 4/B, 5/C.
2. 1/T, 2/T, 3/F, 4/T, 5/F, 6/F, 7/T, 8/T, 9/T, 10/T, 11/T.
3. 1a) differences, b) reshuffle, c) to retain, d) to emphasise, e) office ; 2. protest, abolition, amendment, approval, overthrow, statement, abstention, acknowledgment, denial, claim, complaint, argument, advice, explanation.
4. B/T.

page 109

1. 1/F, 2/G, 3/D, 4/B, 5/E, 6/C, 7/A.
2. 1/B, 2/A, 3/C, 4/B, 5/C, 6/C.
3. 1. a slogan, a catch phrase, 2. (tax) raise, 3. (they) affirmed

RELIGION

page 117

1. 1/E, 2/C, 3/B, 4/A, 5/D.
2. 1/T, 2/F, 3/T, 4/F, 5/T, 6/F, 7/F, 8/T.
3. 1. disaffection, disillusioned, 2. stepped out of line ; 3a) a data bank, b) a bottle bank, c) a blood bank.
4. survey, belief, Catholics, attend, findings, practise, atheists, faith.
5. A/T.

page 120

1. 1/D, 2/G, 3/F, 4/A, 5/B, 6/C, 7/E.
2. 1/T, 2/T, 3/F, 4/F, 5/T, 6/F, 7/T.
3. 1/C, 2/D, 3/F, 4/E, 5/A, 6/B.

ENTERTAINMENT AND THE MASS MEDIA

page 131

1. 1/C, 2/G, 3/D, 4/F, 5/E, 6/A, 7/B.
2. 1/C, 2/B, 3/A, 4/B, 5/B, 6/A, 7/B.
3. 1/E, 2/D, 3/G, 4/A, 5/F, 6/B, 7/C.

page 134

1. 1/F, 2/E, 3/A, 4/G, 5/B, 6/H, 7/C, 8/D.
2. 1/F, 2/T, 3/F, 4/F, 5/T, 6/T.
3. a) hard, soft ; soft (landing), hard (currency), b) advertising, c) ratings, d) cable and satellite.
4. a) programme, b) recession, c) obvious, d) deputy.

CRIME AND PUNISHMENT

page 154

1. 1/E, 2/D, 3/F, 4/B, 5/A, 6/C.
2. 1/T, 2/F, 3/T, 4/T, 5/F, 6/T, 7/F, 8/F, 9/T.
3. 1. detained, 2. hit, 3. staggered, 4. recovered, 5. bruised, 6. suffered.
4. Police launched a murder inquiry after the body of a 70-year-old taxi driver was found with stab wounds beside a country lane at Hampton Gay, near Kidlington, Oxfordshire.

page 156

1. 1/F, 2/E, 3/B, 4/A, 5/C, 6/D.
2. 1/F, 2/F, 3/F, 4/T, 5/T, 6/F, 7/T, 8/F.
3. 1/E, 2/G, 3/F, 4/B, 5/A, 6/C, 7/D.
4. 1/D, 2/E, 3/F, 4/A, 5/B, 6/C.

DRUGS

page 163

1. 1/C, 2/D, 3/B, 4/A.
2. 1/T, 2/T, 3/F, 4/T, 5/F, 6/F.
3. B/T, D/T.
4. 1/D, 2/C, 3/E, 4/A, 5/B.
5. Customs officers seized 50 kg of cocaine worth £5m from a ship which had arrived at Liverpool docks from Chile and Peru.

page 165

1. 1/G, 2/H, 3/D, 4/A, 5/C, 6/B, 7/E, 8/F.
2. 1/B, 2/B, 3/B, 4/C, 5/A, 6/C, 7/A.
3. 1. to make (made), 2. to value (valued), 3. warehouse, 4. to top (topping), 5. to release (released).

DEMONSTRATIONS AND RIOTS

page 172

1. 1/F, 2/D, 3/E, 4/B, 5/C, 6/A.
2. 1/T, 2/F, 3/T, 4/F, 5/T, 6/F, 7/T.
3. 1/C, 2/E, 3/D, 4/A, 5/B.
4. 1. uneasy, fear, 2. prevailed, 3. onlooker, 4. the National Salvation Front, 5. intimidation.
5. stage, flags, procession, address, peaceful.

page 174

1. 1/C, 2/E, 3/D, 4/A, 5/B.
2. 1/B, 2/B, 3/A, 4/C, 5/B, 6/C.
3. 1a) (teargas) grenades or canisters, b) petrol bombs, c) fire engine, 2. pitched, raged, 3. paragraph six.
4. 1/C, 2/F, 3/A, 4/G, 5/D, 6/B, 7/E.

TERRORISM AND REVOLUTIONS

page 182

1. 1/D, 2/C, 3/B, 4/A.
2. 1/F, 2/T, 3/T, 4/F, 5/T, 6/F, 7/F, 8/T, 9/T.
3. 1. to, 2. at, 3. into, 4. over, 5. up, 6. to, 7. on, 8. on.

page 184

1. 1/C, 2/D, 3/A, 4/B.
2. 1/F, 2/T, 3/T, 4/F, 5/T, 6/T, 7/F.
3. 1/D, 2/G, 3/E, 4/A, 5/C, 6/H, 7/B, 8/F.
4. A pro-Iranian Muslim fundamentalist, Fouad Ali Saleh, accused of killing 13 people in bomb attacks in Paris was sentenced to a maximum of twenty years in a French prison yesterday.

WAR AND ESPIONAGE

page 194

1. 1/D, 2/C, 3/E, 4/A, 5/B.
2. B/T.
3. 1/C, 2/B, 3/A, 4/B, 5/B, 6/B, 7/B.
4. a) "illegal", legitimate, b) bribe, blackmail, c) must have had, probably, d) double.

page 196

1. 1/C, 2/A, 3/B.
2. 1/T, 2/F, 3/T, 4/T, 5/F, 6/T, 7/F, 8/T, 9/F.
3. a) Algiers, Tehran, Baghdad, b) Kuwait, Saudi Arabia, c) crisis, d) major concessions.
4. hackers, broken into, network, research, secret, intelligence, discovered, knowledge, danger.

MISCELLANEOUS TOPICS

page 207

1. 1/E, 2/G, 3/D, 4/F, 5/A, 6/B, 7/C.
2. 1/T, 2/F, 3/F, 4/T, 5/T, 6/T, 7/T.
3. a) to intensify (intensified), to perform (performed), stiff, to view (viewed), to outlaw (outlaws), b) fœtus (fetus *US*), c) Utah, d) tightly, profoundly.
4. A/T.

page 209

1. 1/D, 2/F, 3/E, 4/A, 5/C, 6/B.
2. 1/F, 2/F, 3/F, 4/T, 5/T, 6/F, 7/F, 8/T, 9/T, 10/F.
3. 1/H, 2/I, 3/F, 4/E, 5/G, 6/C, 7/D, 8/A, 9/B.

ACCIDENTS

page 219

1. 1/C, 2/D, 3/F, 4/E, 5/B, 6/A.
2. 1/F, 2/T, 3/T, 4/T, 5/T, 6/F, 7/T, 8/T, 9/T.
3. 1. enquiry, 2.a) west of London, b) north of London, c) south of London..

page 221

1. 1/D, 2/C, 3/E, 4/A, 5/B.
2. 1/T, 2/T, 3/F, 4/T, 5/T, 6/T, 7/T, 8/T, 9/T.
3. to do a U-turn, to make a U-turn.
4. 2, 5, 6.
5. died, left, hit, down, taken, happened, minor, released.

NATURAL DISASTERS

page 228

1. 1/C, 2/B, 3/A, 4/A, 5/C, 6/C, 7/A, 8/B.
2. died, disaster, missing, pulled, bus, engulfed, Swiss, unknown.

page 230

1. 1/C, 2/A, 3/B, 4/E, 5/D.
2. 1/F, 2/F, 3/F, 4/T, 5/F, 6/T, 7/T.
3. 1/C, 2/D, 3/A, 4/B.
4. A strong earthquake and a dozen aftershocks struck the Los Angeles area during the morning rush hour, killing at least 5 persons, injuring more than 100 and severely damaging dozens of buildings and forcing the closure of three freeways. It appeared to be the worst earthquake to hit Southern California since 1971, when 64 people died in a strong tremor, measured at 6.4 on the Richter scale.

THE WEATHER

page 238

1. 1/D, 2/E, 3/A, 4/C, 5/F, 6/B.
2. 1/T, 2/T, 3/F, 4/F, 5/F, 6/T, 7/T.
3. 1/E, 2/D, 3/G, 4/B, 5/A, 6/C, 7/F.
4. a) a freeway, b) arrival Thursday, c) meter.
5. 1/C, 2/A, 3/D, 4/B.

page 240

1. 1/B, 2/C, 3/C, 4/B, 5/A, 6/C.
2. B/T, C/T.
3. It seems no let-up is in sight, the forecast is for further moderate snowfalls which could turn into drifts in fresh to strong winds.

TRAVEL AND TRAFFIC

page 248

1. 1/C, 2/F, 3/E, 4/B, 5/A, 6/D.
2. 1/F, 2/F, 3/T, 4/T, 5/T, 6/T, 7/F, 8/T.
3. a) chaos, delayed, b) package tour.
4. paralysed, trapped, deep, abandoned, cancelled, hit.
5. B/T, C/T.

page 250

1. 1/B, 2/A, 3/B, 4/A.
2. 1/F, 2/T, 3/F.

SPORT

page 260

1. 1/F, 2/G, 3/H, 4/E, 5/C, 6/A, 7/B, 8/D.
2. 1/T, 2/F, 3/T, 4/T, 5/T, 6/T, 7/T.
3. 1/D, 2/C, 3/B, 4/E, 5/A.
4. used, fans, watch, urged, home, pitch.
5. B/T.

page 262

1. 1/C, 2/D, 3/A, 4/E, 5/B.
2. 1/T, 2/F, 3/F, 4/T, 5/T, 6/T.
3. 1. took full advantage, handed, inheriting, 2. misfortunes, ill luck, 3. trailed behind.
4. plate, hands, romp.
5. B/T, D/T.

Aubin Imprimeur
LIGUGÉ, POITIERS

IMPRESSION

Achevé d'imprimer en juillet 1994
N° d'édition 1399-04 / N° d'impression L 45854
Dépôt légal juillet 1994
Imprimé en France